NEW FLAGS FLYING

◆

PACIFIC LEADERSHIP

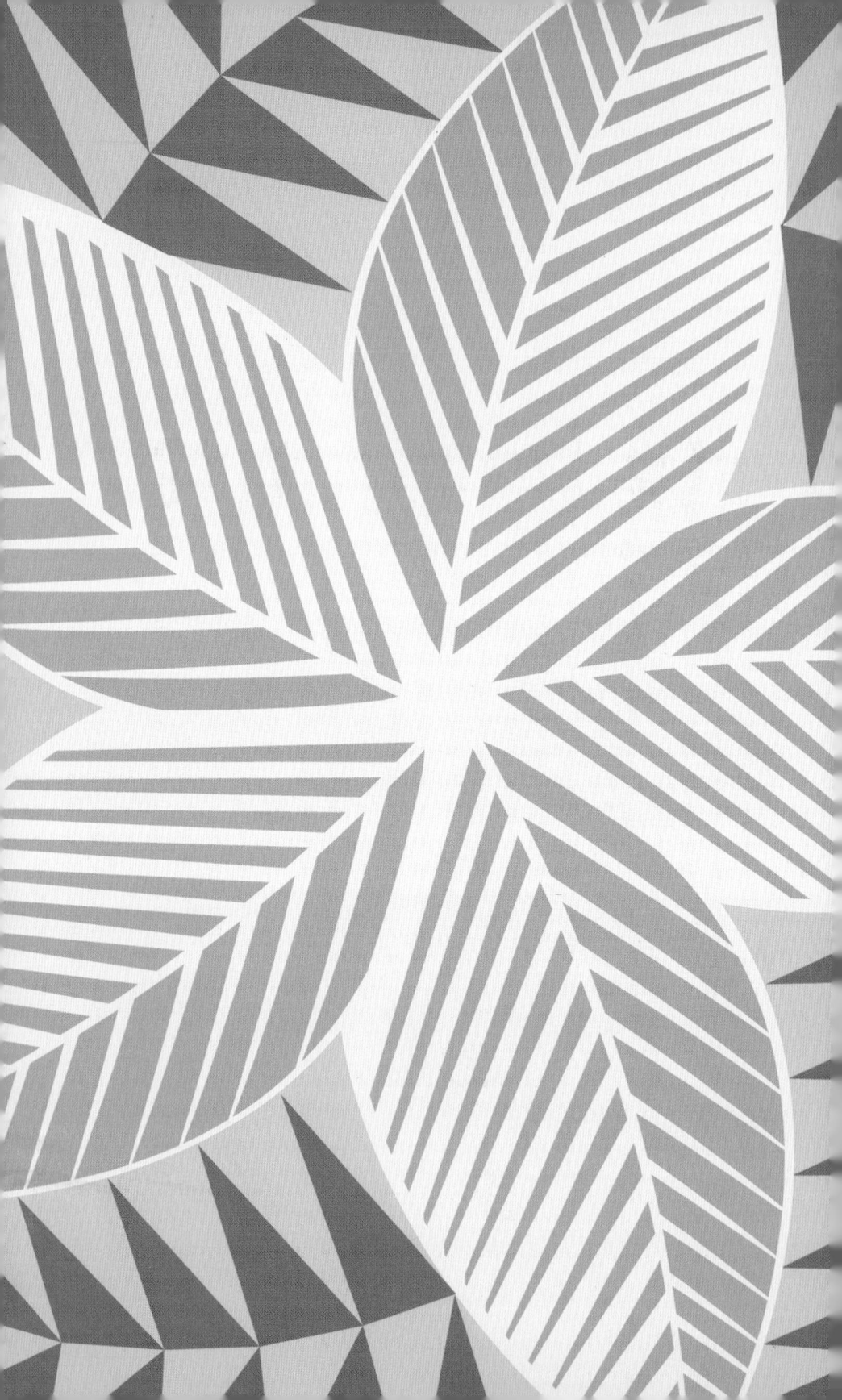

NEW FLAGS FLYING

PACIFIC LEADERSHIP

Edited by Ian Johnstone and Michael Powles

First published in 2012 by Huia Publishers
39 Pipitea Street, PO Box 12280
Wellington, Aotearoa New Zealand
www.huia.co.nz

ISBN 978-1-77550-013-1

Copyright © Ian Johnstone and Michael Powles 2012
CD audio © Radio New Zealand 2011
All photographs in the Julia Brooke-White Collection © Julia Brooke-White
Front cover image © Julia Brooke-White
Back cover, chapter opening pages and CD graphic courtesy of the
Pacific Cooperation Foundation
Flags on chapter opening pages: The World Factbook, 2009, Washington DC: CIA.

This book is copyright. Apart from fair dealing for the purpose of private study, research, criticism or review, as permitted under the Copyright Act, no part may be reproduced by any process without the prior permission of the publisher.

National Library of New Zealand Cataloguing-in-Publication Data
New flags flying : Pacific leadership / edited by Ian Johnstone and Michael Powles.
Includes bibliographical references and index.
ISBN 978-1-77550-013-1
1. Self-determination, National—Oceania. 2. Decolonization—Oceania.
3. Statesmen—Oceania—Interviews. 4. Oceania—Politics and
government—20th century. 5. Oceania—History—20th century.
I. Johnstone, Ian, 1935- II. Powles, Michael.
320.150995—dc 23

CONTENTS

FOREWORD — IX
Sir Anand Satyanand

PREFACE — XIII
Ian Johnstone and Michael Powles

1. **A PACIFIC OVERVIEW** — 1
   Ian Johnstone and Michael Powles

2. **SAMOA** — 17
   Background — 18
   Leader's story: Tui Atua Tupua Tamasese Ta'isi Efi — 21
   Leader's story: Tofilau Eti Alesana — 26
   Some significant events since independence (1962) — 31

3. **THE COOK ISLANDS** — 35
   Background — 36
   Leader's story: John Webb — 39
   Leader's story: Sir Tom Davis — 44
   Some significant events since self-government (1965) — 50

4. **NAURU** — 53
   Background — 54
   Leader's story: Dr Ludwig Keke — 59
   Some significant events since independence (1968) — 66

5. **TONGA** — 69
   Background — 70
   Leader's story: King Taufa'ahau Tupou IV — 74

Some significant events since the return to full
independence (1970)   81

6. **FIJI**   **85**
   Background   86
   Leader's story: Ratu Sir Kamisese Mara   93
   Some significant events since independence (1970)   104

7. **NIUE**   **107**
   Background   108
   Leader's story: Mititaiagimene Young Vivian   111
   Some significant events since self-government (1974)   117

8. **PAPUA NEW GUINEA**   **119**
   Background   120
   Leader's story: Sir Michael Somare   125
   Some significant events since independence (1975)   136

9. **SOLOMON ISLANDS**   **139**
   Background   140
   Leader's story: Solomon Mamaloni   144
   Leader's story: Sir Peter Kenilorea   149
   Leader's story: Solomon Mamaloni again   156
   Some significant events since independence (1978)   159

10. **TUVALU**   **163**
    Background   164
    Leader's story: Hon. Bikenibeu Paeniu   166
    Some significant events since independence (1978)   177

11. **KIRIBATI**   **181**
    Background   182
    Leader's story: Sir Ieremia Tabai   186
    Some significant events since independence (1979)   196

12. VANUATU	**199**
Background	200
Leader's story: Fr Walter Lini	203
Some significant events since independence (1980)	213
13. FEDERATED STATES OF MICRONESIA	**217**
Background	218
Leader's story: John Haglelgam	220
Some significant events since independence (1986)	229
14. MARSHALL ISLANDS	**231**
Background	232
Leader's story: Kessai Note	236
Some significant events since independence (1986)	246
15. PALAU	**249**
Background	250
Leader's story: Sandra Sumang Pierantozzi	252
Some significant events since ratification of the Compact of Free Association (1994)	261
16. PERSPECTIVES OF PACIFIC WOMEN	**265**
Background	266
Leader's story: Hon. Fiame Naomi Mata'afa	270
Leader's story: Dame Carol Kidu	280
17. CONCLUSION	**291**
Ian Johnstone and Michael Powles	
ADDITIONAL READING	**307**
BIBLIOGRAPHY	**313**
INDEX	**317**
THE EDITORS	**325**
NEW FLAGS FLYING — PACIFIC LEADERSHIP: AUDIO CD	**328**

FOREWORD

BY SIR ANAND SATYANAND

The vast Pacific Islands region covers nearly 30 million square kilometres of sea. It is home to some 13 million people in New Zealand and the other island countries, apart from Australia and Hawai'i. The total, albeit sparsely flung, land mass is some 550,000 square kilometres, more than two-thirds being Papua New Guinea. The people living in the Pacific speak more than 800 languages, again most of these based in Papua New Guinea. The area is subject to many natural disasters, such as recurring cyclones, floods, earthquakes and droughts. The man-made difficulties include, without dwelling in detail, differing governance and institutional arrangements, irregular legislation, and the proximity of corruption — yet abiding and substantial coping mechanisms keep things in operation despite these huge challenges.

New Flags Flying – Pacific Leadership brings together in one collection the hopes and voices of many of the region's first leaders following the achievement of self-government or independence during the past fifty years. The editors, each of whom has had some kind of professional or personal association with the Pacific, capture the viewpoints of many of those leaders like Sir Tom Davis of the Cook Islands, Ratu Sir Kamisese Mara of Fiji, Sir Peter Kenilorea of Solomon Islands, King Taufa'ahau Tupou IV of Tonga and Father Walter Lini of Vanuatu, to name just a few.

The hopes and aspirations expressed by these office holders for their people are special.

Many issues, including their own upbringing, are canvassed. These include their description of the attitudes and treatment of the colonial powers, the moves to self-government and independence, and their hopes and fears for an independent future. As new Pacific leaders face new challenges, the hopes and aspirations of their forebears can sometimes provide valuable guidance.

The aspect of continuance of connection is borne out by observing that many of the Pacific's leaders of the present and very recent past, such as Dr Feleti Sevele, former Prime Minister of Tonga, and Tuilaepa Lupesoliai Sailele Malielegaoi, Prime Minister of Samoa, undertook parts of their education in New Zealand.

In my view, as very much a Pacific person myself, the work will make a significant and lasting contribution to knowledge of the issues which faced the region in the past and which in a number of ways endure to the present.

The book will be a valuable resource for students and academics interested in the Pacific and development studies, and will provide a challenge for politicians and policymakers throughout the region to 'play their best game'.

I congratulate the editors and commend their initiative.

Anand Satyanand

February 2012, Wellington

Rt. Hon. Sir Anand Satyanand was born in Auckland New Zealand to parents from Fiji whose own parents had come from India. He also has family links with Samoa. A lawyer, judge and ombudsman in his time before serving as New Zealand's Governor-General for five years, he maintains a number of associations with other Pacific countries.

PREFACE

In 1992, after the deaths of Hammer DeRoburt, Albert Henry and Sir Robert Rex, the Director of the South Pacific Division of New Zealand's Ministry of Foreign Affairs and Trade, Gordon Shroff, wrote to Deputy-Secretary Graham Fortune '... we may be losing the opportunity to record for posterity leaders' views of their countries' progress to independence ...'.

A grant was promptly approved to assist Radio New Zealand International to gather interviews with Pacific leaders.

Radio New Zealand International Manager Linden Clark commissioned broadcaster Ian Johnstone to gather as many interviews as could be arranged with the help of New Zealand's High Commissions in the Pacific.

Over the next three years, conversations were recorded with leaders from Samoa, Cook Islands, Tonga, Fiji, Papua New Guinea, Solomon Islands and Vanuatu. The recordings were broadcast and then lodged in the Radio New Zealand International Archive. With increasing frequency, extracts were re-used in obituary tributes.

In 2009, after Pacific students had told him how difficult it was to find information about the recent history of their countries, Johnstone began to look for ways to make the 'leadership interviews' more widely and easily available. He made no progress until good friend Michael Powles, former senior diplomat and founding chair of the Pacific Co-operation Foundation, volunteered his help as co-editor.

NEW FLAGS FLYING

Over the next two years, with support from the agencies and people listed below, the co-editors interviewed leaders from those self-governing and independent nations that had not been covered earlier (Nauru, Niue, Tuvalu, Kiribati, Federated States of Micronesia, Marshall Islands and Palau). Excellent material was also gathered from three distinguished women leaders (Fiame Naomi Mata'afa, Dame Carol Kidu and Sandra Sumang Pierantozzi).

The contributions from all these leaders, with introductions and explanations by the co-editors, were assembled into a seventeen-part web-site (www.rnzi.com/newflagsflying). Graciously launched in August 2011 by the then Governor-General of New Zealand, Sir Anand Satyanand, it has been warmly received. However, difficult and unreliable Internet access in many Pacific areas means that the stories, experiences and insights carried within *New Flags Flying – Pacific Leadership* are still not fully available to the students, teachers and others who would most value and benefit from them.

It is the great hope of the co-editors that copies of this book and disc produced by Huia Publishers of Wellington will find their way into Pacific and other classrooms, libraries and homes and will inform, inspire and delight all those young people seeking to build on the foundations laid by the leaders who, not very long ago, set new flags flying across our Pacific ocean.

The editors are grateful for help from:

Brian Lynch; Tony Johns; Hugh Laracy; Margaret Pointer; Michael Field; Tahu Hikoroa; Margaret Keni; Rhys Richards; Alison Quentin-Baxter; Annette Note; Teresia Teiawa; John Laming; Christopher Chevalier; Giff Johnson; Roger Clark; Karen McDowell; Anna Powles; Guy Powles; Linden Clark; Gordon Shroff.

PREFACE

UNESCO office in Apia; Radio New Zealand; Pacific Islands Forum Secretariat: New Zealand Ministry of Foreign Affairs and Trade; Pacific Co-operation Foundation; New Zealand Institute of International Affairs, and two agencies whose support has made possible the production and wide distribution of this book and disc – the Pacific Leadership Program of AusAid and the Pacific Development and Conservation Trust.

Views expressed in *New Flags Flying – Pacific Leadership* are those of the contributors or editors and are not necessarily endorsed by any supporting people or agencies. Errors and omissions are the responsibility of contributors or the editors, who welcome comments to newflagsflying@gmail.com

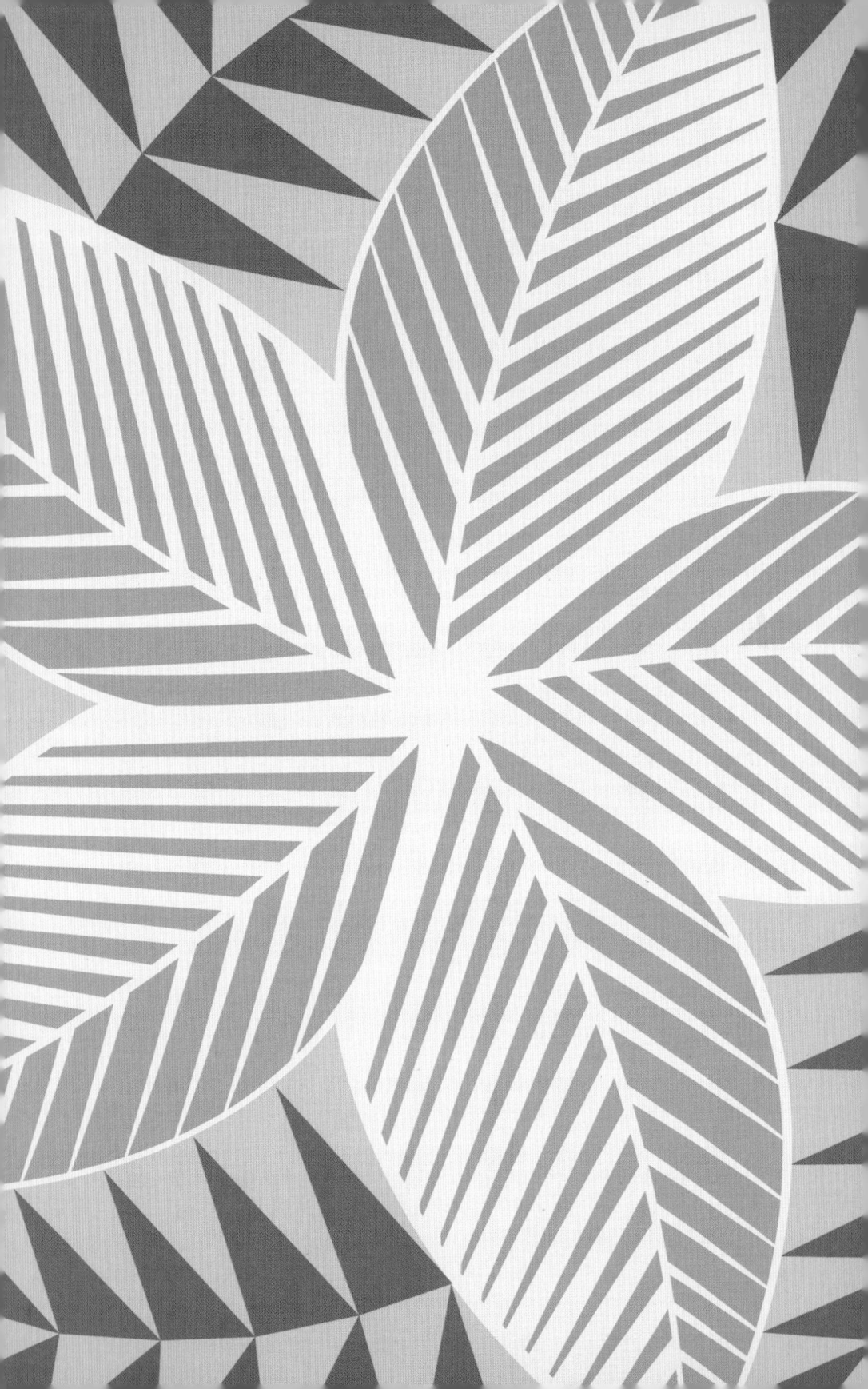

A PACIFIC OVERVIEW

CHAPTER ONE

Ian Johnstone and Michael Powles

I thought, you are as much prepared for it now as you ever will be ...

Sir Peter Kenilorea

PI Forum Secretariat

PREPARATION FOR LEADERSHIP

After World War II, in the late 1940s and '50s, most of the leaders who tell their stories in *New Flags Flying* were away from their homelands studying at schools, training colleges or universities, three or four in Britain and Australia, most of them in New Zealand.

A PACIFIC OVERVIEW

For two sons of influential families, Tonga's future King Taufa'ahau and Fijian aristocrat Kamisese Mara, an overseas education was a matter of course, but most of the others, from humbler backgrounds, had gone away only because they had earned good marks at primary school and won government scholarships. Winning those scholarships, then studying for years in unfamiliar schools and colleges and gaining a degree or diploma earmarked them for leadership. When they came home they would join the tiny group of academically qualified Pacific Islanders and work as economists, doctors, teachers, priests, accountants, and public servants for governments, businesses or church missions.

CHANGES IN THE OLD ORDER

But even as these men returned to Rarotonga, Honiara, Suva, Tarawa and other Pacific capitals to take up those jobs, they must have noticed how the islands they had left as schoolboys were changing.

The established order in the Pacific had been fractured by war. Supposedly great powers had been humbled by the Japanese. Servicemen from the Pacific had travelled and fought for freedom and individual rights. Experiences recalled by Sir Tom Davis in chapter three, and Sir Peter Kenilorea and Solomon Mamaloni in chapter nine, show that old notions of racial superiority were under challenge. In Asia and Africa, the British and French empires to which most Pacific Islanders had 'belonged' were beginning to break down. At first, news of such change was discounted because, as Ratu Sir Kamisese Mara comments in chapter six, 'we thought it was a remote hurricane warning, that would never come to Fiji'.

Julia Brooke-White Collection

NEW OPPORTUNITIES

Other Pacific Islanders were keen to run their own affairs, and ready to take advantage of the new opportunities history had brought them. In chapter two, Tofilau Eti Alesana tells how proud Samoa was to be the first Pacific country to achieve self-government.

Other leaders followed as they began to discern that instead of guiding and helping their people in a hospital ward, government office or classroom, they now had to change direction and learn to be politicians. Through the 1960s, each leader came to realise that his people – or their colonial governors – had decided his country was to become self-governing or independent and, like it or not, his task was to lead his people there.

NEW ROLES

Some, like Hammer DeRoburt, Sir Michael Somare, Solomon Mamaloni and Albert Henry were more than ready to take on that task and pushed their Australian, British and New Zealand governors to follow the example set in Samoa: withdraw and let them take over leadership of their country. Others were less keen. Sir Peter Kenilorea would have preferred to remain a public servant and Ratu Sir Kamisese Mara wanted to become a doctor, until each was instructed that his duty lay elsewhere. Kessai Note and Father Walter Lini seem to have accepted they would have to lead if their countries were to be freed from powerful and intransigent rule. Leaders like Sir Ieremia Tabai, Young Vivian and Sir Tom Davis seemed simply to acknowledge that independence is preferable to servitude, and they were ready to do whatever was needed to bring it about. Bikenibeu Paeniu recalls that for Tuvalu's early leaders that meant facing the challenge of building a nation from half a colony, and with very few resources.

POPULAR RESPECT

The leaders had two very valuable assets. The first was that each could count on the respect and support of his people. In some cases, that was because of their chiefly or privileged background. These included Tonga's King Taufa'ahau Tupou IV, Tupua Tamasese Lealofi IV, a key leader in Samoa at independence, Chief Hammer DeRoburt of Nauru and Ratu Sir Kamisese Mara of Fiji, whose noble rank and personal mana gave him authority among Fijians and Indo-Fijians alike. Others with clear chiefly connections were Sir Tom Davis of the Cook Islands and Sir Robert Rex of Niue.

Some, such as Sir Michael Somare of Papua New Guinea, Albert Henry of the Cook Islands, and Solomon Mamaloni of Solomon Islands were admired for their charisma, political adroitness and ability. Sir Ieremia Tabai of Kiribati and Bikenibeu Paeniu of Tuvalu were well-informed, and respected for their courageous example. Churchmen Father Walter Lini of Vanuatu and Sir Peter

Kenilorea of Solomon Islands inspired confidence through their firm religious belief.

TRUST AMONG LEADERS

The other important asset enjoyed by these distinctively Pacific men (and it is, perhaps, a distinctively Pacific advantage) is that they knew and trusted each other. The patricians of Samoa, Tonga and Fiji were linked by blood and marriage; others had common church connections; a number had forged friendships at New Zealand schools and colleges. All had a common purpose – a successful move to self-government or independence for their country – and it was important, especially for the smaller countries, that they should be able to talk frankly to each other about the challenges they faced.

Opportunities for such talk occurred at gatherings such as South Pacific Conferences (the plenary meetings of the South Pacific Commission, now known as the Secretariat of the Pacific Community) held annually in Noumea or another Pacific capital. Funded by Australia, Britain, France, New Zealand and the United States, the commission provided Pacific territories and colonies with technical help, from agricultural production to language teaching. However, when regional leaders gathered to consider the work programme, discussion of political matters was forbidden. This prohibition was vigilantly policed by the representatives of France, anxious to ensure that talk of self-government did not 'infect' delegates from New Caledonia, Wallis and Futuna, and French Polynesia, the territories France controlled and wished to keep controlling. Not surprisingly, leaders found ways round this ban, discussing topics that were really important to them –

constitutions, timetables, negotiations and the like – informally, vigorously, and sometimes late into the night until the session was brought to a close with Albert Henry's famous ukulele rendition of 'Pearly Shells'.

THE COLONIAL POWERS

Meeting each other at those conferences gave leaders the chance to compare notes about their controlling powers: Australia, ready to grant independence; Britain, keen to do the same for all its colonies; France, anxious to keep control of its territories and delay self-government in the Franco-British Condominium the New Hebrides; New Zealand, itself part of Polynesia, ready to combine self-government with continuing support for its former colonies; and the United States, determined that the other colonial powers should decolonise but equally determined to keep control of most of its Pacific possessions.

The most potent, overarching international impetus came from the United Nations, founded in 1945. The Labour government then in power in New Zealand was strongly committed to decolonisation and its prime minister, Peter Fraser, played a major role in the drafting of a large section of the new United Nations Charter. This section recognised a right to self-determination and established a trusteeship system under which many colonial dependencies and trust territories would achieve independence. Through the 1960s and 1970s, the United Nations was an important source of encouragement and support for Pacific territories, most of whom were among the world's last – and, some might claim, most poorly prepared – to achieve self-government or independence.

NEW FLAGS FLYING

Julia Brooke-White Collection

READINESS TO CHANGE

Some leaders would have been happy to continue under colonial rule. Ratu Sir Kamisese Mara, sometimes a titled English gentleman, sometimes a high chief wholly committed to traditional ways, acknowledges in chapter six that he had no sense the colonial period was ending because 'we were part of the Queen's regnum; we were happy – why should we change things? ... I belonged to the school that believed we should never be parted from the United Kingdom ... we ceded our islands, as far as we're concerned, we've given the authority – how can we bring it back? This is not chiefly.'

Other leaders were more philosophical. Sir Ieremia Tabai of Kiribati and Bikenibeu Paeniu of Tuvalu give the clear impression of accepting as a fact of life that Britain was departing. In chapter ten Bikenibeu Paeniu remembers 'Of course they wanted rid of us as soon as possible, because we know in those days Britain was letting go of her colonies, the empire was breaking down.'

Although Bikenibeu Paeniu believes his country needed more time to prepare for independence, the leaders of Samoa, Nauru and the Cook Islands wanted self-government for their countries as soon as possible. One of the most outstanding leaders in these early days was Tupua Tamasese Mea'ole, in many ways the guiding force leading Samoa to independence. A large and formidable-looking man, able and respected, he was kind, gentle and always courteous. His son, Tui Atua Tupua Tamasese Ta'isi Efi, later to become head of state, explains in chapter two the success of the small group of Samoans and New Zealanders who brought his country to independence: 'There wasn't argument. There wasn't the emotion, the drama. These personalities dealt successfully with the complex issues because of the people that they were.'

The 'small group': L–R, Samoa's first Prime Minister, Hon. Fiame Mata'afa; Hon. Tupua Tamasese; New Zealand Minister of Island Territories, Hon. J Mathieson; High Commissioner of Western Samoa, Mr G R Powles; Hon. Malietoa Tanumafili
New Zealand Ministry of Foreign Affairs and Trade

NEW ZEALAND TERRITORIES FIRST

Samoa led the way to independence in 1962 and the Cook Islands followed in 1965 when it became self-governing in free association with New Zealand. Both were proud of being trail blazers, not just because their freedom came so early, but also because of the unique aspects of the constitutional arrangements that were agreed.

In Samoa's case the original constitution recognised tradition and custom in according suffrage only to *matai*. This unique voting system lasted nearly thirty years.

A PACIFIC OVERVIEW

In a 2006 referendum, citizens of Tokelau voted to remain members of a non-self-governing territory within the Realm of New Zealand.
Photographer Michael Field
Michael Field Collection

The Cook Islands (and later Niue) also broke new ground constitutionally when they negotiated with New Zealand forms of self-government which met their particular needs. As Cook Islands official John Webb explains in chapter three, 'I thought we were very lucky. I saw it as a mark in history and I thought "Good old New Zealand – here's a little country come up with something which I'm sure a lot of other countries will follow"'.

THE OLD MASTERS AND THEIR LEGACIES

Self-determination and independence were just the first steps in empowering Pacific peoples. The early leaders faced many varied challenges. The colonisation of no two Pacific countries had been alike. Some had experienced Spanish rule dating back to the seventeenth century. Indeed, all the major imperial powers – France, Britain, Germany, the United States, the Netherlands – took control of territories in the Pacific and ruled them for periods in the nineteenth and twentieth centuries.

Sometimes Pacific islands 'changed hands' and suffered more than one colonial ruler – although only one, Vanuatu, had the particular pain of being ruled by Britain and France at the same time. Father Walter Lini, prime minister of Vanuatu, recalls in chapter twelve: 'The French and the British did not do anything to develop us. They waited and waited until we saw, ourselves, how we should begin to move to get self-reliance, no, self-government and independence .... I became mad because the French were deliberately trying to tell us lies and deliberately trying to show that they were in control, not us.'

One country, Tuvalu, was in effect sliced from the previous Gilbert and Ellice Islands Colony and had to start life with no central administration or infrastructure. Bikenibeu Paeniu, a former prime minister, remembers in chapter ten that Tuvalu had to 'form a nation of our own and be given no assets and a mere budgetary provision. All the colonial assets were left with Kiribati. We had only one ship.'

Different challenges were thrown up by the different motivations of colonial powers, whose presence in the Pacific was certainly driven by self-interest. Greed was a factor; access to the cheap phosphate deposits of Nauru and Ocean Island being a good example. Security concerns were also important, as with American determination to retain the deep harbour at Pago Pago in American Samoa and to conduct nuclear tests in Micronesia.

Access to resources and the pursuit of trade were clearly behind the activities of Germany and France around the end of the nineteenth century. And more generally, the 'partition' of the Pacific islands was strongly influenced by the ever-changing dynamics between and among the colonial powers of the day. Britain, for example, could not countenance its European competitors stealing a march on it, even in the remote Pacific. Britain was also persuaded by public opinion in Australia and New Zealand to play a more active part in the colonisation of the region than many policy-makers in London might have preferred.

PROFIT AND LOSS

Many subjective comparisons have been made between the respective virtues and vices of the different colonial powers. It has been said, for example, that Germany was known for the efficiency of its colonial administration in the early days; that Britain placed beneficial emphasis on the education sector; and that France actively discouraged the study of indigenous languages.

In terms of colonial exploitation, Australia, Britain and New Zealand reaped enormous benefits from Nauru and Banaba (formerly Ocean Island) phosphate, and France similarly profited from New Caledonian nickel. The United States gained benefit, presumably, from conducting nuclear tests in Micronesia, and the same applied in respect of French nuclear testing in French Polynesia. And today Guam is being developed into a major base to enable the United States to maintain a forward military presence in the wider Pacific. The economic and strategic gains made by the United Kingdom, Australia and New Zealand were smaller but still significant. New Zealand, for example, has benefited considerably from the infusion of hundreds of thousands of Pacific islanders into its society and economy.

Inevitably, colonial rule had an impact, directly or indirectly, on the peoples of the Pacific, but it was unevenly felt. For those affected by nuclear testing in Micronesia and French Polynesia, it was catastrophic. For others it had some benefits – Bikenibeu Paeniu of Tuvalu remembers high educational standards and comments that, compared to its neighbours, '... Tuvalu is far far better off in terms of education. That is one good thing Britain did.'

For many, in the highlands of Papua New Guinea or on remote Pacific atolls, the impact of colonial rule was slight. Overall, it probably influenced the lives of Pacific Islanders less than many Westerners would assume. Although educational opportunities and prospects for advancement have improved in many countries, subsistence lifestyle, family and the ocean remain at the heart of most Pacific cultures. Tongan historian Epeli Hau'ofa acknowledged this when he wrote: 'Nineteenth century imperialism erected boundaries that led to the contraction of Oceania, transforming a once boundless world into the Pacific island states and territories that we know today. ... It was continental men, Europeans and Americans, who drew imaginary lines across the sea, making the colonial boundaries that today define the island states and territories of the Pacific.'

Hau'ofa laments colonialism's 'contraction of Oceania' but is confident that decolonisation can undo those unwelcome changes. Foreign descriptions of Oceania as a Spanish Lake, a British Lake, an American Lake are short-lived '... we all know that only those who make the ocean their home and love it, can really claim it as theirs.' (Hau'ofa 1993: 2–16.)

Here are the stories of the men and women who led Pacific peoples as they reclaimed their ocean and their homes.

A PACIFIC OVERVIEW

Julia Brooke-White Collection

REFERENCE:

Hau'ofa, E., 'Our Sea of Islands' in Hau'ofa, E. (ed). *A New Oceania: Rediscovering our Sea of Islands*. Suva: University of the South Pacific and Beake House, 1993, 2–16.

SAMOA

◆

CHAPTER TWO

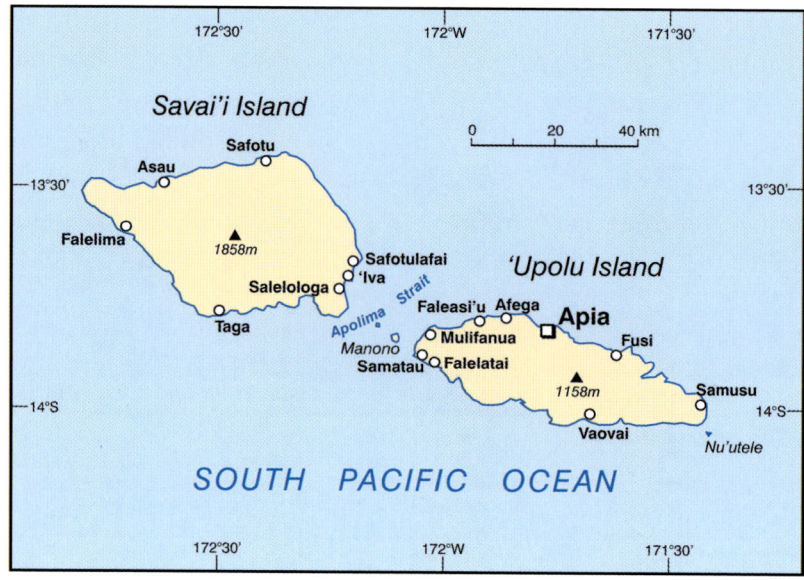

B Bradley, Cartographic Art Company

BACKGROUND

Samoa was one of the first island groups settled by the people later called Polynesians. Descendants of Austronesian language-speakers who originated in East Asia, they arrived in Samoa more than 3000 years ago. Archaeological evidence, tradition and genealogies indicate inter-island voyaging and intermarriage between Samoans, Fijians and Tongans before European explorers reached the Pacific.

Colonial competition

Contact with Europeans began in the eighteenth century. Early French explorer, Louis-Antoine Bougainville, named Samoa the Navigator Islands after witnessing the navigational prowess of Samoans in ocean canoes. The first formalised colonial governments were determined by agreement among competing imperial powers Germany, Great Britain and the United States at the 1889 Berlin Conference. While Britain withdrew in exchange for uncontested colonial spoils elsewhere, the United States annexed the eastern islands (American Samoa) and Germany took what came to be called Western Samoa.

Germany and then New Zealand

German rule continued from the turn of the twentieth century until New Zealand troops, at Britain's request, occupied Western Samoa without opposition in August 1914 until the end of the military administration in 1919. From the end of World War I until independence in 1962, New Zealand governed Western Samoa first under mandate from the League of Nations, and, after 1945, under a United Nations trusteeship. During those forty-three years, two fatal mistakes caused much suffering and understandable ill-will towards the New Zealand administration. Thousands of Samoans died in the 1918–9 epidemic of influenza after infected passengers aboard SS *Talune* were allowed entry by the New Zealand administration in breach of quarantine regulations. Over the following decade, the Mau movement emerged in opposition and in the course of a peaceful Mau demonstration on 'Black Saturday' in 1929, one of the country's highest chiefs, Tupua Tamasese Lealofi III, was killed by New Zealand police gunfire.

Independence – the first in the Pacific

Tensions eased after 1935 when New Zealand's new Labour government introduced a more tolerant administration in Samoa. In *The Pacific Islands – an encyclopaedia*, authors Lal and Fortune note:

Mau leader Tamasese, later killed by New Zealand Police, with his committee outside Mau office at Vaimoso, Samoa; 1929
Photographer Alfred Tattersall
F J Gleeson Collection, Alexander Turnbull Library, Wellington, NZ. PA1-o-795-49

By the end of the World War II the climate had changed, assisted by the influence of American troops stationed in Samoa, and the role of Peter Fraser, New Zealand's Prime Minister and Minister of Island Territories, in the 1945 drafting of the United Nations Charter. (Western) Samoa became a [Trust Territory] of the United Nations, administered by New Zealand, and the process of devolution leading to independence was under way. (Lal and Fortune 2000: 608.)

After a constitutional convention, responsible government was gradually introduced over several years. A draft constitution, approved by the United Nations, was endorsed by a universal plebiscite in May 1961 and independence followed on 1 January 1962.

The constitution and *fa'a Samoa*

Samoa was not only the first Pacific Island country to achieve independence but its constitution remains unique in its initial meld of Western principles of representative government with Samoan custom, or *fa'a Samoa*. A voting system restricting suffrage to chiefly titleholders, *matai*, lasted nearly thirty years until universal suffrage was introduced by plebiscite in 1990. On independence the role of Samoa's first prime minister went to Fiame Mata'afa Mulinu'u II, a descendant of one of the four *tama'aiga*, high chiefly families.

The constitution provided that the two *fautua* (highest chiefs), who had jointly chaired the Constitutional Convention of 1959, should become joint heads of state on independence and continue for their lifetimes. Tupua Tamasese Mea'ole held office until his death in 1963 and Malietoa Tanumafili II until his death in May 2007.

From then on, the legislative assembly elected a head of state for a five year term. Political parties did not emerge until many years after independence and then mostly around the competing personalities of Tui Atua Tupua Tamasese Ta'isi Efi and Tofilau Eti Alesana, the two leaders featured in this chapter (see Crocombe 2001:459–60).

LEADER'S STORY: TUI ATUA TUPUA TAMASESE TA'ISI EFI

Tui Atua Tupua Tamasese Ta'isi Efi is a son of one of the original heads of state, Tupua Tamasese Mea'ole, and a nephew of the leader of the Mau movement, Tupua Tamasese Lealofi III, who died when police opened fire on unarmed marchers in December 1929. He served as prime minister from 1976 to 1982 and was elected head of state in 2007. He has studied and written about the long relationship between Samoa and New Zealand.

◆ ◆ ◆

Tui Atua Tupua Tamasese Ta'isi Efi
PI Forum Secretariat

In the early twentieth century many New Zealand political and professional leaders thought their country should incorporate nearby places including Samoa. Later, under Prime Minister W F Massey, that seems to have become the official New Zealand government view. When the New Zealand army did come to Samoa, in 1914, I don't think there was any great resistance. Despite the overwhelming German presence there was a very strong feeling in Samoa for the Brits, due to British missionaries and British and American entrepreneurs, and New Zealand was a part of the Brit camp. On the other hand, people who had benefited from German patronage sang sad songs about being parted from their ways after they were ousted by New Zealand.

The first significant disenchantment had to do with the 'flu epidemic of 1918 and that demolished the image of British efficiency, British caring. In awful circumstances, a third of the population got wiped out. I think the image of the white man's superiority was greatly set back by the epidemic, by the negligence and lack of caring.

Then there was heavy-handedness during the Mau period and on top of that people like Nelson and others were demonstrating they could run businesses better than the administration. This was most unusual because during the German regime, whatever else, the Germans demonstrated they had the technology and the personnel and the will to show they could run things better than anyone. They ran the plantations well, they ran the stores well, and Samoa was relatively prosperous. When you compare the German record with the New Zealand record, there was certainly a downturn economically under New Zealand and there was no match between the calibre of the people. On top of that, the locals were demonstrating they could handle these things very well.

Pressure for independence developed within Samoa and was influenced from overseas. Nelson and the more enlightened among the independence movement in Samoa had links with Evatt in Australia and Sir Stafford Cripps in Britain. Through them they had links with Irish and Indian nationalists and this tended to create a moral and intellectual impetus. The movement permeated international leadership so that people were united politically and by a shared vision. As a result you had Cripps not only plugging very strongly for us at the League of Nations but also, with others, helping the Indians and the Irish.

I wasn't involved when a new constitution was being devised. I came in when independence was well established, but my father was closely involved. For him it was all quite problematic. On the one hand you had the commercial sector being very suspicious about self-government and independence — as in most other colonies. On top of that you had also traditional rivalries. The great task our leaders faced was how to blend all this in order to find consensus. It wasn't easy.

Bear in mind that we hadn't run our affairs since 1900 and even before then, from the 1880s until the 1900s, there was chaos.

During this period input from the colonial powers was a critical factor in the political equation. People got into power because of patronage from Great Britain, the United States or Germany – and they lost power when the patronage was withdrawn. And later the New Zealanders came. Overall, though, there was the sense that Samoans came out the losers. The big job for our leaders was to sell the idea to people that we are *not* born losers, it's not our fate to keep on losing and that in fact there are prospects of doing better through independence. We were taking a plunge that no one else in the Pacific was.

In some ways Samoans continued to run their own affairs no matter which colonial administration was in operation. Our people had a genius for operating a system that would ensure that by and large the power would still rest with them. That was tolerated up to a point. As soon as they impinged on the interests of the imperial powers then you had a scuffle.

Overall, our constitution served our purposes, although I wonder whether like any other constitution, it requires a bit of refurbishing. I think it was envisioned that it would be reviewed in twenty or twenty-five years and I don't think we've really had that as yet. Maybe we should do it. But by and large I think the Samoan constitution was a pattern that people accepted as something that's worth emulating. People are always going to put in some things that suit their own peculiar conditions, but by and large it was accepted by others as a good example that was worth looking at.

The popular plebiscite figures in 1961 of five to one showed that people wanted to take on independence. I remember on Independence Day feelings of pride, of expectancy and of achievement. And I think these were generally shared by people.

Of the challenges faced then by my father and other leaders, the greatest, considering our history, was whether we could ensure that the constitution would not come unstuck with people going their disparate ways, provoking internecine strife. Judged from that standpoint I would say the constitution was very successful. Its provision for joint heads of state initially had some precedent from the later part of the nineteenth century when in a number of cases Samoans suggested that the honours at the top should be shared.

When asked how well the country was prepared for independence by its colonial masters it's fashionable to say that our patron could have done better by us. There was a general attempt by the administrators, which was not unusual, to keep the level of education of the indigenous people at a certain relatively low point. They did this to ensure they did not invest in potential revolutionaries or disruptive elements. There is always a supposition that if you educate a subject race, potentially you are creating a challenge or a threat to your own authority. It was actually government policy that natives were not supposed to go beyond a certain standard in education. I think that fitted in with the traditional Tory mindset. And in fact even for a long time after the Labour people got in we still had this standard imposed on schools. If you were native and you didn't have a European name or whatever, you were supposed to be educated at a different school or you were supposed to reach a certain standard and no more. In fact the only people who resisted that government edict were the Marist Brothers school. Just about everybody else went along, including the Marist sisters.

In judging how well Samoa has managed since independence, one has to acknowledge people who were brought in from the United States or from the United Nations because their input was quite considerable. But the most significant contribution came from the people who were directly involved, in this case the New Zealanders and the Samoans. On the New Zealand side you had prime ministers and foreign affairs people and then people like Sir Guy Powles, Colin Aikman, Jim Davidson. When you read what I wrote about the New Zealand and Samoa relations there's the temptation to de-emphasise or underestimate the contribution of these people. All these guys, including my father, they had the very practical task of trying to build or construct a blend that was acceptable to people. Now that's not easy. I want to acknowledge their contribution. There wasn't strain or confrontation among them. There wasn't argument. There wasn't the emotion, the drama. These personalities dealt successfully with the complex issues because of the people that they were.

So I would mark the performance quite highly.

LEADER'S STORY: TOFILAU ETI ALESANA

Tofilau Eti Alesana, who died in 1999, was prime minister from 1982 to 1985 and from 1988 to 1998, a total of thirteen years. Although he was born on American Samoa's main island of Tutuila, he was brought up in Western Samoa when it was administered by New Zealand. Tofilau became known as a noted orator, gaining him much respect in Samoan society. He became the youngest member of Samoa's first Cabinet in 1959. As prime minister, he presided over a vigorous drive to prepare Samoa for the economic challenges of the next century.

There had been troubles under German rule, including a rebellion following which the ringleaders were exiled to the Marshall Islands. The Germans had not been very impressed with the way Samoans organised themselves, with the *matai* system. But the Germans implemented one policy — banning the sale of native land to foreigners — which was very advantageous to the Samoan people. The policy was continued by the New Zealanders and on independence it was enacted in our constitution. This policy was especially important because we don't have all that much land to live on and cultivate. We are certainly enjoying the fruits of the policy now.

Tofilau Eti Alesana
PI Forum Secretariat

New Zealand governed us under a mandate of the League of Nations initially and, according to what I heard, they were a bit like the Germans. Samoans in their *matai* system have their own cultural and traditional way of dealing with things. And that is exactly what New Zealand and Germany should have exploited. Unfortunately, the advice to them was not to because it was thought the chiefs, the *matai* system, were primitive. They wanted to educate the people in their ways but there was a clash of systems. Samoan custom and tradition and the *matai* system were our well established heritage. But when the colonialists came they thought what they introduced was best and people should adhere to it. That caused a clash.

Some legislation during New Zealand's regime showed signs of discrimination. I can recall one statute, the Samoa Amendment Act of 1949. In that act, Fiji School of Medicine graduates were prevented from practising medicine on their own. They had to be under the control of a *palagi* doctor — someone who had graduated from the UK or Northern Ireland. It was very restrictive. Samoan doctors were known as 'native medical practitioners'.

Samoa was certainly ahead of many others seeking independence, certainly in the Pacific. But independence was not just handed over – it was through the harsh negotiating on the part of the Samoans.

One of the main things we had to thrash out was economic development. We needed to see more investment in Samoa because there wasn't enough. And the other important aspects we wanted to see developed were education and health. New Zealand provided some assistance with health, every now and then sending patients to New Zealand. But less so with education. When we became independent in 1962, our education was levelled at the sixth form. Samoa College had been established by New Zealand but it was only up to the sixth form, university entrance. After independence we opted to establish our own university. The scholarships offered to Samoa by New Zealand and Australia were totally insufficient to cope with the need.

We had no models to follow – no one else in the region was independent yet. We had a working committee preparing the new constitution. We had to give serious thought to ensuring peace into the future. In our system the royal families of Samoa from time to time select a paramount chief to be their royal son. It was all part of *fa'a Samoa*, with its royal families and an authoritative body of orators. The salutation in Samoa is 'chiefs, orators, the people of Samoa … '

When we became independent, the two *fautua* became joint heads of state. After that, when one passes away, the remaining one would keep on as the sole head of state, for life. When he dies he will be replaced by one successor chosen by Parliament – not by the royal families because in the past that was sometimes a cause of warfare between the royal families. Now it is democratised …

On the Council of Deputies, the working committee on self-government considered the position of the four royal sons at the time and decided two would become joint heads of state. What about the other two? One of these two was prime minister at the time, leaving only one. So we established a Council of Deputies, whose members could deputise for one of the heads of state if that person should be unable to perform his duties.

We didn't go along with the United Nations' desire that newly independent countries should have a one-man-one-vote electoral system. Only the *matais* were entitled to vote under our constitution. And what happened? There was a multiplication of *matais* … only because they wanted to vote. So we decided that maybe the answer to this unnecessary making of *matais* was to opt for universal suffrage. It was not very simple to achieve that. We had to propose that the country undertake a plebiscite referendum and the percentage of those who voted yes for universal suffrage was 57 percent I think.

Our first decision was for Samoa to become a self-governing state – we did not opt for independence. But during the course of our deliberations for our final constitutional convention, it was moved by someone and discussed that the country should become a full independent state. Someone suggested that there must still be a treaty of friendship between Samoa and New Zealand.

While we were the first country in the Pacific to achieve independence we did not adopt the feeling that we were travelling on a one-way street. We thought we were travelling on a multi-faceted street for the future – economically, socially – and with stability. Although we thought that the constitution provided every means and way of maintaining stability in the country,

Daily flag raising ceremony by Samoa police band, Apia; 1996
Photographer Julia Brooke-White
Julia Brooke-White Collection

nobody knew that for sure at the time. As a matter of fact, it was prophesied by some people that on the day of independence New Zealand, still hiding behind their grievance against Western Samoa because Samoa wanted to become independent, was preparing some battleships to come and bombard Samoa. That was the very first day of judgement. So I was looking out to see if there would be a fleet of battleships!

Did independence happen too early or too late? There are two answers to this: in certain aspects it was too early, and in other aspects it was a little bit too late. When I say too early, that is based on insufficient preparation with economic measures. And when I say it was too late, Samoans should have been taught how to run their affairs earlier.

On the continued division of the country into American Samoa and Samoa, when we submitted our petition to the United Nations for Samoa to become self-governing, it consisted of three subject matters. One was for Samoa to become a self-governing state; secondly for the lands that were taken by New Zealand from the Germans as reparation estates to be reverted to Samoa; and thirdly, for the two Samoas to be reunited. So we have completed the first and second parts, but not the third one.

Some people have praised me for our progress since independence, and thanked me, and I said, don't thank me, thank the people because the government's responsibility is to invent proposals and then introduce them. If the people rejected them, what would be the position of the government? So I wholeheartedly give thanks to the Samoan people – to the public – to everyone in the country. It's entirely dependent on the stability of the country. I mean that really is an asset. If you can pacify, if you can stabilise your country, that is the main asset. Because we can never induce developed countries abroad to come to our assistance if they see the country is unstable. They won't waste their resources with a country that is not resting peacefully.

SOME SIGNIFICANT EVENTS SINCE INDEPENDENCE (1962)

1963	Tupua Tamasese Mea'ole dies. He had played a leading role in the preparations for independence and, being one of the two *fautua*, had become a joint head of state in 1962.
1976	Western Samoa joins the United Nations, using the name 'Samoa'.
1990	The constitutional restriction of voting to title-holders (*matai*) is removed by a plebiscite decision to introduce full universal suffrage for all citizens.

1998	Tuilaepa Aiono Sailele Malielegaoi becomes prime minister, an office he continues to hold following general election successes.
2002	New Zealand Prime Minister Helen Clark tenders an apology to Samoans for the failures of the New Zealand administration in Samoa between the two world wars.
2007	Malietoa Tanumafili II, head of state since independence in 1962, originally jointly with Tupua Tamasese Mea'ole, dies aged 95 and former prime minister Tui Atua Tupua Tamasese Ta'isi Efi is elected to succeed him as head of state for five years.
2009	A major tsunami strikes Samoa, causing tragic loss of life, devastation and economic damage, particularly on the south coast of the island of Upolu.

REFERENCES:

Crocombe, R., *The South Pacific*. Suva: University of the South Pacific, 2001.

Lal, B. and Fortune, K., *The Pacific Islands: An Encyclopedia*. Hawai'i: University of Hawai'i Press, 2000.

THE COOK ISLANDS

CHAPTER THREE

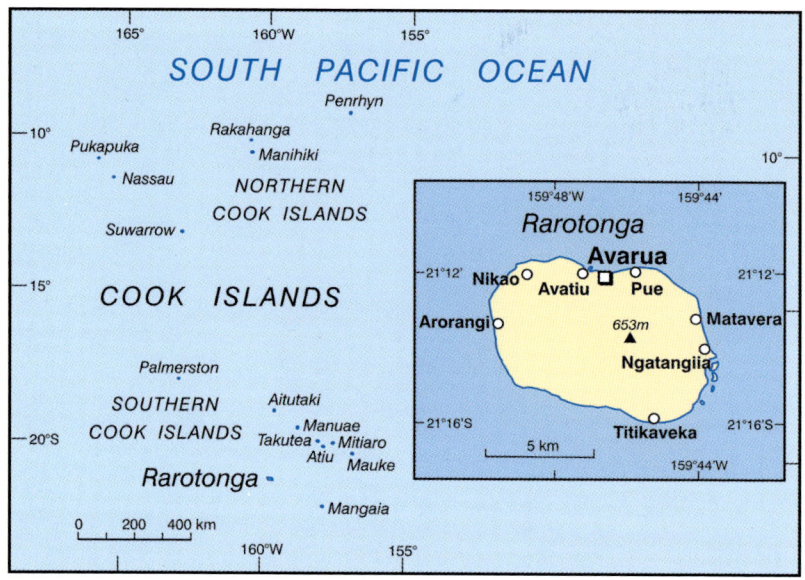

B Bradley, Cartographic Art Company

BACKGROUND

For centuries, the fifteen Cook Islands – seven northern atolls and eight larger, southern islands running along longitude 160 degrees – were separate entities governed by *ariki* (high chiefs). The people were very accomplished seafarers.

The first European visitor was the Spaniard Mendana in 1595. Between 1773 and 1779, James Cook landed on some of the southern islands. In the 1820s, Protestant missionaries arrived and by 1840 many *ariki* and their subjects had adopted Christianity.

British and New Zealand influence

In 1888 six of the larger islands became a British protectorate with Frederick Moss as British Resident. He persuaded the *ariki*

Queen Makea and supporting *ariki* with New Zealand Premier Richard Seddon and Mrs Seddon, Rarotonga; 1900
Alexander Turnbull Library, Wellington, NZ. PAColl-8566-1

to set up a federal government, headed by Queen Makea, which created a Cook Islander identity but little more.

After New Zealand Premier Richard Seddon's visit in 1900, *ariki* from Rarotonga, Atiu, Mauke and Mitiaro asked to join the British Empire.

The other eleven islands followed and New Zealand sent Major W E Gudgeon to be Resident Commissioner. Within ten years the authoritarian Gudgeon had replaced *ariki* leadership with colonial control.

That continued for almost fifty years; social and technical services were improved but political development was neglected.

Gradual moves towards self-government

After World War II, local participation in government was increased. In 1946, half of the new legislative council was elected, but the Resident Commissioner still controlled public works and spending.

Lord Ranfurly reads the proclamation annexing the Cook Islands to New Zealand; 1900
Photographer Malcolm Ross
Malcolm Ross Collection, Alexander Turnbull Library, Wellington, NZ. G-21257-1/2

During the 1950s and 1960s, as more Cook Islanders went overseas and learned about democracy and decolonisation, dissatisfaction grew with low wages and slow political progress at home. Leading that dissent was Albert Henry, an Auckland waterfront trade unionist who'd been born in Aitutaki. Demanding better pay and representation for Cook Islanders at home, he set up and led the Cook Islands Party, which dominated politics for fifteen years.

In 1962, the New Zealand government asked Cook Islanders to choose:

- Independence; or
- Integration with New Zealand; or
- Self-government in association with New Zealand; or
- Federation with other Polynesian groups.

Chief Arikis and Queen Makea of Rarotonga.

Cook Island *ariki* waiting to meet Premier Richard Seddon in 1900. Their leadership was to be restricted by New Zealand colonial administrators.
Alexander Turnbull Library, Wellington, NZ. F-51918-1/2

LEADER'S STORY: JOHN WEBB

John Webb, who held the senior government position of Resident Agent on the island of Aitutaki, was one of the officials who provided information about these options. He had been born in French Polynesia and brought up in the Cook Islands. His job was to travel from island to island, addressing village meetings. He recalls that in the early 1960s, Cook Island residents knew very little about the proposals for political change.

Our people living in New Zealand then were probably more aware about these matters, but it took us in the Cook Islands a while to realise what the people who talked about independence and

John Webb
Cook Islands News

self-government meant. New Zealand was magnificent, saying we could have either self-government in association with them (they would continue to look after defence and foreign affairs) or complete independence, or complete integration with New Zealand. That option was soft-pedalled. In fact, everybody laughed about it, including the chap who came to talk about it.

Although people were pleased that the New Zealand government encouraged people to be independent as far as work was concerned, pouring money into citrus and banana schemes and shipping the fruit to New Zealand, they got a bit impatient with the colonial system. They didn't like having to go to see someone to be able to do this or that. Then they were told that under self-government control would be with Cook Islanders and they'd get lots of money from the sale of fruit.

Pressure for change from New Zealand

People started to say our taxes should be used to pay our own public servants.

Some who came back from New Zealand told workers on the Rarotonga wharf, 'There, we get £5 a day, here you're only paid £5 a week. You're being exploited'. Until then people here had been quite satisfied, but considerable unrest was caused by the unions under leaders like Albert Henry, who came back from Auckland. His one objective was to free the people from what he saw as exploitation. I don't think it was exploitation – it was just the comparison between living standards.

Albert Henry

I liked Albert. I'd been to school with him and we often sat on the verandah and had a few drinks. Politics didn't come into it – I was just talking to a friend. He was a good man, highly intelligent, and very charming with (as we say in Māori) a sweet tongue. Eloquent and forceful, he could have you in fits of laughter, he could control a crowd; he'd pick up a guitar and start to sing and everybody would join in; everybody loved him. He was a fresh wind blowing though the Cook Islands.

He set up the Cook Islands Party and I was sympathetic towards it. All he and his party wanted to do was take over the land which belonged to them. He never talked about bloodshed. Why shouldn't we control our own land? Why should expatriates tell us what to do – where to put the road and so on? Why can't one of our own people tell us, then we can argue with them?

Albert Henry
Alexander Turnbull Library, Wellington, NZ

The Cook Islands Party was looked on with suspicion by the Rarotonga government, most of whom were expatriate New Zealanders who'd just applied for the job and couldn't speak a word of Māori when they arrived. All they thought of was working five days then claiming overtime. They didn't care that local staff didn't get overtime. They didn't want anyone rocking the boat, even though the New Zealand government said it supported the party because the growth of political parties was an important step towards self-government.

Albert did not like the way he was treated by New Zealand politicians. He told me, 'They don't understand what self-government means. I have to tell them what I am going to do'. He had some very rough passages, but he never seemed to lose his temper. A lot of Cook Islanders there were faithful and followed him.

Preparation for change

My job was to make sure the people had the information about what was available to them. With another man from New Zealand, I went in a Sunderland flying boat to Manihiki, Penrhyn, Mangaia and various islands. We didn't persuade or foretell. We just said, 'This is what has been offered'.

All the people of the island were ready for the meeting when we arrived. I heard them talking about what we'd come for. They knew what it was, but they wanted us to say it. We sat at a table. I spoke in English and it was interpreted into Māori, but if the interpreter got it wrong, I'd correct it. Really, just two options were considered — self-government in free association with New Zealand, or complete independence. The other choice, integration into New Zealand, was hardly mentioned because, I think, New Zealand didn't want the United Nations to think it was pushing Cook Islanders into joining New Zealand. I think they went for free association mainly because they didn't want to lose the right of free entry into New Zealand. Nobody seemed concerned about the role of traditional leaders, the *ariki*, after self-government.

We got a lot of questions. Should we put a line through the person we want, or the person we don't want? In Penrhyn, people said, 'Well, who should we vote for?' I said 'You have to decide for yourself if you want this person, or that person — that's the democratic way of doing things'. Literacy wasn't a problem because everyone had been to school and read the bible, but

New Zealand seemed to have overlooked the fact that people here didn't know how to vote.

Peaceful process of change

There was never any hint of violence. A Spaniard called Pradas had been sent by the United Nations. He stayed at my house in Aitutaki. He'd just come from Khartoum, where force of arms had brought self-government. When I said I was going round the polling booths on my jeep he asked if I had police with me. I said 'Good heavens, whatever for?' He gave me a United Nations flag and told me to put it on my jeep. So I did. I've still got it. He was very worried but it all went smoothly.

When he realised there wasn't going to be any trouble he said he'd go and count the votes. I told him I'd already done that. But he insisted on re-counting and got the same numbers that I had. Then we sent the voting papers at three in the morning. Later, on the radio we heard results from all over the country. There was no great celebration. The people chose a new form of government. It was so simple. No waving guns. People clapped and what not. That was it. We all went to bed, and woke up the next morning self-governing, more or less. I thought we were very lucky. I saw it as a mark in history and I thought 'Good old New Zealand – here's a little country come up with something which I'm sure a lot of other countries will follow'.

At the general election, Albert Henry could not stand because of a requirement that candidates had to have lived in the Cook Islands for a continuous period before the election, three years I think it was, and he hadn't done that. His sister stood in his place and everyone knew that if they voted for her they were voting for Albert.

The Cook Islands Party won the election and Albert came in and replaced his sister. I don't think the residence requirement was put there to try to keep Albert out of being premier – it was just a stupid mistake and they realised, 'Good Heavens, we're keeping out the very man the people of the Cook Islands want to lead them'.

With Albert Henry as leader, the Cook Islands Party won general elections in 1965, 1968, 1972, 1974, and 1978. The 1978 result was challenged by the Democratic Party, led by Dr Tom Davis, claiming supporters had been given free flights to come and vote for the Cook Islands Party. The challenge was upheld. Dr Davis was appointed interim premier and held on to that position after his Democratic Party won the second 1978 general election.

LEADER'S STORY: SIR TOM DAVIS

Tom Davis
PI Forum Secretariat

Born in Rarotonga, **Dr** (later Sir) **Tom Davis** spent many school and university years in New Zealand and was the first Cook Islander to qualify as a medical doctor at Otago University. After graduating in 1945 he wanted to work in his homeland.

I applied to the New Zealand government for a job in the Cook Islands Health Service. They turned me down but I kept on applying and the fourth or fifth time I was appointed; they couldn't find anybody else, I guess. I presume they didn't appoint me earlier because they didn't think it was a good idea to have an educated Cook

Islander come back in an important role. I'm afraid that was the opinion of the time.

I had seen evidence of that earlier when I was getting ready to study medicine and they told my family I shouldn't go to Otago University, but to the Fiji School of Medicine, which provided a lower level qualification; they felt that would keep me on the right track, as it were. I rebelled and said I would do a full medical course, or nothing at all. I had to work my way through, which wasn't easy, but I managed it.

Senior appointment

In 1948 I was promoted to Chief Medical Officer (CMO). The New Zealanders running the Cook Islands government seemed to look on me quite favourably personally, but there were problems. Instead of living in the CMO's quarters, they wanted me to be housed 'at home' which must have been because of sheer racism. I had to suffer a fair bit of that. I was asked by the Resident Commissioner not to worry so much about the sick people – I was spending too much money! Eventually, it made me think we really need to be free of this. Our people had much more intelligence than they were being credited with; they were being trampled on.

When Albert Henry came back to Rarotonga in 1947 we talked about how Cook Islanders should have more say in running their country. Albert had come home with the intent to disturb, and he caused some trouble on the waterfront. I talked him out of it and persuaded him we should not push for full independence, but for more say in our own affairs. Then we got the legislative council. As CMO I was a member, but it was a bit of a façade. People from each island met once a year. We were listened to, but that was it. But I have to say New Zealand supported my medical programme fully. I started with a budget of £12,000 – £15,000 and within three years it was £45,000 and we had a good medical service.

Recruited by Harvard University

The Harvard School of Public Health was recruiting people from all over the world and had been impressed with some of the programmes I'd introduced. In 1952 I was invited to go there. While I considered the offer, the Cook Islands Resident Commissioner said, 'If you accept that, you'll never get a job here again'. But I accepted the Harvard offer and decided to sail to America with my family. Quite an adventure; extremely cold. I'm never going into the roaring forties again in winter!

I was attached to Harvard's nutrition department. I taught and researched in my physiological field of altitude, heat and cold. I had about twenty years in the USA and in 1965 I heard about the choice of self-government back at home. I thought that was a good step. We would make mistakes, but we could live with our mistakes. Why should we have to live with New Zealand's?

Before 1965, I couldn't have come back as a doctor. New Zealand kept the promise that the Resident Commissioner had made. I once made an approach and was offered a medical job in Kiribati. I heard Walter Nash didn't like me.

Return to the Cook Islands

Then in 1968 my cousin Makea and old friends I'd worked with asked me to come back. The USA had been very generous to me – I was one of the top couple of hundred when I was working for the government there – but despite my great fondness for

America, nowhere caught my attention more than my own home. When I got back I thought the way Albert Henry and his Cook Islands Party had handled self-government was rather sad. The economy was going backwards 10 percent a year. They tried to make the Rarotongan Hotel work at the expense of everything else, preventing ordinary Cook Islanders from using their own land and resources to get into tourism. I fought against that policy.

Despite the undercurrent of rivalry, Albert Henry and I continued to be friends and reminisced about our times together in the late 1940s before he went away for seventeen years and I went away for about twenty. One thing I have to say about him, I could talk about anything with him. He kept confidences well and I did the same. There are some I won't tell even now. He tried to get all his supporters to talk me into supporting him, but I was determined to set up an opposition – the Democratic Party.

Election to Parliament

It was a long hard slog, but I got there. First, of course, I had to get elected to Parliament. It was my first time in politics, but I did enough to get in and stay long enough to be useful – to the majority, I hope – and be a problem to others. I'm proud that we took one of the lowest Pacific economies to the top, above Fiji and other independent states. Nobody can take that from me.

In 1980/81 we made big changes which took us forward. We had to overcome New Zealand's wish to be paternalistic. David Lange (the New Zealand prime minister) wanted us to give up all the economic gains the country had made and have equal dealings with France, USA and Japan. He wanted to take over all our foreign affairs; of course the constitution still says New Zealand has charge of our foreign affairs but it's nothing like that. We run our own economy, our own foreign affairs and that's the way it's going to stay.

Colonial attitudes

I've always loved New Zealand, but any country with a colony treats it the way they treated us. Look back in Polynesian history; the Tongans, the Samoans, the Tahitians, they've all been climbed over. Look back to the Romans, they did it and New Zealand didn't act any differently from the Romans. It's the nature of colonial power and it's no surprise that during those years Cook Islanders lost a sense of their own worth.

Confidence and culture

It's not all corrected yet, but 90 percent of people really believe in themselves; they have self-esteem, they do things on their own. I wasn't so happy about the proposal that Filipinos be brought in to run the Sheraton. How we turned the economy around was by our own people getting in there and owning tourist-associated industries. I hope we keep that. This government has tended to go towards a few elites instead of saying 'C'mon fellows, lets build an industry; if you feel you've got the resources to do it with your own hands, with your own family, your own money – go ahead and do it'. I think Premier Geoffrey Henry has done pretty well in rebuilding among Cook Islanders that sense of being independent, with a strong culture – and I hope I did, too.

My area is voyaging and I put everything I can into knowledge of our maritime history, types of canoes, Polynesian navigation. Culture is not a government department; it's what you adapt for yourself of what you are and what you have been. It's a progression of what you do culturally that suits you.

Sir Tom Davis (by mast, wearing cap) aboard ocean-going canoe Te Au-o-Tonga, Apia, Samoa; 1996
Photographer Julia Brooke-White
Julia Brooke-White Collection

I'm a great believer in free enterprise; I do not believe in restrictive legislation. I believe it's hard enough for our people to say 'What can I do to make a living for myself and family – how can I do better?' without restrictions blocking them.

We went from about 200 businesses, mostly European owned, to almost 1000, with very few new European ones, and our people heard my call 'Use your creativity, learn how to make a better living for yourself. Whatever you do for yourself is good for the country; the country is no good with poor people – it needs rich people'.

Cook Islanders have made good progress since self-government. They are responsive to what is good, reasonable and logical. They've done so well that I don't think leaders can take them backwards now – at least I hope they can't.

'Whatever you do for yourself is good for the country ...' Avarua; 1992
Photographer Julia Brooke-White
Julia Brooke-White Collection

SOME SIGNIFICANT EVENTS SINCE SELF-GOVERNMENT (1965)

(Note; The Cook Islands are part of the Realm of New Zealand; its citizens are also New Zealand citizens and have right of entry to New Zealand. Cook Island internal affairs are controlled by a parliament of twenty-four members elected for a maximum four year term. In the years since self-government, the Cook Islands Government has increasingly managed its own external relations.)

1965	The Cook Islands Party (CIP), led by Albert Henry, wins the first general election.
1967	House of Ariki created (twenty-four members from all islands) for a ceremonial/advisory role.
1968	CIP defeats United Cook Islanders (UCI) in general election.
1972	Tom Davis returns to the Cook Islands, forms Democratic Party (DP), joined by UCI.

1974	CIP defeats DP in snap General Election. Albert Henry knighted.
1978	CIP defeats DP in General Election; 1000 plus voters are flown from New Zealand; court voids seats won by bribery/corruption.
	Tom Davis regains seat; becomes premier of DP government.
1979	Albert Henry stripped of knighthood.
1981	Albert Henry dies aged 73; Tom Davis knighted.
1983	(April) CIP wins general election; PM Geoffrey Henry.
	(November) DP wins general election; PM Sir Tom Davis.
1987	DP wins general election; PM Pupuke Robati.
1989	CIP wins general election; PM Geoffrey Henry.
1999	Democratic Alliance Party (DAP) wins general election; PM Terepai Maoate.
2002	DAP wins general election; PM Robert Woonton.
2004	DAP wins general election; PM Jim Marurai.
2005	Cook Islands First Party wins general election; PM Jim Marurai.
2006	Democratic Party wins general election; PM Jim Marurai.
2007	Sir Tom Davis dies.
2008	Failure of political coup attempt by some members of House of Ariki.
2009	Cabinet Ministers resign after dismissal of Finance Minister Terepai Maoate.
2010	CIP wins General Election; PM Henry Puna.

NAURU

CHAPTER FOUR

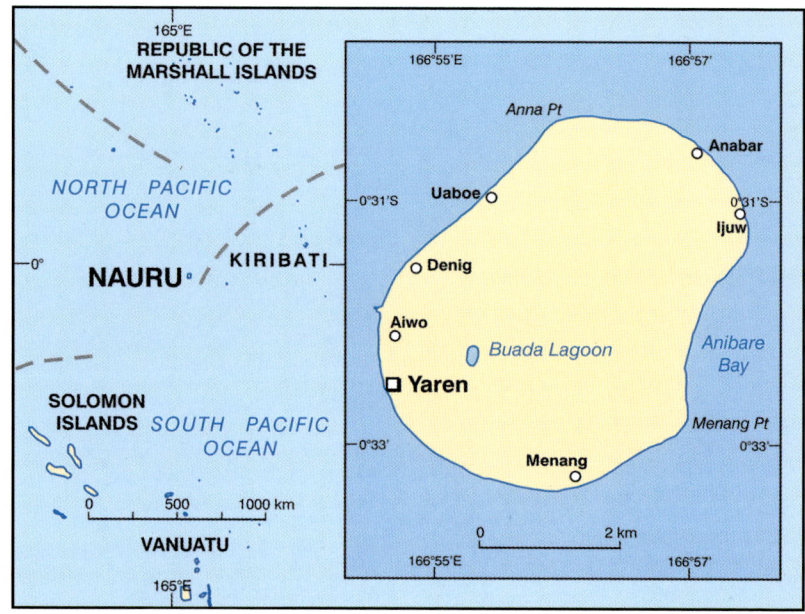

B Bradley, Cartographic Art Company

BACKGROUND

Nauru is a small, uplifted coral limestone atoll, about 4 kilometres across and 5 kilometres in length. Its barren interior plateau had extensive deposits of phosphate from many centuries of bird droppings. It is believed to have been settled by both Micronesian and Polynesian voyagers about 3000 years ago. Their descendants belong to one of twelve matrilineal tribes or clans on the island.

European contact

The first European contact occurred in 1798 between a British whaling ship and a flotilla of Nauruan canoes. The British captain named it 'Pleasant Island'. From the 1830s, whaling ships visited the island to re-supply and trade with Nauruans. This brought about the introduction of guns and alcohol which resulted in a decade-long war among the twelve clans and the almost halving of the population from approximately 1400 (1843) to 900 (1888).

In the mid-nineteenth century German traders on the island agitated for German government protection. Major imperial powers, including the United States, were competing for colonial acquisitions, and following the Anglo-German Convention, Germany annexed the island in 1886.

Rich phosphate deposits were discovered and mining started in 1906. An Australian force took over in 1914 at the beginning of World War I. The German colonial legacy is still evident in the use by many Nauruans of German first names

War suffering – and phosphate development

In 1919, after World War I, Nauru became a mandated territory of the League of Nations with Australia as the administering power and Britain and New Zealand as co-trustees. The three governments formed the British Phosphate Commission which took over the lucrative phosphate industry.

In World War II Nauru was attacked by German ships and Japanese aircraft and, in 1942, captured by Japanese troops. Nauruans suffered heavily, approximately 1200 being sent to work as labourers in Truk (a Micronesian island now called Chuuk) where at least a third of them died. Remaining Europeans were executed by the Japanese. (A memorial referring to wartime atrocities remains to this day.)

A United Nations trust territory

Australian forces recaptured Nauru in 1945, and in 1947 it became a trusteeship territory under the United Nations, again

Bags of phosphate delivered to Waipawa, New Zealand; ca 1918
Photographer Thomas Shackleford
Bibby Family Collection, Alexander Turnbull Library, Wellington, NZ.
PAColl-2838-1-10-1

administered by Australia with Britain and New Zealand as co-trustees. The British Phosphate Commission re-established the phosphate industry and large-scale exporting resumed.

Pressure for independence — and phosphate compensation

In the 1950s Hammer DeRoburt, who held chiefly status, emerged as the pre-eminent political leader. First in the Nauru Local Government Council and later in the new legislative council, DeRoburt became a powerful advocate of independence.

Mining operations caused such devastation that Australia proposed the resettlement of Nauruans on an island off Australia's northern coast, just as the Banabans (Ocean Islanders) had been

Strip-mining phosphate, 2009
Photographer Michael Field
Michael Field Collection

resettled on Rabi in Fiji. DeRoburt rejected Canberra's proposals and after hard bargaining obtained Australian agreement to full independence, which was formally achieved in 1968. Hammer DeRoburt became first president of the new republic.

In 1970 agreement was reached on passing control of the country's one valuable resource from the British Phosphate Commission to the Nauru Phosphate Corporation. For a short time, phosphate returns gave Nauruans the second highest per capita GDP in the world. During the 1980s, debate

Hammer DeRoburt
PI Forum Secretariat

Karst following phosphate mining, Nauru; 2002
US Atmospheric Radiation Measurement Program

intensified over compensation for the environmental degradation that had devastated much of the island, and the issue of rehabilitation of mined land.

The farming fertiliser consumers of New Zealand and Australia had benefited enormously from the cheap phosphate: Nauru was seen by many as the Pacific's prime example of colonial exploitation.

In 1989 Nauru began legal proceedings against Australia in the International Court of Justice seeking compensation for past phosphate exploitation. In 1993 a series of payments was agreed. However, declining phosphate returns and financial mismanagement brought Nauru's economy near to collapse in the late 1990s.

LEADER'S STORY: DR LUDWIG KEKE

Dr Ludwig Keke served as a member of Nauru's Constitutional Convention before independence, as parliament's speaker and deputy speaker, and was an associate of President Hammer DeRoburt, Nauru's first president. Dr Keke is Nauru's current ambassador to Taiwan.

My involvement in the political affairs of Nauru started in 1967 when I returned from Brisbane after graduating as a dentist from Queensland University. At the end of 1966 or early '67 was when the Constitutional Convention started being formed.

At that time, the Nauru Local Government Council (NLGC) was operating on behalf of the Nauruan community. We had an election for a member of the Constitutional

Ludwig Keke
Private collection

Convention and although others were better qualified, I was fresh from Australia and became a member of the Constitutional Convention in 1967.

Independence

The prospect of independence was being widely discussed at that time, not only by the head chief but also by the members of the NLGC and amongst the community. Hammer DeRoburt was head chief and had been unanimously elected chairman of the NLGC. Talk about independence had probably been going on since the mid- or late-50s. Hammer and a couple of his colleagues were moving in and out of Australia, and to the United Nations and attending Trusteeship Council meetings to push their view to the council.

Recollections of wartime experiences when Japan occupied Nauru would have been a factor in the desire of Nauruans to run their own affairs. Also the knowledge of foreign domination of Nauru for many years, centuries actually, was a factor. It started with the Germans, then Australia under the League of Nations, then the Japanese in World War II, and then Australia (with New Zealand) under the United Nations Trusteeship Council.

When I came back from Brisbane about 1967 or so, there was dissatisfaction with the way the British Phosphate Commissioners, and the Australian government, had been administering the island. Half of the population were aware of the NLGC proposal to go for independence, half would just cruise along with the rest of the community. That's the feeling that I got. In some ways the dissatisfaction was more to do with the British Phosphate Commission (BPC) than the Australian administration. The BPC was very powerful. Sometimes they almost overruled the administration, or ran the administration, because they controlled the shipping which brought in supplies, and everybody depended on the BPC. The BPC was one camp, the Australian administration was another camp, and the rest of the community was a third camp. In some ways Nauru was run like a company town.

A quote used often by some NLGC members was 'Nauru is for Nauru'. Their main idea was to have Nauru completely independent, looked after by the Nauruans themselves. Associated with that was the second issue, the control of the phosphate industry which had been under the control of foreign companies. The NLGC thought it was about time, in the sixties when independence seemed to be sweeping through the Pacific, that Nauru should be capable of running its own show, to look after Nauru, and take over the phosphate industry and run it themselves, rather than have a foreign country running it.

Compensation for mining damage

The issue of possible compensation from the three governments, Australia, Britain and New Zealand, which had benefited from the phosphate mining, was also being talked about during council meetings, during independence and afterwards. I was also involved in a meeting with members of parliament and our legal counsel on the issue of compensation. Of course, Australia, New Zealand and Britain refused to discuss the issue. They thought it wasn't part of their mining activities, which is perhaps not quite correct. That's why Nauru took Australia to the Court at The Hague, seeking compensation.

Leadership

Through all this, Hammer DeRoburt was a natural leader in many ways. A very hardworking person and to me, a man of great principle and vision. During meetings with the administrator who often, not always, attended NLGC meetings, the issue of independence and later the takeover of the phosphate industry was very much discussed. The programme of rehabilitation of the mined areas was to be undertaken by the three governments [Australia, New Zealand and Britain] which they refused, and that led to the Court at The Hague.

Hammer DeRoburt tried very hard through public speeches to encourage public support for independence but there were mixed feelings in the community, especially with two members of the NLGC, who were not quite agreeable with the method of independence. They were trying to get the council to run a referendum for the people to decide whether they wanted independence or not. Their aim was to continue an association with Australia. It was not a clear-cut case of everybody wanting the colonial power to depart. My recollection is that the NLGC wanted Nauru to be run by the Nauruans, but with the relationship with Australia remaining. Australia at the time of independence offered to look after the military defence of Nauru. It was not really a matter of removing everybody, of saying 'goodbye' to Australia. No, the idea was that the Nauruans would run Nauru, and the phosphate industry. But still associated, the friendship would still very much be associated, with Australia and New Zealand.

There was no public bitterness in our dealings with the Australians during the negotiations. I think people were aware how difficult it was for us because the Australian government and New Zealand and Great Britain at the time were not prepared to discuss independence on Nauru. My feeling, and what I gather from some of the people, was that naturally Australia and Great Britain did not want Nauru to be independent.

Friends and neighbours

Samoa was the first country in the Pacific to become independent, followed by Nauru in 1968. With Samoa, Nauru was one of the pathfinders. From 1968 on there's a flow-on of independence going on across the Pacific. In 1970, I think, Fiji.

I remember meeting Professor Jim Davidson who advised Nauru after advising the Samoans. Hammer was also at that time very friendly with the leader of the Samoan government, Mata'afa.

Nauru's new flag: L-R Mr D J Carter, New Zealand Government; Mr C E Barnes, Australian Minister for Territories; Sir Charles Johnston, United Kingdom Government; Mr Hammer DeRoburt, Head of State, Republic of Nauru; 1968
New Zealand Ministry of Foreign Affairs and Trade

Professor Davidson and a lady who came with him assisted Nauru with the Constitutional Convention.

Thinking back about Hammer DeRoburt, I found him a man of vision and certainly of great principle. He was a workaholic, really hardworking, and had the interests of Nauru really at heart. He demanded perfection of himself and his staff. As I said earlier, he seemed to be a natural leader for Nauru at the time. Despite the war, he had no hatred for the Japanese people; like everyone else he had hatred for the war. In fact after the war, Hammer made a trip, his first trip to Japan, and he looked for some of the Japanese friends who had helped Nauruans on Truk during the war. Nauruans had been taken to Truk by the Japanese to do forced labour there. Not only had Hammer made friends with Japanese but during this time he formed the Japanese Nauru Association. Then later on he developed a relationship with Japan whereby he obtained the Japanese government's agreement for Air Nauru to fly to Japan once weekly. After the war, many of his friends were Japanese whom he had met during the war and later on. There was no hatred of Japanese people because of the war.

Dissatisfied with compensation

When eventually the International Court ruled in favour of Nauru and awarded phosphate reparations, there was still great dissatisfaction among the members of parliament because the amount of compensation was far too low. Many of us had been thinking in the vicinity of $300 million. The Australian Prime Minister, Paul Keating, came up to Nauru for a Pacific Islands Forum meeting. I was present at the handover of a cheque to President Bernard Dowiyogo (Hammer had passed away by then) and it turned out that the amount was rather meagre, $190 million or something, and conditions had been set whereby Nauru didn't really get all the money, it was discharged on a monthly or yearly basis.

Limited prospects

Today there's a sense of pessimism on Nauru. The legacy Hammer DeRoburt left behind was to make Nauru a happy and prosperous society. His vision in creating all those investments worldwide was to cater for Nauru's future. We knew that there would be a period of time when the phosphate industry would wind down. I remember bringing up the issue in the late '60s, early '70s, that we should be looking for a second or third income-generating industry. But we so heavily indulged ourselves with the phosphate industry that we missed out on the fishing industry, which was a big thing at the time. Years later we thought about it, but it's too late. So no fishing industry really brought in any benefit at all.

There had been talk about establishing canning and the transportation and export of fish to Guam. The fishery started at one time but did not continue. Our resources are such that we cannot involve ourselves and cannot get engaged in huge industry. But the fishery people more or less are becoming our guardians for the fish around the Pacific. As a result we just rely on the fishing licence fees, not the big industry itself. We could not even find time to find out what would be our third income-generating industry.

The phosphate industry is dwindling down but I believe there is the possibility of secondary mining. We don't know the actual quantity or how much and how long and what income it would bring, although the president of the Nauru Phosphate Corporation is also trying to find out what other income they could get, not out of phosphate, but out of generating industry in relation to the coral chips or coral slag.

So, there are some further possibilities but don't forget at that [earlier] time the population was [less] and so the income was quite high simply divided by the number of people. But the population's getting high, and with a very large youth sector of the population and currently many of them are unemployed. So looking for employment facilities is another issue that the Nauru government is looking at. But the Nauruans are taught to be hopeful. Unless we can rally ourselves up it's going to be a very difficult life ahead, unless an industry or something else comes up.

Tourism has been around since as long as independence or even before that. Tourism is a big word, used for everyone in the region. Nauruan tourism is non-existent in terms of actual organisation. Apart from using Nauru as a stepping point to other tourist areas like Fiji and maybe Kiribati, there's not much potential for tourism.

I think the future for Nauru is to look ahead and try our best with what is available – and we'll see what happens after that.

SOME SIGNIFICANT EVENTS SINCE INDEPENDENCE (1968)

1987	Nauru begins legal action against Australia for phosphate compensation, finally settled in 1993.
1992	Following Hammer DeRoburt's death in office, Bernard Dowiyogo elected president.
1997	Political instability with five presidents in office in the course of one year.
1999	Nauru joins the Commonwealth and the United Nations.
2001	Australia-bound Tampa refugees sent to Nauru for detention there as part of Australia's 'Pacific Solution' to its problem with 'boat people'.
2002	Nauru establishes diplomatic relations with Taiwan, switching back and forth between China and Taiwan in the following years; relations currently with Taiwan.
2006	Experts report Nauru's phosphate reserves almost exhausted.

TONGA

CHAPTER FIVE

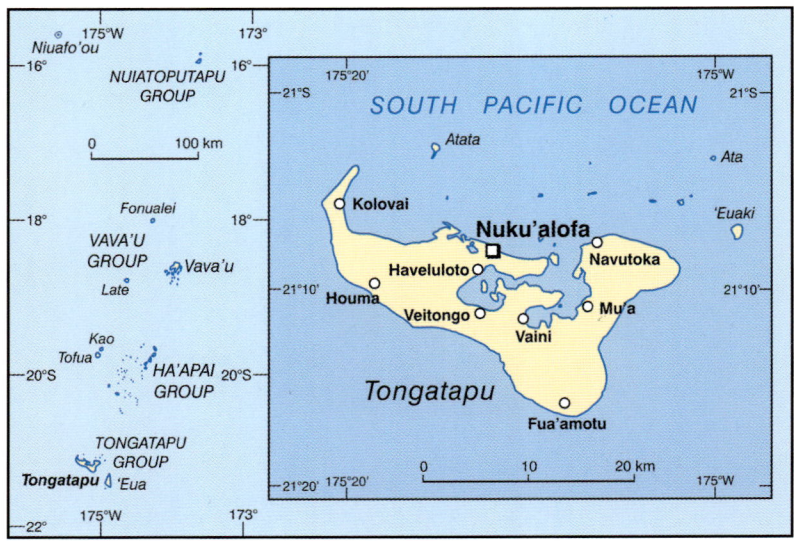

B Bradley, Cartographic Art Company

BACKGROUND

Tongans have long pointed to the fact that theirs is the only Pacific Island country never formally 'colonised' by a foreign power. Tonga also remains unique as the only remaining kingdom in Polynesia.

Said to be one of the most centralised and highly stratified societies in the Pacific, its chiefly system has been supremely aristocratic. The traditional system was weakened by internal strife, and then further by the arrival of Wesleyan missionaries and European merchants in the 1820s. In 1845 a Protestant leader was proclaimed King George Tupou I.

Big powers: influence and treaties

European powers were annexing or interfering in other Pacific Island groups and in 1855 Tonga was harassed by the French

TONGA

Royal palace, Nuku'alofa, Tonga; ca 1884
Photographers Burton Brothers
S P Smith Collection Alexander Turnbull Library, Wellington, NZ.
PA1-f-071-04-2

navy and forced into an unequal treaty with France. Germany, increasingly active commercially in the region, was keen to establish a coaling station on the island of Vava'u. King George took advantage of this interest and a treaty of friendship was concluded in 1876. The treaty not only recognised Tongan nationhood but also prompted Great Britain to seek a treaty on similar terms. A treaty of friendship with Britain was ratified in 1879.

British involvement in Tongan affairs developed and a new treaty of friendship resulted in Britain declaring Tonga a British protectorate in 1900. This followed protracted negotiations between the colonial powers over potential spoils in the Pacific. Eventually, in 1899, Germany annexed Western Samoa and the United States took Eastern Samoa.

HM King George Tupou II on his way to open Tonga's parliament; 1900
Photographer Frederick Sears
Alexander Turnbull Library, Wellington, NZ. PAColl-9061

In the early twentieth century Tonga continued to be governed by its own constitutional monarchy.

The constitution, dating back to 1875, gave the king virtually absolute power. But the third monarch, Queen Salote Tupou III, recognised that the constitution and laws not only protected her rights and powers but also provided a stable framework within which she could exercise many of the traditional powers of a ruling chief.

The arrangement with Britain under which Tonga was declared a British protectorate in 1900 gave the British 'Agent and Consul' virtual veto rights over most important matters of government. In 1970, a new agreement with Britain terminated this arrangement and Tonga, in its own words, 're-entered the comity of nations' as an independent monarchy within the British Commonwealth.

TONGA

HM Queen Salote reviewing her troops, Nuku'alofa; 1940
Alexander Turnbull Library, Wellington, NZ. F-82384-1/2

In the late twentieth century and the early twenty-first century, pressure grew for political reform to move the country towards a form of government respecting the democratic rights of citizens. The late King George Tupou V advocated and supported reform.

A Constitutional and Electoral Reform Commission Act of 2008 appointed a commission of that name, which described its purpose: 'This is an historic opportunity to build on HM King George V's wish to devolve many of his powers to the Legislative Assembly and, by reform of the electoral process, grant the majority voice in the Assembly to the people of this country' ('Tonga Constitutional and Electoral Reform Commission Final Report' 2008).

Following electoral changes, Lord (or 'Noble') Tu'ivakano became Tonga's first elected prime minister in November 2010 by winning the support of fourteen of the twenty-six politicians in Tonga's new parliament, edging out his only rival for the post, veteran pro-democracy campaigner Akilisi Pohiva, who secured twelve votes.

LEADER'S STORY: KING TAUFA'AHAU TUPOU IV

Although significant constitutional change was not considered by the late King Taufa'ahau Tupou IV, it was during his reign that Tonga's special relationship with Great Britain was ended.

King Taufa'ahau explained the background in this way:

Tonga's relations with other countries have always been by treaty; we are the only country in the region never to have been colonised. In the nineteenth century, when larger powers – mostly European – were taking control of Pacific Islands, they had to deal with Tonga as an orthodox nation because it already had a constitution and a government of its own.

HM King Taufa'ahau Tupou IV
Government of Tonga

Our first national treaty was with France in the 1850s and then with the German Empire in 1876 and with Britain in about 1900, also America. All these treaties have been renewed, generally on their hundredth anniversaries. So we have continued with treaties with France, Germany, Britain and America into this century. All except America originally wanted to absorb us into their empire, but they couldn't do that once we were recognised as an independent nation by one of them; that set the precedent for treaties with the others. However, we were caught up in the dealings between and amongst the European powers.

European naval rivalry

During the 1880s, which was a period of naval rivalry between Great Britain and Germany, the British Admiralty was doing surveys of islands and reefs all over the Pacific. Our treaty with Germany involved letting them have a coaling station in Vava'u, which has a very good harbour. The famous admiral, Tirpitz, was head of the German Imperial Navy and it became an important objective for the British government, no doubt egged on by the Admiralty, to dislodge the Germans from Tonga.

Germany was also keen to take over Samoa, but Britain had secured agreements with the authorities in Western Samoa and America had American Samoa, so the three powers were arguing backwards and forwards about the administration there. Suddenly, the British offered to withdraw from Western Samoa altogether, on condition that the Germans hand their treaty rights in Tonga, including control of the Vava'u coaling station, to Great Britain. That's how Britain came to Tonga.

Pacific wishes not considered

Neither Tonga nor Western Samoa had any say in these decisions; they were part of a deal between the British and the Germans, who each wanted sole control of any country they absorbed into their sphere of influence. They consulted between themselves about who would take control of which island group, but the Germans had been annoyed by the British for a long time and were glad to give up their treaty rights in Tonga in exchange for a free hand in Western Samoa. They were already trading there, and

DH&PG, a subsidiary of Godeffroy in Hamburg, came from Samoa to Tonga to establish a store, and later became the country's biggest company. There is an interesting trace of that time in the Tongan language, because when we want to speak, for example, about 3:30, we don't say 'half-past three', but 'half-four', which is the German way of counting. So they must have sold us the first alarm clocks or something!

I think our first treaty with Britain was signed in 1890 or thereabouts, after some years of disorder. My great-grandfather, King George Tupou l, assumed the throne in 1875 and a few years later appointed as prime minister Rev. Shirley Baker, a missionary from Australia who had set up the Free Church of Tonga, in opposition to the established Wesleyan church.

Missionary prime minister

Baker, who introduced most of the kingdom's early laws and governmental systems, was accused of favouring supporters of his church when appointing public servants, and of receiving money to help set up his church from German firms, in return for advancing their interests in Tonga. In 1887, some opponents tried to assassinate him and wounded one of his daughters and, it is said, another child, but Baker himself wasn't shot. He had the assassins executed. After the failure of efforts to restore harmony, Baker was deported to Auckland in 1890. I think everyone was pleased to see him go.

The British Consul in Nuku'alofa supported the appointment of my grandfather as prime minister after Baker – the British always thought Baker was pro-German. Incidentally, we renewed our treaty with the federal republic of Germany in 1976 and I was the first foreign head of state to visit the federal republic after German reunification.

TONGA

My grandfather, as prime minister and later as King George Tupou II, had a lot to do with the administration of the Treaty of Friendship and Protection with Britain. There are copies in the library and references in the Tongan law books. The aim was to keep out other foreign influences, and see that affairs were well administered, with appropriate practices to deal with bankruptcy and so on, and no further religious or political trouble.

Tonga pro-British

By the end of World War I relations between Tonga and the British had become very positive and settled. My father (Queen Salote's consort) came from a family that traditionally supported Britain and he was educated in Australia.

In 1932, when I was fourteen years old, I too was sent to school there and remained away for ten years. In fact Pearl Harbour was bombed while I was in Australia. General MacArthur had to make special arrangements to get me back on an American bomber from Queensland, refuelling in New Caledonia, to Fiji. I waited there a few days in an American camp, and then flew from Fiji to Tonga on an American seaplane. I was coming back to live in Tonga and work in the government.

They made me minister of education and health and then, after a while, prime minister. In foreign affairs and so on we were advised by the British consuls. They were appointed after discussion with us and most of them were personal friends of mine.

No colonial government

Our system was different from that in British colonies, which were directly administered by British officers. In Tonga, consuls were paid by the British foreign office and we paid our own officials, so we had the right of hire and fire. Because the relationship was by treaty and Tonga was always recognised as a state in its own right, the Union Jack was flown only at the British Consulate and nowhere else.

Tongans had no rights associated with British citizenship. They travelled on Tongan passports and the British foreign office would get visas for them if they needed to visit other countries. Some interesting officials were appointed here. I recall a judge from South Africa who tried to interfere in politics and was eventually sent packing. Another judge had a Russian wife who was a really good singer and used to sing Tongan folk songs.

At the start of World War II we had to make agreements with the USA because they stationed forces in Tonga and improved the airport so it could handle fighter planes. Later, they had aircraft

Tongan dancers celebrate; ca 1995
Photographer Julia Brooke-White
Julia Brooke-White Collection

carriers and so didn't need a land base. Before the Coral Sea battle an American taskforce of fifty warships including aircraft carriers came here to rest after the voyage from Pearl Harbour. For the week they spent here, Americans outnumbered Tongans on this island of Tongatapu. They had to go on leave in relays because the small wharf couldn't take all the launches.

Pacific neighbours

We have always had good relationships with our near neighbours, helped by a certain amount of intermarriage. My second son is married to a granddaughter of Malietoa in Western Samoa, so I have four Samoan grandchildren. We've played our part in regional matters. We backed the Fijians in their 1987 coup. The coup leader, Sitiveni Rabuka, came here when we agreed to jointly charter a small jet, a Boeing 737. It had Royal Tongan Airline on one side and Air Pacific on the other side and when it came to Tonga, the Royal Tongan side faced towards the terminal building, and when it went to Fiji, the Air Pacific side was towards the terminal building!

We never discussed independence or self-government with any of our neighbours — we saw that as an internal matter for each of them. Of course we could see the Fijians were hesitant about independence because they feared being swamped by the Indians. In fact they were already swamped because they had 'given themselves away' and so had no say in immigration policies. The Indians were really important to the sugar industry; without them there would be no sugar. They should have brought Indians to Fiji for a term of years and after that repatriated them, but they were never repatriated from Fiji nor from the Caribbean and Malaysia, Singapore and so on. It could not have happened here because we had a law prohibiting it.

End of the treaty

In about 1970 we decided it was time for Tonga to move out of the treaty relationship with Great Britain and return to full independence because we had shown we could take care of our own affairs and had done very well. There was no feeling that the British should go away. We never had any anti-European feeling of any kind, because we got on with people, whoever we were dealing with. We talked about it, and they talked about it in London as well. It was agreed that it was just a question of taking care of the legal process. Tonga was a protected state, so they had to pass an act in the British parliament to remove us.

There was no special occasion to mark the end of the treaty. On its last day I went along to the British Consulate when the Union Jack was lowered, but that was a normal event; it was evening and time for the flag to come down. Our friendship with Britain has continued, and so has friendship with other countries like France, Germany and America. Most of our dealings in trade and so on have been with Australia and New Zealand because they are closer. They bought products from Tonga and we bought supplies from them. Right now our chief trading partner is Japan. We just started a fund for the earthquake victims after the Kobe earthquake. That relationship is not new because Japanese trading companies were operating in Tonga before World War II. When they got involved on the other side in the war, they were interned and their property sequestered and administered by the custodian of enemy property. But we always had good relations with the Japanese.

Good relations internationally

It's counterproductive to have enemies, but you can't have too many friends, the more the better! The main thing our treaty with Britain achieved was to discourage other great powers from interfering with Tonga and allow us to just do what we liked to do. Our original treaty was with France under Napoleon III. It allowed Catholic missionaries to come to Tonga. They were only interested in the protection of their church, but since then we have maintained very good relations with the French Pacific territories. In fact I opened a new French university in Papeete.

Tonga is now building relationships beyond the Pacific. There are Tongan plantations in Malaysia's state of Sarawak which is nearly the size of New Zealand's North Island, but with just 1.6 million people. They are allowed to cut down only four trees per acre per annum, so their forest will regenerate; it will be everlasting.

We have 2000 acres there for cultivation, but we're starting with an eight acre plantation to see how the crops we like to plant will go. It's a high rainfall area, so we have to put in drains before planting. We're halfway through that and if it goes well we will expand. It is much closer to the Japanese market than Tonga itself so we might be able to supply a lot of things to Japan, and grow taros for the Polynesian communities in places like Sydney and Auckland.

SOME SIGNIFICANT EVENTS SINCE THE RETURN TO FULL INDEPENDENCE (1970)

1999	Tonga joins the United Nations.
2006	(March) Feleti Seveli is appointed as the first non-noble prime minister of Tonga since the nineteenth century.
	(September) King George Tupou V becomes king of Tonga.
	(November) Nukualofa riots cause fires and serious damage.

2008	Constitutional and Electoral Commission created.
2010	Lord (or 'Noble') Tu'ivakano becomes first elected prime minister.
2012	King George Tupou V dies aged 63 and is succeeded by his brother King Tupou VI.

REFERENCE:

'Tonga Constitutional and Electoral Reform Commission Final Report.' Nuku'alofa, 2008.

FIJI

CHAPTER SIX

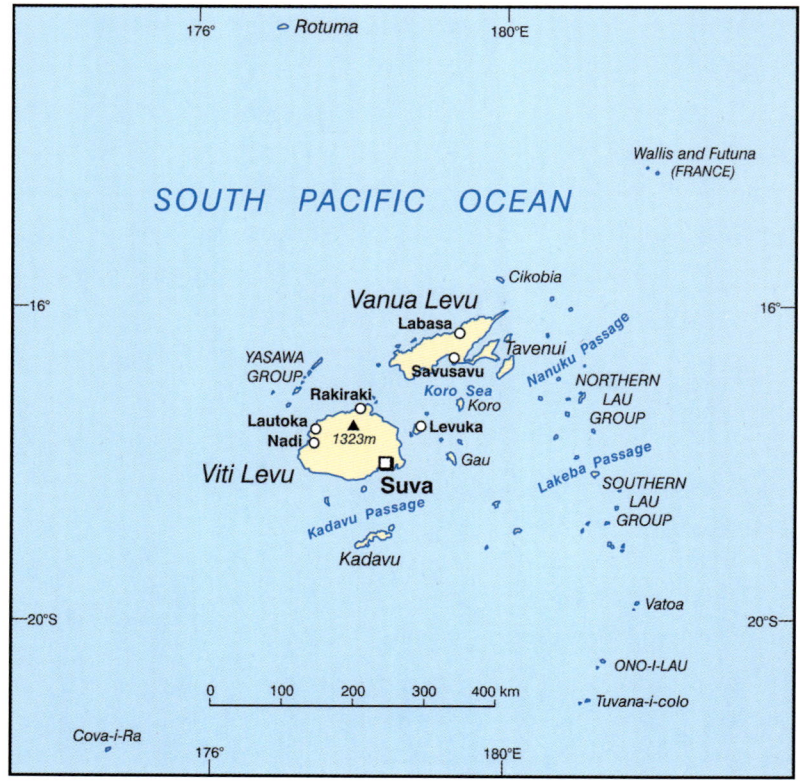

B Bradley, Cartographic Art Company

BACKGROUND

British annexation

The eastern Melanesian island group of Fiji was brought into the British Empire in 1874 when Paramount Chief Ratu Seru Epenisa Cakobau, known as Tui Viti (King of Fiji), signed a deed of cession to Queen Victoria. Troubled by challenges from fellow chiefs and Tongan leader Ma'afu and by lawless settlers, Cakobau looked to Britain for peace and stability. He wrote: '... it is our mind to give the government of our kingdom to the Lady Queen of Great

Britain ... we trust in her goodness; we give ourselves this day to her'. (Burns 1963, 97)

Despite a measles epidemic in 1875, which killed about a quarter of the population and produced famine and riots, Cakobau's hopes were gradually realised. British annexation of Fiji resulted in cannibalism being renounced, settler behaviour checked, and Fijian rights to communally owned land (some 83 percent of the national total) confirmed.

The colony's first governor, Sir Arthur Gordon, was unpopular with many Europeans but admired by Fijians, of whom he wrote, 'If you separated them from their land the race will die out and that would be a violation of the express conditions on which alone we took possession'. (Burns 1963, 107)

He also believed the best way to govern was through the chiefly *ratu* – aristocratic leaders of the hierarchical social system imported long ago from Fiji's Polynesian neighbours. In 1876 the Great Council of Chiefs was created to advise the governor.

Living in Fiji in those days were several thousand indigenous Fijians, a scattering of European and American settlers, traders and missionaries and a few thousand labourers from other Pacific islands, most imported by slave-trading 'blackbirders'. To restrict this traffic, Gordon recruited labourers from India – a common imperial policy which resulted in large Indian populations in Mauritius, South Africa, West Indies and Fiji.

Arrival of workers from India

In 1879 the first 481 workers arrived and over the next thirty-seven years, 44,000 men and 18,000 women, most from India's rural areas, were brought to Fiji under indenture. After five years of work at agreed pay rates they were entitled to free passage home, but two-thirds chose to stay.

In 1880 the Australian Colonial Sugar Refining Company (CSR) bought land and sugar mills and soon controlled a valuable industry built around the cane grown mostly on 10 acre blocks leased by Indian farmers whose interests were represented through their Kisan Sangh union.

As numbers grew, Indians branched out into other agriculture, transport, shopkeeping and small business.

By 1963, 205,000 of Fiji's inhabitants were Indian. The fact that they would soon outnumber Fijians was said by Sir Alan Burns to cause a 'general Fijian fear of domination by sheer weight of numbers' (Burns 1963) and particular anxiety that political change might remove Fijian rights to land ownership which had

Sugar cane harvesting Viti Levu; 1986
Photographer Julia Brooke-White
Julia Brooke-White Collection

Indo-Fijian owned shops and businesses, Suva; 1986
Photographer Julia Brooke-White
Julia Brooke-White Collection

so far been guaranteed by the Native Land Trust Board. These concerns remained, despite assurances from Indian leaders that their people did not want to own land and were satisfied with the leading part they now played in the country's economy.

Separate administration

Until the 1953 introduction of a legislative council including some elected members, Fiji was ruled by a British governor and a civil service staffed largely by expatriate district officers and technical specialists. Alongside this was the Fijian administration. Directed by the Council of Chiefs, its duty was to 'ensure continuance of the Fijian communal system … customs and observances … subject to such modifications as may appear desirable'. The value of this separate administration was much debated.

Villagers carry gifts to Great Council of Chiefs, Viti Levu; 1986
Photographer Julia Brooke-White
Julia Brooke-White Collection

Military tradition

An influential chief who contributed much to this debate was Ratu Sir Lala Sukuna (1888–1958) a great uncle of Fiji's first prime minister, Ratu Kamisese Mara. After schooling at Wanganui in New Zealand, Sukuna was wounded and decorated with the Croix de Guerre while serving with the French Foreign Legion in World War I. He studied law at Oxford University then came home to serve as Secretary for Fijian Affairs.

The British saw Ratu Sukuna as a fine exemplar of military prowess and loyalty to Crown and country – attributes which made Fijians very good soldiers. There had been little recruitment for World War I, but in World War II's Pacific campaigns Fijian soldiers, led by officers including Ratu George and Ratu Edward Cakobau, were awarded several medals including a Victoria Cross. Eleven

FIJI

Ratu Sukuna Statue, Government Buildings, Suva; 1986
Photographer Julia Brooke-White
Julia Brooke-White Collection

Troops rehearse for Queen's Birthday parade, Suva; 1987
Photographer Julia Brooke-White
Julia Brooke-White Collection

thousand men, predominantly Fijian, served under arms between 1939 and 1945. In the 1950s another Fijian battalion fought in the Malayan Emergency.

From then on, Fiji's army gained an international peacetime reputation for its music, parades and professionalism.

Many units served with the United Nations and the British Army recruited hundreds of Fijian men, whose remittances supported families at home. Fiji became the only Pacific Island country with a strong military tradition and a standing, revenue-earning army – factors which would have a profound influence on the nation after independence.

Preparation for independence

By 1964, main government responsibilities had been passed to three Fiji-resident Executive Council members: J G Falvey, of European stock, Indian A D Patel and Fijian Ratu Kamisese Mara, who was also leader of government business and, it was generally acknowledged, the man who would lead negotiations about self-government and almost certainly become Fiji's first prime minister.

LEADER'S STORY: RATU SIR KAMISESE MARA

Born in the south-eastern Lau island group into an aristocratic family with Tongan and Samoan connections, Ratu Mara held the titles of Tui Lau, Tui Nayau and Sua ni Vanua, an impressive pedigree reinforced by his wife's chiefly rank in her home island of Viti Levu.

Fiji Sun Billboard, Suva; 15 May 1987
Photographer Julia Brooke-White
Julia Brooke-White Collection

Dutifully responding to Fijian and British arrangements preparing him for leadership, Ratu Mara did well at schools in Fiji and universities in New Zealand and the United Kingdom. An accomplished sportsman, he could reach across cultures and he earned the respect of the communities of Fiji as leader of the country's dominant political party, the Alliance.

Kamisese Mara
PI Forum Secretariat

No-one was better equipped to lead the country into independence, and at the age of fifty, he accepted the task as an inescapable chiefly duty. But politics was not his chosen career. In the 1940s he had gone to New Zealand intending to qualify as a doctor.

My time at Otago Medical School I always thought of as the best years of my life. I played a lot of sport, made a lot of friends, and was able to get through my exams without much difficulty. I eventually played for Otago in cricket and rugby; in athletics I got a New Zealand Universities record for the high jump; and won the drinking blue in Dunedin – I created a record of 1.8 seconds, which stood for some time!

It was a bolt out of the blue when I got a letter from Ratu Sir Lala Sukuna. They'd been discussing my future with the Warden of Wadham College, Oxford, Mr Bowra, and thought I'd be more useful to Fiji if I left medicine and studied economics. The letter instructed me to report at Wadham on October 13th. My passage would be arranged by the Bank of New Zealand in Fiji. I arrived prepared for the course and went to see Mr Bowra. 'Ah, yes, Mara, you're Sukuna's nephew ... we did decide you should read economics, but I've contacted him and you should read modern history – best course for you. So there you are.' So I said, 'Modern History ... how long will that take?' 'You must take the Honours course, that will take three years.'

As well as that I completed the 'Devonshire Course' which was training to be part of the colonial administration anywhere in the empire. Malaysia and Kenya were highly paid places and I think the best of us went there, and I would probably have liked to go there for three years or so, but they found out I came from Fiji, and I had to come home.

My first appointment was as 'Governor' of Navua! My senior officer, a Mr Sykes, said, 'If you do well you'll get a pat on the back ... if you don't, you'll get a kick in the BTM!'

I didn't feel any awkwardness serving the colonial power here in Fiji. I enjoyed it and I thought the people enjoyed it, too. I was very proud to sit there as a magistrate (third class, in small letters). Fijians called me 'Magistrate of the Europeans'.

Content to be a colony

Surprisingly, I had no sense here in the fifties that the colonial period had to end. We thought we were not going to become independent. We were part of the Queen's regnum; we were happy – why should we change things? We heard about the winds of change overseas. You could see it on television, CNN at that time, but we thought it was a remote hurricane warning, that would never come to Fiji. I belonged to the school that believed we should not be parted from the United Kingdom, and there were countries like the Isle of Man and the Channel Islands who were on their own yet they were part of the UK. And I think there were still some small islands in the West Indies; I think the Virgin Islands was still a virgin! Our first reaction was that we should adopt that status. We said why should we ... we ceded our islands, as far as we're concerned, we've given the authority – how can we bring it back? This is not chiefly.

The move to get the United Nations to come in was in response to the desire of the Indian community. In the Legislative Council they were banging the table, saying we should be independent and have a common roll. And there were remarks against CSR

[Colonial Sugar Refinery] and big firms who were 'exploiting the people'. I felt in the early days that was the legitimate reaction of a people who've been exploited by their employers. They want to get rid of them. It only came later that they really wanted those people to move out and leave us. It wasn't until the Kisan Sangh [Indo-Fijian sugarcane farmers' association] wanted to strike and stop sugar-milling that Fijian members got together and formed the Fijian Association and declared support for the government and the CSR. That's how our first political organisation started. Then the Alliance was formed before the 1965 conference in London.

Negotiating independence

I enjoyed both London conferences. Of course, everything was new. At the time I didn't realise that the destiny of my nation was being discussed. I was trying to score points across the table from the other people. We did a lot of work as an Alliance. We studied all the constitutions of colonies from India onwards, put them on the table and said, 'We like that ... but not that'. By the time we finished we thought we had a good constitution, and put our work down and the others just criticised it. They had no alternative.

I never thought a common roll was a starter. Swamping was at the back of my mind if we had a common roll, and the population figures were changing, one moving up, the other stationary or being surpassed and who knows, in ten years' time it was indicated that we would be a minority in our own land. The amazing thing was I think we were the first country that became independent, in the 1970s, without a common roll.

During this time we did a round-the-world trip and the first country we went to was the United States. We were entertained by a Mr Samuels, I think, of the State Department and over drinks he asked where we were going. I told him from here to the West Indies, to Jamaica, Trinidad, Guyana, then on to England, India, Malaysia, Singapore. 'So you're going to the old colonies.' 'Yes,' I said 'that's why we're starting right here'.

During this period, the 1960s, A D Patel and I were political enemies. We were both in charge of ministries and there was a strong undercurrent of rivalry: I'm going to do my job better than he does his, a friendly rivalry, with a lot of consultation in council meetings. But I didn't have a lot of time talking to A D Patel outside work. There was some relationship, though, because during the difficult times of the war, 1943–4, when there were cane strikes, when I came back on leave Ratu Sukuna used to take me round to talk to A D Patel and S P Patel and have meetings with their group and I got to know them. I found out later of course that he went to the London School of Economics.

Westminster-type constitution

I wasn't worried that a Western-style constitution with a government and an opposition might fracture the country along racial lines because we were already fractured. We had already the Indian view and the Fijian view. They were not co-incidental and therefore they were in opposition. It was not violent but it was already fractured. Indeed, the Westminster system was the only parliamentary system I knew. If we were to move to independence, it had to be with this system. There had to be an opposition and a government side.

The late 1960s were a difficult time. But when I started the Alliance I thought I'd found the solution: get all the races together and we could run Fiji with all races well represented and playing their role in the governance of the country.

Election poster, Fiji, 1987
Photographer Julia Brooke-White
Julia Brooke-White Collection

But when I failed to attract Indians to my side, and those who came were regarded as traitors by the rest of them, that was the time when I think the scales fell from my eyes, so, well, what's the next solution? I was still looking at a way of getting people together.

I found people who were willing to come together. At first the novelty of the ideas brought a lot of people in but I must admit we ourselves were not clear in articulating the needs of all the races, because we were feeling our way: what would the Fijians say about this ... and what would the Indians say about this ...? They wanted to know exactly – what about our desire for equal representation? We couldn't come up with that. I had to say, we have to go now to the Council of Chiefs ... I think we didn't play our role as well as we could have done.

In spirit the various communities of Fiji wanted to work together. I believe this because we very nearly ... I'll just go ahead another ten years. In 1981 I proposed a government of national unity before the election because I wanted the two parties to agree on that and then go to the election and say after the election we'll have a government of national unity To me that would be the best construction of two different groups. There was a lot of detail to be filled in. I assumed it would be a Fijian prime minister and an Indian deputy and more or less equal numbers of ministers, each with particular expertise – going back to the experience I had with A D Patel and John Falvey.

The 1970 constitution was certainly complicated. As I said, much of our work wasn't well done. For instance, we did not translate that 1970 constitution into good Fijian. We didn't succeed in doing that, but for the constitution, I believe it was the best Fiji could have – and I still think that today.

Independence was achieved on 10 October 1970. It was a great day.

Albert Park, Suva; 10 October 1970 – Fiji Independence Day
Fiji Times

NEW FLAGS FLYING

We decided that we shouldn't follow the others by getting up at midnight when people are rather sleepy, to see one flag going down, another going up. We decided to lower the British flag one day, with a Retreat, then at ten the next morning, raise the new flag. I still feel it today; the thrill; the expectation of great things to come; all the people of Fiji there; all the religious people and bodies were there; and the Prince of Wales handing over to me, and I accepted and knelt down and performed the *cobo*.

The most heart-warming day was the Sunday when we had the ecumenical service with all the religions there, Christian, Muslim and Hindu and I think all those religious leaders really meant what they said when they were coming together to form a new nation.

Prince Charles and Prime Minister Ratu Sir Kamisese Mara; 10 October 1970 – Fiji Independence Day
Fiji Times

We continued with the old governor as our new governor-general, partly because of the person concerned. Personality counts a lot. Foster was a gentleman and we thought he could carry on and if there was any conflict he could tell us. He was very free and open with his advice. Anyone who wanted to discuss matters could do so. The appointment had the consent of my colleagues. I had a wonderful person, a great facilitator, in my early leadership – Ratu Edward Cakobau. He seemed to find the solution to any difficulty. People looked to him. In cases like the appointment of a governor-general, I would talk to him and he'd say, 'Leave it to me. Don't worry, I'll see the others'.

The Indo-Fijian community

In the early days I spent time with Indian communities in Fiji. It was the result of my district officership. As DO I had to manage Fijian and Indian schools. Although Indians at the time were starting their own schools, we liaised with them about government subsidies and health. I was chairman of the Native Land Trust Board District Committee, a very important committee. It felt the pulse of the Indian people as far as land tenure was concerned. We received applications for new leases and for renewal of leases; we had to go into their homes. For the first time I realised you can't just terminate a lease and move people out – because there's a school and a temple [nearby] and people would be completely lost if you removed them from that environment. It was a great lesson in human affairs. I've always been comfortable in Indian communities – found no difficulty whatsoever, surprisingly. I cannot speak Hindi, I understand some words and the drift of the conversation. But I felt my district was my kingdom and I must serve it. I think Indians like firm leadership and I can give it to them.

In the years following independence, leading by example was important. Right from the early days I've always thought that even if you can't talk well, at least your example can be more loquacious than you are. Leading by example was the greatest thing I have, I think.

And we were aware in the early seventies that Fiji itself could set an example to others. I attended my first heads of Commonwealth meeting in 1971 in Singapore. In a discussion, I made a remark that we were the only multiracial country in the world. Lee Kuan Yew pulled me up very very quickly and very very quickly I said yes, I agree, you're right! His country, Singapore, was another example. I became very friendly with him. We seemed to have great empathy in discussing our development. He was all for doing things yourself and not relying on other people for help, unless there is some unique way in which only they can help you. But do it yourself and then you'll find the right people will come to help you. What I admired in Lee Kuan Yew was his strict adherence to principles, and to law and order. I found that was the way you ought to run a multiracial country. Be firm, be tough, people will respect you. Different religions, different races will respect you if they know that is the way you behave. If you waver ...

First Cabinet

By the time we selected the first Cabinet, we'd already formed the Alliance with European, Indian and Fijian sections. I just found out who in the various races would be good for this or that. Doug Brown – former principal of Navuso Agricultural School – who better for Minister of Agriculture? Charlie Stinson, although he didn't stand for us, had been a successful businessman, so I put him in Finance. Ratu Edward was Home Affairs and deputy. They seemed to fall into place ... Attorney-General was John Falvey ... We had no problems working together. Ratu Edward was my facilitator and if anything became difficult, he'd say don't worry.

Regrets?

Looking back to independence I have no regrets at all. I thought we were lucky to come the way we did. Many other countries had difficulties. We didn't. Mauritius is a prosperous country now, but soon after independence they had a bit of a hiccup, and we didn't have any. The Indian representatives walked out of the Legislative Council in 1968, I think, on [the] common roll [issue]. We carried on. I was advised at the time not to fight the by-election when all the Indians walked out. But I wanted to test the water. I wanted to find out how many Indians will stand for me. And we had 31 percent I think, and that's the highest percentage of Indian support I ever had. Later, it went right down to 8 percent and I lost.

Looking back fifty years to my days at Otago, time and again I've regretted I didn't complete medicine. And I think if I did complete medicine I would have opted out of the administration, like my uncle Ratu Dovi. My ambition, as well as becoming a doctor, was to be district commissioner and district medical officer at the same time for the Eastern Division. That was my ambition. When I got there, the government would provide a boat and I'd visit all the islands and be a doctor and also a magistrate – what more do you want? This is Moses coming down from heaven!

But I had to work on a rather larger scene than that. I can't say, honestly, at any time I thoroughly enjoyed this job. It has been a struggle from the day I left medicine. Particularly the contrast. When I thought I was going to slide down the slope and get a degree, and then I had to go and struggle on a subject that's such a contrast from precise, scientific studies ... every book you pick up is different from the one you read next. It's been a struggle right through.

SOME SIGNIFICANT EVENTS SINCE INDEPENDENCE (1970)

1972	General election won by Alliance led by Ratu Mara.
1977	General election won by National Federation Party (NFP); Alliance reinstated after NFP leader fails to command majority of MPs.
1982	General election won by Alliance led by Ratu Mara.
1987	General election won by Fiji Labour Party led by Timoci Bavadra. Colonel Sitiveni Rabuka seizes control in two military coups and declares Fiji a republic with former Governor-General Ratu Sir Penaia Ganilau as president and Ratu Mara as acting prime minister.
1992	Ratu Mara appointed president. General election won by Fijian Political Party led by Sitiveni Rabuka.
1993	Death of Ratu Sir Penaia Ganilau.
1999	General election won by Fiji Labour Party led by Mahendra Chaudhry.
2000	Bankrupt businessman George Speight seizes control, takes prime minister and Cabinet hostage, declares himself acting premier. Ratu Josefa Iloilo appointed president by Great Council of Chiefs.
2001	General election won by SDL Party led by Laisenia Qarase.
2004	Death of Ratu Mara.
2006	Commodore Voreqe Bainimarama seizes control in a coup.

2008	Bainimarama appoints himself chairman of Great Council of Chiefs; postpones election scheduled for 2009.
2009	President Iloilo sacks all judges, establishes 'new legal order' and sets 2014 deadline for election.
	President Iloilo retires. Ratu Epeli Nailatikau sworn in as president.
2011	Lieutenant colonel Uluilakeba Mara is charged with sedition; escapes to Tonga; accuses Bainimarama and regime of torture and failure to advance promised reforms.

REFERENCE:

Burns, Sir Alan, *Fiji*. London: HM Stationery Office, 1963.

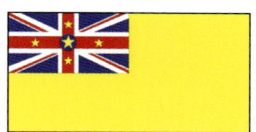

NIUE

CHAPTER SEVEN

B Bradley, Cartographic Art Company

BACKGROUND

The island of Niue was settled more than a thousand years ago by voyagers from eastern Polynesia. A second migration is said to have happened in the sixteenth century when a war party from Tonga took control of the island, leading to extended hostilities. Two centuries later Captain Cook thought the Niueans seemed warlike and called Niue 'Savage Island'.

Missionaries visited from 1830 onwards and Christianity was gradually accepted. The first Niuean king, Mataio Tuitoga, was elected in 1876.

From protectorate towards self-government

In 1900, after several approaches, London agreed to declare Niue a British protectorate; a year later it was annexed to New Zealand as part of the Cook Islands.

King Togia of Niue with New Zealand Premier Richard Seddon, Alofi; 1900
Photographer Frederick Sears
Alexander Turnbull Library, Wellington, NZ. F-19636-1/2

A separate Niue administration was set up in 1904 and by 1960 a legislative assembly had been established. Its leader was Robert Rex, son of a Niuean mother with royal connections and an immigrant English lawyer. In 1974 Niue became self-governing, a status still evolving. Robert Rex was elected first premier in 1975 and continued in office until his death in 1992.

A full member of the Pacific Islands Forum, Niue was a founding member of the forum's small island states group (Cook Islands, Kiribati, Marshall Islands, Nauru, Niue and Tuvalu).

Tourism, one of the country's few economic resources, attracts some investment and revenue, but aid from New Zealand, guaranteed by law to continue, is the mainstay of the economy.

Niuean platoon ready to serve Britain in World War I, Auckland; ca 1915
Photographer William Beattie
Peter Gordon Collection Alexander Turnbull Library, Wellington, NZ. F-42997-1/2

Population decline

In the 1950s the island's population was over 5000, but has steadily declined since then. Following self-government in 1974, Niueans retained New Zealand citizenship. Former premier, Mititaiagimene Young Vivian, estimates that some 25,000 Niueans now live in New Zealand; fewer than 1400 remain on their island.

As its people have moved away, there have been suggestions Niue may need to consider moving more closely into New Zealand's orbit to access the range of services Niueans now consider essential. As Young Vivian underlines later in this chapter, such a step would be a great disappointment to the many Niueans who have worked for a more independent homeland.

Niue does have ample space. The land area of its single island (259 square kilometres) is greater than that of all fifteen Cook Islands (238 square kilometres). But immigrants brought to Niue to increase the population tend to move to New Zealand or beyond once they have gained citizenship. Niue's future may be tied to a possible future rationalisation of travel and residence entitlements throughout the region, including New Zealand and Australia.

LEADER'S STORY: MITITAIAGIMENE YOUNG VIVIAN

Young Vivian, formerly leader of the Niue People's Action Party and premier of Niue in 1992/3 and then from 2002 until 2008, is very aware that for a long time, many Niueans have been attracted overseas.

When I was at primary school on Niue, everybody on the island aspired to go to New Zealand, which we thought was rich and exciting. I went there in my early teens to attend St George's preparatory school in Wanganui and then I went to Wanganui Collegiate where another Niuean boy and I used to cut our schoolmates' hair to get pocket money to go to the pictures. Among the other Pacific Island boys were David Toganivalu who became a minister in the Fiji government and Geoffrey (later, Sir Geoffrey) Henry, who became premier of the Cook Islands.

Young Vivian
Photographer Margaret Pointer

International influences

I trained at Ardmore Teachers' Training College and then went back to Niue because I felt I had to go and help my people. After teaching for nearly ten years, I came back to Victoria University of Wellington to undertake a course in the teaching of English as a second language. The Colombo Plan group I was with – people from Vietnam, Malaysia and Uganda – told me about decolonisation in their countries and that made me think that Niue, too, should be decolonised, just like the countries in Asia and Africa.

Apart from one episode when we had a resident commissioner with a most unfortunate, crude and unacceptable approach, Niue's colonial period was free of deliberate prejudice or racism, but I thought it was time for us to get away from the few bad incidents we'd experienced and control our own affairs.

When I came home to Niue in 1969 I went into politics and there was talk about self-government. I think New Zealand had already sounded people out in Niue and the Cook Islands. There was some discussion about whether we two should become self-governing together, as one nation perhaps, but we insisted on keeping our own identity as a country and on taking time to ensure we got the conditions we thought were essential.

Preparing for decolonisation

We were visited by experts in constitutional development. Dr Aikman, Vice-Chancellor of the University of the South Pacific and Jock McEwen [Secretary of Island Territories] came and explained the decolonisation process. Then Quentin Baxter [Professor of Constitutional Law at Victoria University of Wellington] came and wrote a report and explained to us what it meant. I think New Zealand was genuine in trying to decolonise Niue, but it was difficult to find a solution which met our needs.

Guarantees by New Zealand

At first, I thought we should sacrifice our right to live and work in New Zealand and become completely independent, but the people in the villages didn't like that. They were apprehensive about decolonisation and they wanted to secure the relationship with New Zealand. So I had to modify my view and work to achieve the sort of self-government my people wanted. Even though I think they were a bit hesitant at first, New Zealand's government bent over backwards to reassure the Niuean people by agreeing to three important things:

1. Niueans would always have the right to live and work in New Zealand;
2. New Zealand was legally obliged to assist Niue financially and administratively;
3. Niue's Public Service Commission would be based in Wellington.

In the end Niuean people accepted the plan for self-government and I went to New York with our leader, Sir Robert Rex, to explain what we had agreed to the United Nations' Committee of Decolonisation (the Committee of 24).

Robert Rex
PI Forum Secretariat

Sir Robert's reminiscence of the New York visit can be heard on the disc accompanying this book and at www.rnzi.com/newflagsflying (Part 7).

Their attitude was that ideally, colonies should become completely independent, but when both New Zealand and Niue put forward the view that Niue would never be economically viable and would always have to depend on New Zealand, the committee accepted the constitutional package that we had agreed on. Overall, I think New Zealand did a very good job, and some members of the Committee of 24 told me they liked the solution we had achieved.

When we became self-governing in 1974, it was obvious Sir Robert Rex had to be our first premier. I was Minister for Economic Development and Education, and also Agriculture and Tourism. People were excited. They had hope and faith that their lives would change and they would be in control of their country. We

UN Mission to Niue greeted by Robert Rex, Alofi; 1974
New Zealand Ministry of Foreign Affairs and Trade

moved forward and achieved the things they had dreamed about. We were very successful at that particular time. There had been no water reticulation, so we introduced it, then power reticulation and better housing and roading. The education system improved a great deal. More teachers were trained and more people were getting degrees.

Party politics

After that, I established the NPP (Niue People's Party) and brought in party politics because that seemed part and parcel of the Westminster-type system we had adopted and because I thought it might help to stimulate people to debate a bit more deeply about some of the issues concerning their lives. I believed in democracy, and the Westminster system, but as I look back and try to evaluate them now, I believe we didn't think deeply enough before throwing overboard some of our traditional ways of making decisions, for example by village councils, which still play a major role in developing villages.

A big problem in the early days was that the resident commissioners were always fighting against the resident missionaries, arguing about control of the people. The missionaries were very strong, and churches are still strong, stronger than government. I was a lay preacher and I have been a pastor now for over a year and I am sure churches bring in more dollars, and use those dollars more effectively than the government does. The churches help build bridges with people in Australia and New Zealand, who come in groups to the island. They bring money in and help people to establish businesses or ventures in Niue.

People say we have failed – but we haven't. There are excellent projects that we have built and developed all over Niue.

Niuean flight

Our big problem is we don't have the people to increase productivity. There are 1400 of us on Niue and 25,000 Niueans living in New Zealand. Our people are leaving because with a good education they see their degrees and diplomas as opportunities to have a better lifestyle elsewhere. Maybe we need a different kind of education or different kind of mindset. What they're doing now with the United Nations in terms of food security and self-sufficiency is a better way to think more deeply about how we can go forward. The only things we have are the land and the sea and we have to look after them as we try to build a country and a nation. The sad part about it is that most of our highly trained people are not in Niue, they are in New Zealand.

I fear our people are leaving our little country because of those guarantees that people insisted on when we became self-governing in 1974. We don't have the full commitment to nation-building that I originally wanted us to have. Our halfway house is a compromise, with consequences we are experiencing now. With full independence, total control would have been with us, and I am sure that many good people and a good country like New Zealand wouldn't let us float away.

We will find a way out, depending on how we handle economic development and education. A key problem, I guess, is that when you educate people, they want more, they want opportunities and benefits, but we will never be able to provide substantial benefits such as New Zealand has.

Disappointment

One suggested solution is that we build Niue up as an old folks' destination with homes for retirees. But you can't build a nation like that. You must have people of all ages, young and old, and healthy. We have been going through a dark period for quite some time because you cannot have a nation with very few people and we are not able to keep our people in our little country. Both my children are living in New Zealand and my disappointment is I cannot persuade them to come back. We are trying to keep alive our language and our traditions – but what for?

SOME SIGNIFICANT EVENTS SINCE SELF-GOVERNMENT (1974)

1979	Serious hurricane strikes Niue.
1989	Cyclone Ofa strikes, causing serious damage.
1992	Sir Robert Rex dies after serving as Niue's first premier from 1975 to 1992.
2004	Cyclone Heta, one of the strongest hurricanes ever to strike Niue causes immense damage.
2004	New Zealand's foreign minister, Hon. Phil Goff speculates that Niue's self-governing status in free association with New Zealand might come into question if too few residents live on the island for basic services to be maintained. Soon afterwards, Niue's then premier, Hon. Young Vivian, rejects the possibility of altering the existing relationship with New Zealand.
2006	Smaller Island States Unit established at the Pacific Islands Forum Secretariat, Suva, to serve the Cook Islands, Kiribati, Marshall Islands, Nauru, Niue, Palau and Tuvalu.
2008	*Lonely Planet* says Niue's population has fallen to about 1300.

PAPUA NEW GUINEA

CHAPTER EIGHT

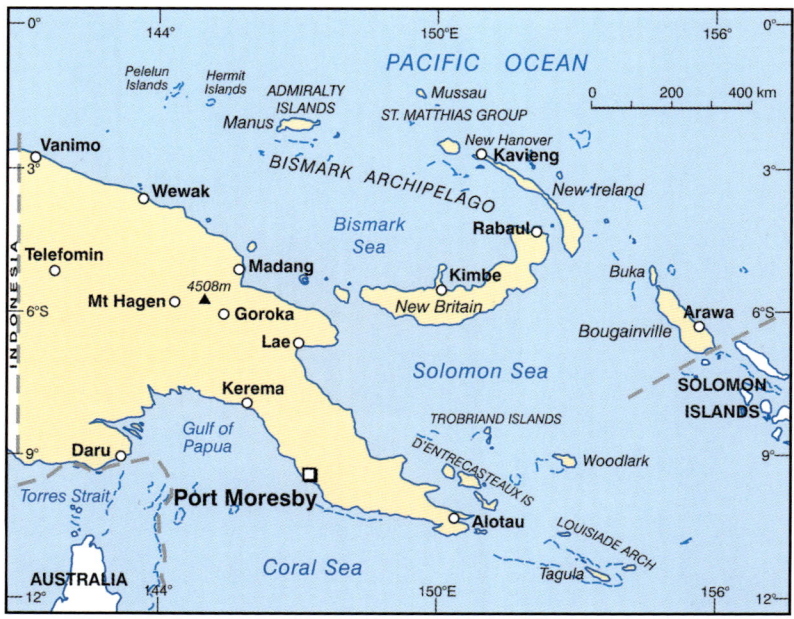

B Bradley, Cartographic Art Company

BACKGROUND

Sometimes called the 'giant of the Pacific', Papua New Guinea (PNG) has twice as many people (more than five million, mostly Melanesian) and twice as much land (462,000 square kilometres) as all the other tropical Pacific islands added together.

Richer than its neighbours in minerals and agricultural production and with diverse languages, cultures and flora and fauna, it is the only Pacific country to have a land border (with Indonesia's West Papua – to its west). Papua and New Guinea used to be separate entities, influenced and colonised over 250 years by the Sultanate of Tidore, Holland, Germany, Britain and Japan. In 1885 Germany annexed the northern coast, 'New Guinea', and Britain annexed the southern regions, 'Papua'. In 1906 Britain transferred the Territory of Papua to Australia, and in World War I Australia invaded German New Guinea and assumed control under a League of Nations mandate. Under a United Nations trusteeship agreement, Australia took control of both territories in 1945. In 1949 they became one – Papua New Guinea – and achieved independence in 1975.

Early European contact – and colonisation

Four hundred years earlier, these highlands and islands in the western Pacific between the equator and 10 degrees south, reminded Spanish explorer de Doda of Africa's Guinea coast. Setting a pattern for all 'discoverers' of Melanesia he gave the archipelago a foreign, second-hand name, New Guinea.

By the 1800s Dutch skippers were trading round the coast from what is now Indonesia and unscrupulous blackbirders (slavers) were transporting *kanaka* slaves to Queensland and Fiji. Some 20,000 were taken until 1884, when the trade was stopped. After a 'divide and swap' deal in 1889, the northern highlands and islands became the German colony of New Guinea while southern, largely coastal, Papua was declared a British protectorate. To mark the accession, Sir William McGregor and his bagpiper climbed, claimed and named the 4000 metre Mount Victoria. The skirl of the pipes is still heard today when the PNG police are on parade. British rule continued in Papua until 1906 when it was passed to recently federated Australia.

'South Seas' – a German commercial syndicate – was responsible for New Guinea but was hampered by malaria and tribal hostility and in 1899 the German government took over and increased trade and agricultural production until World War I began in 1914.

For the next thirty years the two territories were run by Australian administrations. Papua made some economic progress but New Guinea stood still.

Impact of war

World War II brought dramatic change. By 1942 Japanese troops were within 50 kilometres of Papua's capital, Port Moresby, and some quarter of a million men were killed or wounded before the invaders were repulsed.

Papua New Guinea soldiers, trackers and bearers made major contributions to the war effort and were so changed in the process that it became inevitable, according to commentators,

Villagers examine New Zealand tank, Nissan Island, Papua New Guinea; ca 1943
War History collection Alexander Turnbull Library, Wellington, NZ.
PAColl-5547-030

that they would soon demand political equality and even independence.

Slow political change — but pressure for independence

The first steps in that direction came in 1946, when the United Nation's Trusteeship Agreement required Australia to give the people of Papua New Guinea 'a progressively increasing share in the administration and other services of the Territory' (UN Trusteeship Agreement, 1946).

Progress was very slow. By 1961 Papua New Guinea residents were being elected to the legislative council but indigenous people still could not vote. The next year a visiting United Nations Mission recommended that 'Australia should make more rapid, radical changes in the Papua New Guinea constitution.' (Todd, 1974,40). After African, Asian, Commonwealth and even United States of America pressure, a House of Assembly with more voters and more members was established. By the early 1970s, PANGU (the biggest political party, led by Michael Somare) was calling for early self-government, with strong support from Gough Whitlam's Australian Labor Party which came into power in 1972.

But eighty years of political stagnation followed by ten years of hasty preparation had not laid a sound base for the move to independence. More than half the population was illiterate and only a few Papua New Guinea citizens held significant commercial or public positions. Apart from some coffee farmers, Papua New Guinea citizens generally lived by subsistence farming or low paid work; many had had little contact with government or outsiders and concern for tribe or clan far outweighed any sense of national responsibility or nationhood; inter-racial relationships were often soured by arrogance, envy and resentment.

Independence eventually achieved

In 1971, after copra prices fell and unemployment rose, riots broke out around Rabaul. A district commissioner was murdered and confidence in the church and the police weakened. On the mineral rich island of Bougainville long-standing mistrust of central government was growing into a secessionist movement. There was also widespread apprehension that independence would give powerful tribal groups, and foreigners, more opportunity to take land from its present owners. After agreeing on a fair and effective policy safeguarding land rights and transfers, leaders like Michael Somare, John Guise, John Kaputin, Albert Maori Kiki and Julius Chan were able to persuade their followers to

PNG citizens celebrate anniversary of their Independence while in Apia, Samoa; 1996
Photographer Julia Brooke-White
Julia Brooke-White Collection

set dissatisfaction aside and work confidently together towards self-government. That was achieved in 1973 under Chief Minister Michael Somare.

On 16 September 1975, Somare's Pangu Party joined Julius Chan's People's Progressive Party to form the first government of independent Papua New Guinea.

LEADER'S STORY: SIR MICHAEL SOMARE

Sir Michael Somare, born in 1936, was to be prime minister for some seventeen years (1975–80, 1982–5, 2002–11) and would lead two political parties, PANGU and later the National Alliance Party. He began working towards independence in the early 1960s.

It was in the early 1960s that I was brought in with a group of teachers, some working at broadcasting, others in administration, to be interpreters in the reconstituted legislative council in Port Moresby. I was doing the radio commentaries and simultaneous translation for the members of the legislative council, MLCs. That prompted me to start thinking about politics; it was my early introduction to political education. I was called with other young teachers and people in the Australian civil service, to go out and explain to people political education particularly on the electoral college system before the legislative council was reconstituted. Sir Paul Hasluck, who

Michael Somare
PI Forum Secretariat

was then the minister, decided that universal suffrage should be extended to indigenous people in the country. I was involved because I understood a bit of English and they decided I should do the translation.

Looking back, independence really came about in my mind, I think, in 1962. Some of us, all civil servants, were asked to go back and try to, probably not indoctrinate, but give some kind of secondary education. And quite a number, including myself and Sir Paulius Matane, were asked to go back, so that we can be qualified for the Australian third division of the public service. We were given a four year course in one year, in Sogeri in 1962, to sit the Queensland junior certificate public examination. About thirty-five of us were successful in that course. We did some secondary correspondence studies before, so that enabled us to be qualified for the third division.

And then, Sir Paul Hasluck and Bob Menzies, the then Australian prime minister, and other Australian politicians, visited Sogeri and opened the Sirinumu Dam. That prompted me to start thinking about, you know … I even told them that when I go out from Sogeri, I'll probably become your first prime minister. Some of those people laughed at me, my own colleagues!

Leaders selected

I think several of us were ear-marked by the colonial administration for future leadership. That's what Sir Paul Hasluck did, with Les Johnson who was then Director of Education. In the education system as well, I think that was the aim. Sir Paul Hasluck's policy on universal education for Papua New Guinea is one of the things that made the Australian administration start thinking about picking a group of people and Sir Paulius Matane was one of the group of people, with myself and others, who were selected to go and do this training because their aim was to get us, when we finished, to come back to go into the public service system. Sir Paulius became chairman of the Public Service through the system, and of course I decided to step out and go into politics.

Papua New Guinea people did not have any feeling of imposition. But, what other alternatives were there to the Australian system? Who were the other people around to give us alternatives? There were no other alternatives. Only the Australian system was offered to us at that time, so we were made to follow the system.

My shift into politics was gradual. I think I exposed myself to the political system. I had been reading and decided there was something I could do in politics. Particularly being an observer to the legislative council. The teaching profession is something that I wanted to do. But then I thought, well maybe a greater thing I could do is go into politics. And that really put me into that area. It was awkward being engaged in politics while still being a public servant. It was. We were being watched by the Australian Special Branch. Even going to school, going back to do matriculation at the Administrative Staff College. A number of us civil servants were brought back, Sir Paulius and others were brought into the teaching service to be given specialised training for Inspectorate of Schools, secondary inspectors, and primary inspectors of schools. I opted out of that area of education, I decided to go into much more flexible areas, where I can boss myself, you see, and become a politician, that's what I thought. So I opted out.

Planning for independence

And of course I met people like the late Albert Maori Kiki, people like Oala Raroa, Gavera Rea, John Kaputin, and all these people, and I thought, it's a new club altogether, completely new club.

And we formed kind of gatherings in the evenings, after lectures. And talk about what we need to do for Papua New Guinea, as Papua New Guineans. And eventually, you know, organise ourselves. Talking about how we can best organise ourselves, to be the masters of our own destiny. So that's how we got that.

This involved the famous Bully Beef Club in the Administrative Staff College. The principal didn't like the idea, but I think in his own heart he was favouring this type of gathering by Papua New Guineans who, for the first time, could stand up in a forum, and talk, express their feelings. And in those open discussions and seminars quite a number of us were brought in. Trade Union leaders like Oala Raroa, Albert Maori Kiki having exposed themselves in Australia and Fiji, they were coming out and starting to talk about some kind of freedom for Papua New Guinea.

Politics

All this was in the mid-60s. In 1968, when I was elected to the House Assembly – I'd decided to leave the public service in '67 and I went and ran for East Sepik electorate, which I hold up to now – I was talking about, you know, being cut out as prime minister. When asked the question, would you be the first prime minister? I said, 'Well, I don't know. You have to organise yourself before you start talking about dates for independence'. And I was asked to go and talk at a Sir Hubert Murray Memorial lecture in Sydney in 1968. And I said, 'Well, I may not be cut out to be Prime Minister'.

I could see things would be happening. And I said, we should set a date for independence. At that seminar I said we should set the date. Of course, I became very unpopular. I came back here and Maori Kiki, who was the general secretary to Pangu Party, started kicking me and saying you shouldn't have said these things when you got to Australia, and I said, 'I had to say it'. That began to set the agenda.

The real idea of starting a political party goes back to 1965, and we started organising in 1966. People, the likes of Obed Boas, were talking about a grassroots organisation: you need to have organisation if you want to start talking about independence. And the Pangu Party started, formally announced and launched on 13th of June, 1967. And when we went up to policy, we said, you know we are going to run a few candidates for the House of Assembly elections. We ran them and we only had nine seats, we won nine seats.

Independence was definitely one of the aims of the Pangu Party. I had been talking about self-governing and independence. I appeared before the United Nations Trusteeship Council Mission which came to Angoram in April 1968, and said, yes, if I was elected to parliament, certainly I would be pushing for independence for Papua New Guinea.

Too early?

The majority of the people in the villages, with the influence of the churches, were not prepared for early independence; most of them were speaking against independence – even some of our elected leaders were speaking against independence; people who came into the 1964 House of Assembly, the majority of them from the Highlands, anyway. And some from the Papuan coast, New Guinea coast, New Guinea islands were saying we were pushing for it too early. But I said maybe earlier is better than leaving it too late.

Papua New Guinea Dancers at South Pacific Arts Festival, Apia; 1996
Photographer Julia Brooke-White
Julia Brooke-White Collection

You will never be ready for independence until you start doing something about it. Like anything else that you do: you cannot say I won't be able to write, unless you learn to write. It's exactly the same thing with a country.

Other options besides independence were discussed. There were quite a number of people who suggested we should be the seventh state [of Australia]. There was a political party called the Christian Democratic Party. They wanted Papua New Guinea to be the seventh state. But I've never believed in the seventh state. I said, no, if we're going to be independent, we'll have a great association, we can have association with the countries that we want.

Overseas examples

I travelled in 1970 to African countries, and also people like the late Tom Mboya and others visited our colleges and told us about independence. And I read about independence in those countries and I felt it would be far better that we should be independent and on our own. I suggested we should go and look at Africa and some of the Pacific countries; so we had two groups who travelled. Some of us went to Africa. Paulius and his group, and Oala Raroa, travelled the Pacific, and looked at the concepts in the Pacific, what was happening, particularly the American Trust Territories and what New Zealand was doing with Western Samoa. Australia's plan, Britain's plan for Fiji, and things like that.

I went to Kenya. I went to Uganda. That was the time when they had Idi Amin, in 1971. The little corporal started firing at the Foreign Affairs building while we were still in there. They stopped us from going to Nigeria because there was a military coup by then. But I went to Tanzania. And I was more interested in the Tanzanian system. There was the village concept – and that somewhat relates to the provincial government system that we have.

And then we went to Sri Lanka. At the time they had a bicameral system but they were abolishing the Upper House in 1971. The vote was actually taken when we were in the Chamber. So, when we came back, that framed my mind, that we should not have two Houses. When John Guise went out he wanted two Houses and I said no, we have a single unitary system of government so it's easy to control, you have one person. And the legislation is much easier for legislative processes than two houses. I was never for two Houses. We only have one chief in the traditional village – he says it and everybody runs ... They echoed that in the constitution. So, that really helped. We went around, to see what other places did, like what Fiji did, we had exactly the same. But, then, when we were going forward we did not want to adopt any one system: we said, we will develop our own constitution.

Compared with the problems we saw in Africa, we were fortunate in Melanesia. We were very small groupings. We never had huge ethnic groups. We have, but they're all separated. Whereas in Africa, the leaders who emerged from their own tribes – like South Africa for example – you have the chief who comes from the bigger tribe who has the control over things. The first Kenya Prime Minister – Kenyatta – comes from a very, very big tribe. And of course that big tribe dominates over the others. And in our country we did not have that. We have smaller tribes.

Australia

What the Australian government did was unify us by bringing us together in one central place, one focal point, to say we are Papua New Guineans. And that's why I got to know the likes of Paulius, having been born, brought up and working in his area. But I also got to know the likes of people like Vincent Eri, people from different parts of Papua New Guinea. When we were brought together we felt we belonged to this country.

The Australians never had a preferred agenda that they wanted to impose: a lot of credit to the Australians. I hope one day, the Australian government will give credit to people like Les Johnson through their honours system. Les Johnson spoke for Australians but he had Papua New Guineans at heart. He decided that this is what you do. You know, normal administration, he would be an administrator. But from time to time, over a cup of tea, he would say, this is how we should do it. He travelled with us. He was in Kenya, he was in Tanzania, because he was chairman of the Constitutional Development Committee. And he really prompted people like myself, and others, to say, you have to decide what you want for your country. Australia never had a prepared programme, no.

Of course, quite a number of Australian people were not supportive. I mean, they were coming out saying Papua New Guineans cannot run the country. They used the simplicity of people like 'Oh Papua New Guineans, you can't even fly your aeroplanes; Papua New Guineans, you can't even do this, how come that you are now talking about independence?'

Promoting confidence

Well, people who had some kind of education were able to help their own people, and we were doing that. We had this propaganda machine through radio, and I travelled a lot. When I was a member of the House, and the Works Committee, I also went around exerting influence: 'Hey independence is OK for you fellas, come on'. I had a lot of public servants who, through the education setup were working for the colonial service, but indirectly passing the message on, maybe good news was coming, you see. So, it all helped.

NEW FLAGS FLYING

We were all united, we were all united for one cause: independence for Papua New Guinea. Now we are all divided, Chan, myself, and everybody, we are divided but before, we had one cause. I said this is what we wanted for PNG and everybody followed.

We were conscious that there were others in the Pacific whose progress was very slow. We encouraged them. Mara and myself, the Pacific leaders, we were spokesmen for those people who were not independent at the time, Solomon Islands, Vanuatu, Kiribati and these places. We were saying, these countries of the Pacific will be independent one day and we need to expedite and accelerate the process.

Prime Minister Michael Somare introduces New Zealand Prime Minister Robert Muldoon (second right) to Papua New Guinea political leaders, Port Moresby; 1983
New Zealand Ministry of Foreign Affairs and Trade

PAPUA NEW GUINEA

Physically and geographically Papua New Guinea was an awkward country. But I think, you know, if we had the infrastructure we could have united the country. We were divided, but of course it's not our making, it was the making of other people, the British, the Germans, the Dutch, they divided our country. And of course now we've got to try to put it together, and we have put our country together. Indonesia of course came before us, and they had the other part of the country.

I never believed that Papua and New Guinea should separate. When I formed the Pangu party I told them I wanted to unite Papua New Guinea. Those were the colonial names imposed on us. I would rather have a name for the nationality, the name that we should have for this country as one. You know there's a lot of words in your mouth when you say 'Papua New Guineans'.

We didn't really have enough people to run the country. But I think the talent in Papua New Guinea was there, and Papua New Guineans didn't have the opportunity because our universities started very late, in 1967. Australia over a long period, only had produced three graduates; John Natera, Joseph Awai, Kipling Wiari, and later in the time, they had Henry de Robert and Bernard Narokobi, and in this long period you only have about ten people who graduated from Australian universities.

Early problems

The biggest problems of the first few years of independence were the public service and the economy. I think in politics we were getting the message across. People have a much better grasp of information in our country and I think with our radio system, with the messages we carry mouth to mouth, it did go very well, because we had the field officers who were able to go out and explain to people the concept of government, what we were doing, the policies that we were trying to implement, to push through for them to be implemented and we were able to do this. The message was gradually getting to the people.

I felt I had to do something to build a new Papua New Guinea. I think my aspirations came about when I travelled around, when I was exposed, when I watched what was going on, I thought I'd better do something. And, well, I don't regret now that I have done what I could. And I'm hoping that the next generation of Papua New Guineans will be able to carry on and make it a better place for all of us because I will have great grandchildren, and I will have my great grandchildren's children, and I hope we can make Papua New Guinea a better place to live.

SOME SIGNIFICANT EVENTS SINCE INDEPENDENCE (1975)

1977	Government of Pangu, People's Progressive Party, Mataungan Assn and independent re-elected under PM Michael Somare.
1978	Somare introduces Leadership Code stating MPs' responsibilities. PPP quits coalition; Pangu continues to govern backed by United Party.
1980	PPP and three coalition partners form government under PM Julius Chan.
1982	Pangu wins general election under PM Somare.
1985	After no-confidence vote, five-party coalition forms government under PM Paias Wingti.
1987	Coalition wins general election under PM Wingti.
1988	After no-confidence vote, Pangu forms government under PM Rabbie Namaliu.

1989	Bougainville Revolutionary Army close down Panguna copper mine, declare Bougainville independent.
1992	Wingti elected PM.
1994	After no-confidence vote, PM Wingti replaced by Chan.
1997	Bill Skate elected PM.
1998	Tsunami kills 1,500 people on north coast. Permanent cease fire signed and Autonomous Bougainville Government established under President Joseph Kabui.
1999	After no-confidence vote, PM Skate replaced by Mekere Morauta.
2001	Law prohibits party loyalty shifts by MPs.
2002	Michael Somare re-elected PM.
2003	Limited preferential voting at general elections introduced.
2007	Somare re-elected PM: now Commonwealth's longest-serving parliamentarian.
2010	John Momis elected President, Autonomous Bougainville Government.

◆

REFERENCES:

Todd, I., *Papua New Guinea: Moment of Truth*. Sydney: Angus & Robertson, 1974.

United Nations Trusteeship Agreement, Agreement approved by the General Assembly of the United Nations, 13 December 1946.

SOLOMON ISLANDS

CHAPTER NINE

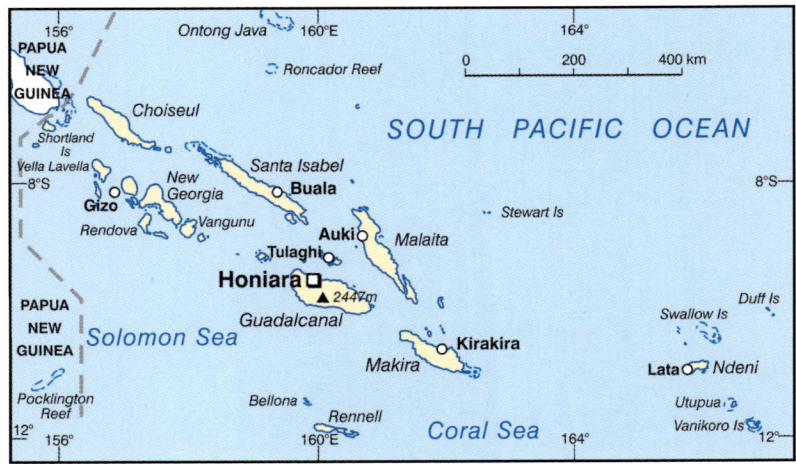

B Bradley, Cartographic Art Company

BACKGROUND

For centuries many self-governing communities speaking separate languages lived on the six big volcanic islands and scores of atolls in this central Melanesian archipelago. The islands were originally settled by Papuans from New Guinea in a migration which began about 30,000 years ago.

Spanish explorer Mendana sighted them in 1568 and named them the Solomon Islands, in the mistaken hope of mineral riches matching those of the biblical king.

The islands continued largely unbothered by foreigners until the 1800s when people from Europe, America and Australasia arrived to barter, evangelise, and settle.

Big powers were then competing for influence in the Pacific and in 1893 the captain of HMS *Curacao* declared the islands under British protection. Britain wanted to protect not so much the

Solomons people, but the supply of workers to sugar estates in Queensland and Fiji.

Between them, officials and missionaries quelled squabbles and attracted planters and entrepreneurs. Many policies favoured foreigners ahead of Solomon Islanders.

Land profiteering

Disease and tribal wars had depopulated many areas and large so-called 'waste lands' were leased to foreign companies to produce rubber, copra and vegetable oil. European planters and traders bought freehold land from their Melanesian neighbours then sold it at huge profit to big companies such as Levers. In 1912, the British government decreed that it alone could buy and lease land, so cutting traders' profits and increasing official revenue.

The slave trade

Solomon Islanders had only their land and labour to sell. For years, young fit men had gone – or been forcefully taken by 'blackbirders' – to Queensland, Fiji and Samoa, and many now enlisted on Solomons' plantations. Often brutally treated, their poor housing and food led to outbreaks of dysentery and similar diseases.

By the 1920s conditions were better, but wages remained low and men's absence at work weakened village and family life. Living together on plantations gave men the chance to learn about each other in a common language – pijin English. By the mid-twentieth century, many Chinese had come to settle, sometimes displacing European traders and plantation owners.

There were few opportunities for Solomon Islanders to advance and in 1939 village headmen asked the government and

Men taken from Solomon Islands to work on plantations in Samoa; ca 1910
Photographer Alfred Tattersall
Tattersall Collection Alexander Turnbull Library, Wellington, NZ.
PAColl-3062-3-08

missions to build schools and dispensaries, increase wages and copra payments and move towards 'a native parliament'. These requests were dismissed by officials and missionaries, whose authority diminished from 1941 to 1945 as Commonwealth and United States forces fought the Japanese in central Solomon Islands.

Pressure for change

Impressed by the generous and open attitudes they had observed among American troops, many Islanders resented the post-war return of planters and officials. 'Maasina Rule' — a brotherhood

SOLOMON ISLANDS

RNZAF Corsair fighter planes, Guadalcanal, Solomon Islands; 1944
Evatt Collection Alexander Turnbull Library, Wellington, NZ.
F-106417-1/2

movement seeking local control — spread from Malaita to other islands. After several arrests, but without bloodshed, Maasina Rule and similar groups lost impetus when island councils were introduced in 1953. The protectorate then experienced 20 years of relative calm until the early seventies, when, as historian Judith Bennett comments '... Britain's gentle amble towards self-government rapidly escalated into a breakneck gallop towards Independence' (Bennett 1987, 311).

In preparation for that independence, island and legislative council members were elected by popular vote, aid was increased and policies were controlled by committees of elected MPs.

LEADER'S STORY: SOLOMON MAMALONI

Solomon Mamaloni, MP for Makira, served on one of those policy-making committees. He went on to become chief minister (1974–6) and prime minister for three terms (1981–4, 1989–93, 1994–7). Mamaloni's interest in government and public service began when he was at school.

◆ ◆ ◆

Solomon Mamaloni
PI Forum Secretariat

I took history, geography, English language and literature and mathematics at King George VI Secondary School here in Honiara and when I won a government scholarship to Te Aute College in Hastings (we had to go to New Zealand for Form 6 because here we only went to Form 4), I broadened my studies into colonial history. I was very interested in things like the Boston Tea Party, the French and English conflicts in Canada, people like Lord Delaware, people who shaped the governments of the world. I read about the black hole of Calcutta and then got a library book about Mahatma Gandhi and was so absorbed that I stole it and brought it back to Solomon Islands. I read about the way Tito handled Yugoslavia and realised he had some exceptional leadership qualities. I looked at the things President Kennedy set up, extending American concern to the world, questioning foreign aid, establishing the Peace Corps.

Studying how the British system was transplanted across the Commonwealth to countries like Australia gave me a broad understanding of constitutional changes, authorities and government.

Work in the public service

The first time I heard talk about self-government was when I was working as an executive officer in the secretariat division responsible for 'protectorate affairs' as they called them. Later, I made a verbal submission to the 1968–9 Constitutional Committee about the governing council system, which had first emerged in Ceylon. I had come across it in my studies so I mentioned it. It was adopted here later, and I was elected as a member.

I had left the public service when the British gave me a hard time following some unpleasant exchanges with my bosses. Most public officers were confirmed after two years' probation, but after five years I still was not confirmed. They saw me as a troublemaker because as a young officer I went round villages in Guadalcanal, Russells and Savo checking the everyday life of people and meeting head men, and the reports I wrote to my boss were not very sympathetic or sentimental. I think that is when they decided I wasn't a good administrator.

Still, they appointed me assistant clerk to the Legislature and then I replaced an expatriate officer as Clerk. Our section shared a photocopier with Finance and I had priority for its use. I was producing copies for the Legislature one morning when the financial secretary's assistant – she was South African – came over and asked 'Who told you to do this?' She pulled out my papers and took over the copier so I swore at her.

My boss dressed me down. 'You shouldn't be doing this. You have big potential. We're thinking of sending you to Westminster to learn how to be clerk to Parliament.' But that never happened.

Later I met the head of Protectorate Division going down the stairs as I was going up and he greeted me, 'Good morning, Solomon' so I replied the same way, 'Good morning, Douglas'. He was a senior officer, but I saw nothing wrong in addressing him by his first name, as he did to me. I had been in the office long enough, taking big responsibilities to the extent that we could say, OK, we are colleagues, fair and square. But he took me into his room and said 'You can't call me by my first name, I'm your boss. I've served HMG for more than twenty-four years. I'm forty-five and you must address me as "Sir"'.

Another expatriate officer, a Scotsman who ranked above me, saw me crying and asked what had happened then challenged me, 'You're from Makira, be strong. When you next meet him, say what you want'.

Douglas Freegard, the man who'd told me off, walked with a bit of a waddle and when we met later he said 'Good afternoon, Solomon' and I replied 'Good afternoon, penguin'.

I was severely reprimanded; my wages were cut and my probation was extended again.

Now, I make fun of those incidents and tell them when we have a function or a party.

I left the public service to go into politics round about the time our first university graduates were starting to come home. There was strong feeling against British colonial servants who had been posted here after the African country where they used to work had become independent.

Family history of service to Makira

An important reason why I moved was to try to help people in my province of Makira, almost the backwater of Solomon Islands.

SOLOMON ISLANDS

My father was the first member for Makira, followed by my uncle Jack Campbell. They thought I should stay in the public service and were unhappy about my taking up politics.

It was the late 1960s when I was elected to the Governing Council. We were preparing for self-government and independence and the first thing I was concerned with was human rights. I had a few books on that and I was interested in the Canadian approach so I moved motions in the Legislature – I think in 1972 – one for improved education and one for further constitutional changes. Then a small committee consisting of David Kausimae, myself, Rev. Fugui (I think) and the Attorney-General was appointed. From various documents including those from Canada, which I was well versed in because I had studied North American history, we built up the embryo of what Solomon Islands human rights should be and some of that is entrenched in our constitution.

Preparation for self-government

In 1974, when I was elected chief minister, we were preparing for self-government and then independence. Britain's Assistant Minister of State, Miss Joan Lester, came here and we began discussions on the timetable for Solomon Islands. I said we wanted self-government by 1976 and she almost fell over 'That early?' I said 'Yes, I think we can make it'. I wanted us to move quickly because I had some worries. I did not want Solomon Islands to have to fight over independence. I think that was one of my misconceptions. At that time we were dominated by African affairs, where people had fought for their independence and I thought there might be similar trouble here. There was much diversity and a history of divisions in the Solomon Islands, with some in the east who had been involved in anti-colonial movements like 'Marching Rule [sometimes known as the 'Rule of Brotherhood'], being opposed by pro-colonial people in the west. We called them 'Yes' people.

There was a possibility the western islands would try to secede and go it alone. Their main grievance was they weren't getting enough returns from their resources. I got the Ministry of Finance to calculate exports from each province over the past two years, then I went to the west and spoke to a big demonstration at the wharf at Gizo. I told them the idea of secession would never work because living in the west were many people from other islands like Malaita and Makira, so they could forget any idea of 'West for West only'. And by a bit of fiddling with the export income figures, 'specially for timber from the western province, I was able to promise them a bit more in their copra returns. That seemed to quieten things down.

I was also concerned about relations with Bougainville, which has always been part of PNG even though its people are ethnically closely connected with people from our Shortland Islands. Many Solomon Islanders – from as far away as Malaita and Honiara – were benefiting because of the Bougainville copper mine and the trade it generated. When there was trouble at the mine and serious disagreement between Bougainville and PNG, it was the most awkward position a prime minister would find himself in because my minister for Prisons and Justice was from the Shortlands with relatives in Bougainville, and the head of state had land in South Buin (PNG) and the minister of Finance's uncle was from Kieta and others like the minister for Provincial Government had similar connections. I just said 'If you want to shoot your mouth off about Bougainville, do it – but not as a minister of the Crown. We have to maintain relations with Papua New Guinea. If you want to make a statement, make it as an MP'.

Britain had insisted that if a leader wanted his country to become independent he had to tell the Cabinet, start campaigning for independence and take the issue to the polls. If you win the majority, that's it. We still had colonial bosses in the government departments, so I replaced them with the first bunch of Solomon Island permanent secretaries. Francis Bugotu, now dead, Aser Golon, Leonard Mainu, and Bobbie, still here. Foreign Affairs remained a colonial responsibility. We had a bit of luck and were given self-government in January 1976.

From then on I thought the best way to go back to the people was to establish another constitutional committee so I appointed a big one, chaired by Sir Fred Osifelo who canvassed the country again on the question of independence. We had a competition for the national anthem, and finally, after much controversy and arguments with Governor Luddington we approved the national flag. In 1976, we had the general election to decide who would be prime minister to complete negotiations with Britain and then lead Solomon Islands into independence. I was defeated by a man with whom I had worked very closely and who, like me, had left the public service to enter politics.

LEADER'S STORY: SIR PETER KENILOREA

Peter Kenilorea led Solomon Islands into independence in 1978 as first prime minister and held that post until defeated by Mamaloni in 1981. He led the country again from 1984 to 1986.

I am from southern Malaita and I went to King George VI School where I was fortunate to get, under the Commonwealth Colombo scheme sponsored by the New Zealand government, a scholarship

Peter Kenilorea
PI Forum Secretariat

to Wesley College in New Zealand, then went on to Wanganui Boys College. There I rubbed shoulders in hostels with people from Fiji, Cook Islands, Vanuatu and Western Samoa, which was independent by then. There was some talk about that and the idea was around the school corridors and that sort of thing. I went on to Ardmore Teachers' College, came home and went school teaching.

From teaching to administration

In 1974, the financial secretary in the colonial government, John Smith, suggested I move into public service administration because there was a need for senior officers to be put in the right places as independence approached. I was a little taken aback, but I said, whatever the nation wanted me to be part of in the transitional period, I would be willing to do it, if I could. Since Solomon Islands did not have to fight for independence but was going to be given it, we felt we should rise up to our responsibility.

British sense of superiority

Relationships with our British colleagues were sometime strained. We were equal in terms of designations and positions, but the attitude that 'some are more equal than others' was always there. There were certain places one was not able to go to, like the hotel. We didn't go there, we didn't have permits to drink – no bother for me, I didn't drink anyway. There was a sense of them being superior, you know, opening the door without knocking and bashing into your office, but when you did the same to them, they did not like it. That kind of attitude. There was usually mutual respect at the official, professional level, but the element of colour, race, and differences in understanding were still very much there. We're talking about individuals, not about the system. But I had some good friends among them, like a very good colonial administrator called Tony Hughes, still here. I suppose, when you consider colonial experience in other parts of the world, we did not have it bad at all. There was no physical harassment.

Career dilemma

After a while I was appointed Secretary to Cabinet and to Chief Minister Mamaloni. In 1975 I was presented with two opportunities – I got a letter from a senior colonial administrator asking me to go in for diplomatic training to look after our foreign affairs, and Malaita people asked me to stand as a candidate for Parliament.

I'm a Christian and I prayed, asking the Lord for some tangible direction – did he want me to serve the country or the state? I didn't want to cause ill feeling among my people, who didn't really know what an election is about, you know, some people win and some lose in politics, so I decided, 'If I am nominated unopposed, I will take it as a clear direction that's where I'm being led at this time'. When I asked who else was likely to stand for my constituency, a friend said 'There were six, but when they heard you were interested, they all pulled out'. So I took that as a lead and that's how I entered politics.

Leadership

In our traditional society I was pretty young for leadership, which belongs to the chiefs and the old people, but I was greatly helped by the old political leaders then who accepted and recognised me for leadership at that time and it wasn't difficult to switch. We had to deal with administration as it applied in other countries, so being a public servant was a good stepping stone for me. Our traditional leaders know their leadership is confined to tribal respect, whereas when you talk in the context of the nation, quite honestly that is beyond the bounds of traditional leadership. At national level they must give way to people with some education who can think widely. Our national constitution provides specifically for traditional leaders to play their role at provincial level.

Another mentor and encourager was my contemporary Francis Bugotu and when I became political leader I asked him to look after our international relations. He did that well, but paid a heavy price because he spent much time away from home and had a lifestyle halfway between our own people and the colonial masters. Later when he wanted to enter politics, he was misunderstood by his own people who saw him as a stranger.

Politics – parties and communities

In the period when we were self-governing and moving towards independence, we tried to run the country under a governing council with a number of committees and much consultation. In my view it was quite close to the way we run things under communal arrangements but it was done away with in the mid-70s when political parties began and it was agreed the party with a majority under the democratic system should run the government. I see that as important for purposes of political democratic decision[-making].

Party politics isn't the real problem in this country, the problem is understanding the principles party politics operate on, and getting personalities out of politics. Our Solomon Islands communal system hinges on a socialist lifestyle. We live for each other, communally, but at the same time I'm right wing in terms of democratic ideas and free market forces. I think going to school in a free atmosphere gave me reasons for my position, but essentially, it's my own Christian principle – every man is born free.

In hindsight and with due respect, it's obvious the British hadn't done very much for Solomon Islands. Their main emphasis had been on law and order, no emphasis on economic development – that was almost nil. Only a dozen of us had tertiary education; there was only one secondary school, King George VI; most education was in the hands of the churches. We had the feeling the British had had enough and just wanted to go away. I told them as much at the constitutional negotiations in London when I said we wanted extra money, above what they had agreed to, because they had not done anything and we would have much work to do after they had gone.

Citizens and their land

The two main constitutional issues were citizenship and land ownership. They wanted a clause stating that anyone who had been here for seven years should have 'belonger' status and equal rights to land ownership. I said that's not possible. Land is owned by tribes and some of our expatriate friends do not understand our customs about land ownership. I fought hard over that very important issue. I feared they were going to force it on us that non-indigenous people would have equal rights to land and that was just not on as far as I was concerned.

They also wanted to make it easy to get citizenship here. I said there's no problem with that, but please do not relate it to land ownership, which is to do with our affinity and affiliation to our custom rights and traditions. We still have bad memories of the days when the traders and colonial masters came and bought our land with empty bottles, a piece of cloth, a bush knife, that sort of thing.

Solomon Islands ferries, Honiara; 2009
Photographer Michael Field
Michael Field Collection

Eventually we agreed that the former 999 year land leases would be reduced to seventy-five years. I remember someone came and cried in the office saying that was very tough, but seventy-five years is long enough, and they could extend and still use it after the seventy-five years.

National identity

Isolation and differences in our islands, tribes and communities made it difficult to think nationally at that time and that is why our national thinking had to be safeguarded in our constitution. We had to have a strong and clear written document if we wanted to create a nation out of so many diversities.

I felt for Solomon Mamaloni when I ousted him and became the first prime minister. We'd been close, we'd gone to New Zealand for schooling at the same time and then worked together and he had been my boss. When we had to race against each other for the leadership of this country, I'm sure he knew the competition was not personal, it was for the leadership.

Joys and challenges

The moment when our new flag flew for the first time was very joyous but also very challenging. We had never been alone before. There was the fear of the unknown. But the other leaders were very helpful and I thought well, you are as much prepared for it now as you will ever be. The mass of people were saying 'Are we doing the right thing?' but there was no argument among the political leaders. There were comments and songs about 'We're not ready' and 'We don't have enough money'. But I felt then that independence is not about money, but deciding about being yourself – which is your right.

We looked to PNG, already independent, and if little Nauru could have its independence, I couldn't see why Solomon Islands, better blessed, couldn't go the same way. As I said, every human being is born free and to be shackled by a system which is outside of yourself is not human, in my view.

I was very close to New Hebrides Chief Minister, Father Walter Lini. He rang me when his independence was coming up. 'How did you do this?' and so on. And I respected Ratu Sir Kamisese Mara. I think being a chief helped his political career, but I valued his fairness, particularly important given Fiji's situation, which is difficult for anybody.

Looking back

If I had my time again, I would allocate a lot more resources to education. An enlightened society is more authentic and can hold itself up, as it were. And I would have made constitutional provision that an MP who leaves his political party has to go back and face a by-election. There's a lot of fluidity about political affiliations and it causes instability. I hope government will have a strong look at that and improve the constitution.

Overall, we have great resources and we'll either make it or break it ourselves. After seventeen years we're still together despite our diversities and we can be a very successful country of beautiful happy people. Although I would rather have stayed as a professional public servant and only took on political leadership out of duty, because I felt I had been called into it, I'm very proud of independent Solomon Islands.

LEADER'S STORY: SOLOMON MAMALONI AGAIN

Solomon Mamaloni, who became chief minister in 1974 at the start of self government and, later, prime minister for three terms (1981–4, 1989–93, 1994–7) had not expected to be defeated at the 1976 election.

Away from politics

I resigned after Peter won. I needed a rest because I had a hell of a time as chief minister. Nineteen seventy-five and 1976 were the worst two years with fights for wages; conditions were very bad, and people yelled their heads off about the terms and conditions for MPs. Then there were protests against self-government when they smashed all the buildings along the road and the police had to use tear gas. And, according to some sources, people from Langalanga wanted to terminate my life. They didn't understand that Peter and I were schoolmates and almost part of the same family – his wife was a cousin of my sister's cousin. Despite all the politics, we still maintained cordial family relationships. Peter took the same studies as me – colonial history and all that – and was a much more respected fellow, even at school. When he took over, there was no problem.

Solomon Mamaloni
PI Forum Secretariat

I did have problems with the opposition; this firebrand Bart Ulufa'alu was marching in the streets and wanting to become the leader of the opposition. So I decided I'd better leave politics for a while and look after my business. But rumours that people were marking me to knock me off still continued and I remember around Christmas my house was surrounded by friends of the family, people from Sande Islands, Reef Islands Tikopia ... all saying they are going to kill you – we are here to protect you. I never feared for my life. People create rumours. It was a typical Solomon Islands situation, believing in superstition and all that. But anyway I left the political scene and I was looking after the plantation on Independence Day.

The colonial legacy

One of the best things the British left was the Land Act, preventing owners of customary land from selling their land to foreigners. That is the only thing we're hanging on to now. Had we been able to sell customary land, some crazy people would be selling plots of land for cans of beer in the suburban areas of Honiara.

But the British did little to help our economic advancement. As in most of their former colonies, they set up companies and agencies to deal with resources which assisted British industries. Here they did well with social facilities, education, medical and health services, the courts and Christianity. And they built a very good road on Malaita!

In terms of accepting changes and appreciating difficulties I think we are ahead of most, 'specially African countries, but I always thought that in the negotiations for an independence financial settlement, we should have done better than we did. But it's no good for Solomon Islands to blame the colonials whenever something goes wrong. We've only ourselves to blame.

The British colonial system isn't like the French, who actually impose assimilation of cultures and therefore the people become francophones and French in taste and culture. The British left all our culture intact and said if you're going to become a modern nation you've got to improve health services, have more education, more exports and all that, leaving the culture and traditions to the people themselves. In Solomon Islands, having seen Fiji and PNG go through it, we said OK, it's about time we governed ourselves.

Leadership

Since I entered politics, the only time I enjoyed was when I was an ordinary MP without responsibilities except for my constituency. After appointment as chief minister, life was not fun any more, as I began to realise how heavy is the responsibility for the nation. So many times, despite what every political critic has been saying about me, the leadership lot has fallen on me – and I don't know why. Could I have some secret things that people see in me? I don't know. Maybe the only way out is to retire. There are some up and coming young leaders and I've told them that after a few more years, they will be ready.

Any leader we get needs two qualities – one, you must be a worker; two you've got to have the respect of the whole nation. So far, we've got that respect through Peter Kenilorea. As for me, I'm just a workman, I try to get things done.

SOME SIGNIFICANT EVENTS SINCE INDEPENDENCE (1978)

1980	Sir Peter Kenilorea re-elected PM.
1981	Solomon Mamaloni elected PM.
1984	Kenilorea elected PM.
1986	Ezekiel Alebua elected PM.
1989	Mamaloni elected PM.
1993	Francis Billy Hilly elected PM.
1994	Mamaloni elected PM.
1997	Bartholomew Ulufa'alo elected PM.
1999	Ethnic strife breaks out on Guadalcanal Island.
2000	Malaita militia detains PM Ulufa'alo; replaced by Manasseh Sogavare.
	Mamaloni dies.
2001	Sir Allan Kemakeza elected PM.
	Negotiations to end violence unsuccessful.
2003	Solomon Islands Government asks Australian-led Regional Assistance Mission (RAMSI) to restore order.
2006	After Snyder Rini elected PM, violent protests are directed mainly against Honiara's Chinese residents.

	Rini resigns; replaced by Manasseh Sogavare.
2007	Major destruction in Western Solomons after earthquake and tsunami.
	Vote of no confidence in Sogavare government after Julian Moti, facing criminal charges in Australia, appointed Attorney-General. Derek Siku elected PM.
2010	Danny Philip elected PM.

REFERENCE:

Bennett, J.A., *Wealth of the Solomons: A History of a Pacific Archipelago, 1800 – 1978*. Honolulu: University of Hawai'i Press, 1987.

TUVALU

◆

CHAPTER TEN

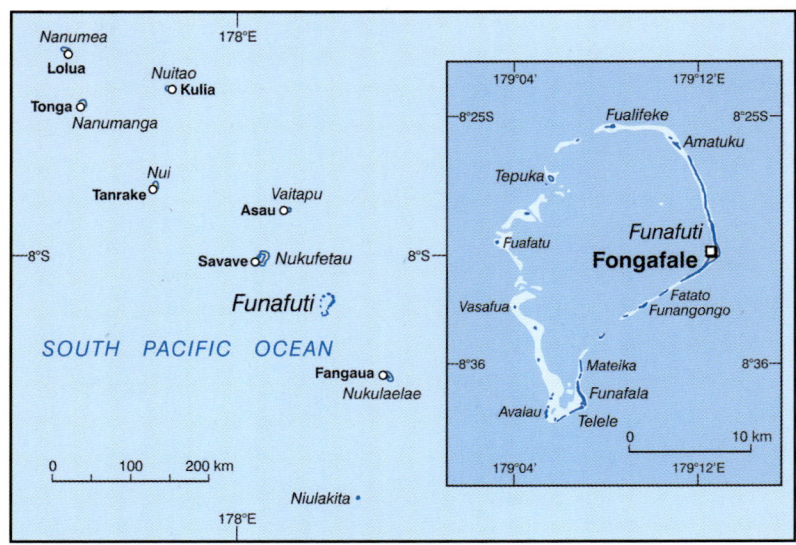

B Bradley, Cartographic Art Company

BACKGROUND

Voyagers from Samoa, Tonga and Uvea (Wallis Island) were believed to have settled Tuvalu about 2000 years ago. However, in 1986 scuba divers found evidence suggesting possible human habitation more than 8000 years earlier.

European contact – and World War II

Spanish explorer Alvaro de Mendana de Neira was the first European to sight Tuvalu, in 1568; next was a Spanish trader in 1781. From the 1820s they were followed by whalers, traders, blackbirders (slave traders), and, later in the century, London Missionary Society missionaries from Samoa. Britain colonised and named the Tuvalu island group the Ellice Islands in 1892 when they became part of the Gilbert and Ellice Islands Protectorate (later Colony). During World War II, American military bases were set up on several islands and Funafuti airfield was used to launch raids against the Japanese in both the Gilbert and Marshall Islands. Funafuti became the administrative centre of the colony during the war and suffered Japanese bombing raids in 1943.

Separation from the Gilbert Islands, now Kiribati, and independence

After the war, numbers of Tuvaluans migrated to the Gilbert Islands in search of education and work. Their growing numbers in the public service created tensions and rivalries between Micronesian Gilbert Islanders (I-Kiribati) and the Polynesian Ellice Islanders (Tuvaluans), many of whom favoured separation and an independent future. A referendum in 1974 resulted in a clear preference for separation. Tuvalu accordingly was granted self-government in 1975 with its own constitution and full independence in 1978.

Few resources, but good management

With a population of some 10,000 spread over nine small atolls, Tuvalu has few economic resources. Many Tuvaluans have sought work overseas, including on German ships, Japanese fishing vessels and, earlier, at Nauru's phosphate mine. Unlike other small Polynesian island groups, Tuvalu has no special relationship with a larger economy to which its citizens could freely move, although New Zealand has accepted some immigrants from Tuvalu over the years. Recognising Tuvalu would have to fend largely for itself, early leaders promoted the idea of a trust fund to generate investment revenue. In 1987, New Zealand agreed to start such a fund. Australia, Britain, Japan and Korea also contributed and Tuvalu added $A1.6 million. Twenty years after independence the fund was worth $A57 million. It has been described by historian and commentator Ron Crocombe (see Ref) as a significant success.

The challenge of climate change and rising sea levels

Rising ocean levels present the greatest threat to Tuvalu. Its atolls are approximately 4 metres above sea level and a number of them are already uninhabitable. It is estimated that in fifty years, Tuvalu as a territorial and inhabited land mass will not exist. As sea damage increases many Tuvaluans doubt their homeland can remain their home for long; they are likely to become the first entire population of environmental refugees. Presumably countries like New Zealand (home already to hundreds of thousands of Polynesians, both Māori and Pacific Islanders) and, if necessary, Australia, will accept Tuvaluans forced from their homelands. Every Tuvaluan worries what will happen as the ocean rises.

LEADER'S STORY: HON. BIKENIBEU PAENIU

Bikenibeu Paeniu, the country's prime minister from 1989 to 1993 and again from 1996 to 1999, is a graduate in agricultural economics of the University of the South Pacific. His name comes from the place where he was born in 1956 – Bikenibeu in Tarawa, capital of neighbouring Kiribati. His parents moved there when Kiribati and Tuvalu were jointly ruled by Britain and known as the Gilbert and Ellice Islands Colony.

Both my mum and dad were from Tuvalu, from Nukulaelae, the country's southern and smallest island. During my school days in Kiribati, I never felt different because I was Tuvaluan, from my I-Kiribati friends. There were times in school that there was fighting between the two races, but it really did not spark, or plant a seed of fear or discriminatory feeling that you are being discriminated against and all that. From my own knowledge the separation was instigated apparently through an underground movement by the Kiribati nationals because of a fear that the Tuvaluans were dominating and actually holding the top positions.

Nation of two races

It was a view of the Brits, their vision, that the two island groups should be thrown together and administered as one. But certainly it wasn't right for us. Looking back, I voted against separation, but I think our elders made the right decision to move

Bikenibeu Paeniu
PI Forum Secretariat

on because there's nothing wrong with Kiribati people, nothing wrong with us, we just are two different races altogether, two different cultures. I want to take you further back, too. Although we went together when the British said let's lump them together because they are side by side, at one time before then we were together with Tokelau. Tokelau was part of Kiribati and Tuvalu as a protectorate. We basically have the same language, same culture with Tokelau — we speak dialects — and our ties go back to blood ties as well. But the Tokelaus were annexed back to New Zealand by Britain, leaving us with Kiribati.

For some unknown reason, the British civil servants in the days when their empire was flourishing, maybe because they saw the potential in the Tuvaluans to help them run the phosphate mining on Ocean [Banaba] Island and the Tuvaluans were perhaps people they could rely on, and depend on them to produce or whatever. They had their reasons, but I think what they did in lumping us together to continue as a nation of two different races was not appropriate.

Forgotten Polynesians

There were other options besides separation and full independence for Tuvalu. But unfortunately our leaders and the Brits weren't really that cooperative in providing us options. Our leaders should have at least taken time not to rush things into independence, because there were other options. We could have gone back to the United Nations and requested to be incorporated like the Tokelaus. Because why was Tokelau given away, and why not Tuvalu, to New Zealand? When we were together we were Polynesians and that was a point I tried to make at the 2011 Pasifika Festival. We are the only Polynesian country formerly under British rule that has no formal ties with New Zealand. All the other Polynesian countries have formal ties by way of treaties; they are citizens of New Zealand, like Cook Islands, Niue and Tokelau; Samoa has a treaty, Tonga I believe has a similar arrangement. But none for Tuvalu. We are the forgotten Polynesia.

I don't regret of course that we're not like Tokelau; I think Tuvalu has done a lot of good on its own. I mean we are a nation now, independent in 1978 and now thirty-three years old. I can be proud that we still are a nation. But still the question is there, why annex Tokelau to New Zealand, leaving Tuvalu with Kiribati when we are two different people altogether?

Inventing a nation

Looking back now, we were inventing our own nation. Not just becoming independent but separating from Kiribati. Obviously traditionally we were long there; our eight islands used to be kingdoms of their own, linked with the same language, culture and all that, but to have to form a nation of our own, given no assets and a mere budgetary provision. All the colonial assets were left with Kiribati. We had only one ship. We had no share of the royalties from the British phosphate on Ocean Island so we started off with nothing.

Of course I pay tribute to the fathers of my nation; the government who started off. New Zealand and Australia helped us, and Britain. But the terms were very harsh. In fact in my time as prime minister, my political cronies were pushing me to take Great Britain to court for treating us so badly. I even took several trips to London to discuss that but in the end I came to the conviction 'Why cry over spilled milk?' The British gave us such harsh conditions with the hope that would discourage us from separating, but without the British I don't think people like us would have had the standard of education we did in our day. Compared to our sister countries in the Northern Pacific for instance, the French territories, the American former territories, Tuvalu is far far better off in terms of education. That is one good thing Britain did.

Talking of my own education, I must go back to the history of King George V and Elaine Bernacchi school. None of its students had ever won the Division One O Level Cambridge School Leaving Certificate. In our year, the class of 1974, five of us won the Division One, for the first time in the history of the Gilbert and Ellice Islands Colony. But those of us from the Tuvalu islands couldn't be given the medical scholarship because there were so many Tuvalu doctors at that time, so those scholarships were given to the Kiribati Division One students. I ended up pursuing a different course altogether, first a diploma in fisheries at the University of South Pacific [USP], but I didn't like it and shifted to agriculture and managed to get my Bachelor's from USP. But my point again, coming to university from King George V School was very easy in our first year. The quality of education then at KGV was really excellent.

At the time of independence, Tuvalu had only two university graduates. One was working at the University of the South Pacific in the registrar's office; the other, Alesala Pia, was sick at the time but he's back to normal now, as smart as he used to be. Apparently I was the first Tuvalu student to graduate with a degree after independence, and the first Tuvaluan citizen to come back with a Masters after independence.

I did have an affectionate regard for the British, probably because of what I believe the education system had done to me and people of my age and beyond. I think we were very fortunate to have had British teachers. But in those days some British officials were a bit arrogant and patronising, mostly, I think, the bureaucrats. If you talk to the British of nowadays, and I have the opportunity to converse with a number over the past five or six years, their attitude is totally different. I think in the days of our separation and independence, they were real bureaucrats I would say, they go by the books, very little flexibility, very narrowly focused I would say. I think they just served by following the general Administrative Orders, regardless of anything else. I would say there could have been sparklings of racism amongst a number of them.

Support for independence

Independence was wanted by the people of Tuvalu. In the referendum I think 99 percent voted for separation. At that time it was the wish of the people of Tuvalu to separate. The elders wanted it. I recall the reasons then were the fear of loss of our identity and our culture; the younger generations were gradually being absorbed into the Kiribati culture. But economics and sustainability, in terms of adequate finances and infrastructure, were not considered at all. The wish was just to get out and be on our own, to run our own affairs.

TUVALU

There was no second referendum about what sort of constitution Tuvalu would have. There were earlier visits to the islands to explain the options, I think the United Nations team came twice. The second time was dealing with the referendum, the first time was for two or three months, going around the nation explaining to the Tuvalu people the process, the outcome, the procedures and all that.

The possibility of becoming a republic was considered. But the decision was to remain a constitutional monarchy. It was not through a national convention or referendum, but through negotiations among the political leaders. I still believe enough time wasn't allowed by our early leaders to really map out the destiny of Tuvalu. Two years after separation, then self-governing, then independence. No time for nation-building, for proper planning at all. I would say Britain also did not help out in that. They could have given us time. Of course they wanted rid of us as soon as possible, because we know in those days Britain was letting go of her colonies, the empire was breaking down.

Choice of a new flag was done through a competition, and the Parliament of Tuvalu chose it, under the leadership of our first prime minister who still is alive, the Right Honourable Sir Toaripi Lauti. That flag was the choice of the people of Tuvalu, from day one of independence. So in 1996, when our fourth prime minister came in, the Right Honourable Sir Kamuta Latasi, he changed it because he's a strong supporter of a republic and he basically did not want to see any sign of British in there, especially the Union Jack. So he had a new flag in, which lasted for about a year or so. When I came in I had to change it back, on the principle that you just can't keep changing things like that. To pay tribute to the founders and the father of our nation we flew the flag of their choice, so what matters if the Union Jack is there? Really the flag is the flag of Tuvalu

NEW FLAGS FLYING

Tuvalu dancers
Photographer Julia Brooke-White
Julia Brooke-White Collection

so I opted to bring back the old flag, legislate it, so that any changes to the flag has to go through Parliament and all that, and it will not be a political choice of any particular leader. I saw it that way.

In October 1978 I was at university in Suva and went back to Funafuti for the independence celebrations. The depiction of the Tuvalu culture was excellent and it was so nice to see the people of Tuvalu there with all our traditional leaders and to see the culture of Tuvalu alive and very strong at the independence celebrations. I can still see it vividly in my mind now.

I can remember how it went: the Union Jack is pulled down and the new flag comes up and flew until today and continues to fly. I remember for the British royalty, it was Princess Margaret who came for the independence [celebrations]. And, of course, in any Tuvalu national celebrations, there must always be a church service accompanied by the singing of hymns, and of course the dancing and feasting. I danced myself – I was the choreographer of our dancing group from Nukulaelae.

Politics and the constitution

At that time there were no political parties, just groupings. Each member of parliament is independent. It was gentleman's groupings and agreements and all that. Of course, a prime minister when forming a government has to have the numbers, it's a numbers game. So you have to choose from within the numbers that supported you.

Adopting the constitution was an interesting occasion. The people of Tuvalu, and even, I would say, most of the leaders, hardly understand what the constitution was. Of course, they knew about the constitution but how to live and work by it, there's really very limited knowledge.

So what I would say is, constitutionally, it's a culture imposed on another culture, because the constitution of course is a Western ideal which I don't reject because human rights is important and all that. But how can we ensure it marries well with our culture so that our people know and are able to work within the approved constitution? In addition, the constitution actually requires a process of dialogue, consultation, culminating in a national convention to adopt the changes in a systematic manner, not in a piecemeal approach, the way it has been so far.

Looking back at what we had at the time of independence, there were our eight islands, the ninth island of Niulakita to the south, just north of Rotuma, Fiji. Our ocean, of 1 million square kilometres. where we know it's very rich in fish, there may even be manganese down there, so our assets were there. Our people, our clean white sand beaches, our crystal clear lagoons, of course our own traditional food crops. Copra was not valuable then, while it was still important, its market value was declining already. Money-wise, financial-wise we had just the taxes raised and the budgetary allocation from the British. I said earlier we had no share of the royalties of the British phosphates mined over Ocean Island. Had we a share there, we could have had lots of money by now.

Our country hasn't gone broke, thanks to our former leaders' proper management and careful spending of the funds. The British budgetary provision went off in 1987 and in that year under the government of Prime Minister Sir Puapua Tomasi and then his Minister of Finance, the late Henry Naisali, they formed the Tuvalu National Trust Fund. Contributions came from Britain, Australia, New Zealand, and of course Tuvalu. I think we started off with a capital of about $A27m. The fund, managed by fund managers overseas, and when market conditions work out well, provides distributions annually that supplement our national budget. That is one of the main institutions sustaining Tuvalu all these years.

Economic strengths

The sale of '.tv' was a baby I initiated. Tuvalu had been pursuing the abnormal to bring about benefits, and one is the dot-tv, our internet top level domain. When the internet was becoming a reality and there was big potential, I happened to be prime minister. I started pursuing it then, because TV obviously was an international language. We believed it was a blessing from God for us to have the dot-tv because we could have been TU but Turkey took that so we ended up having the TV, and it is still now making money. The first years I instigated that, the forecast was that Tuvalu could earn annually $A50 million, which could have been the case, but unfortunately, through different governments and different people helping us, we weren't able to reap the real benefits of that. At one time from the dot-tv we reaped up to $US40m – money coming out from heaven. Just from this dot-tv.

It's one of Tuvalu's strengths that some of our people are able to work out of Tuvalu and send money back. But I also caution that my people are relatively immobile, they do not come out in mass numbers to emigrate, and it's a personal choice for Tuvaluans who leave Tuvalu to come overseas. But we've tried over the years to build a knowledge-based economy in a way that we are among the highest per-capita qualified and well-educated people in terms of population.

Climate change refugees

On climate change, we don't have a formal policy that I'm aware of in terms of mitigation – it's so far a personal choice for people to leave. Though our people are well cognisant of the fate they are facing from climate change, we need the support of countries like New Zealand, Australia, in allowing our people to come in. I think we should be really treated as environmental climate change refugees, because we are.

Tuvalu now is host for king tides, which started about two or three years ago. People come to Tuvalu and they see mass acreage of our land and houses coming under sea water at times of king tides, so it is happening. We need to sit down and plan. I don't think it is really good to spur the wide scare amongst our people, but it's their free choice.

We need the cooperation of all to cut down on greenhouse gas emissions and control the emissions so that levels of CO_2 can be reduced and so forth.

I'm now coming to accept that probably in my grandchildren's lifetime, maybe even earlier, they may not have a nation to live in. I have championed action on climate change from day one. I wanted the debate started way back in 1990, culminating in the Climate Change Convention Framework in 1992 in Rio, where I was also the one signing for Tuvalu. I believe that God will never let Tuvaluans leave their homeland. The Bible speaks about only one flood, Noah's flood, but given the rate of what is happening right now, we see the tsunamis, we see all these earthquakes, we see industrialised countries not even really coming genuinely to commit, also with China and India. I think sooner or later, according to the IPCC, International Panel on Climate Change, Tuvalu will eventually be submerged underwater.

Regrets?

In terms of its performance as an independent nation, I would mark Tuvalu at about seven out of ten for now, referring 'specially to the years from independence, the first and second prime ministers, then when I came in. But things started going off balance from 1994 onwards, which is sad, because of all these political turmoils, in terms of votes of no confidence and all that. Otherwise, because of the trust fund and its board and how things are being managed, I will put seven out of ten.

I don't have regrets, looking back, that I was not able to be a doctor. I think I was probably destined for life in politics. When I was in KGV School on Tarawa I was deputy head boy, then when I went to the University of the South Pacific and finished off my two years' Bachelor of Agriculture at the University's School of Agriculture in Apia, Western Samoa, I served as president of the students' association, so I tend to have been kind of coached until I came into politics in 1988. So I don't have regrets. Now, of course I am an economist, and a lot of people will say that is dangerous because it breaks nations and all that, but I will say I am a people-centred economist, a welfare economist. I try all the time to put people first.

In Tuvalu lots of people believe that anybody can do the prime ministership. Unfortunately that is not the case. We need a leader who goes in there to serve the people; articulate, able to perform and produce and of course foremost, to sacrifice and serve the people.

SOME SIGNIFICANT EVENTS SINCE INDEPENDENCE (1978)

1979	Treaty of Friendship formally ends US claims to Funafuti, Nukufetau, Nukulaelae and Niulakita islands.
1987	New Zealand, Australia, Britain, Japan, Korea and Tuvalu contribute to Tuvalu Trust Fund.
1990s	Tuvalu begins selling internet domain rights to '.tv'.
2000	Tuvalu becomes 189th member of the United Nations.

2006	Smaller Island States Unit established by Pacific Islands Forum to serve Cook Islands, Kiribati, Marshall Islands, Nauru, Niue, Palau and Tuvalu.
2008	PM Apisai Ielimia addresses UN General Assembly on Tuvalu's vulnerability to the consequences of climate change.

REFERENCE

Crocombe, Ron (1929–2009), Emeritus Professor of Pacific Studies, University of the South Pacific; Founding Director, Institute of Pacific Studies.

KIRIBATI

CHAPTER ELEVEN

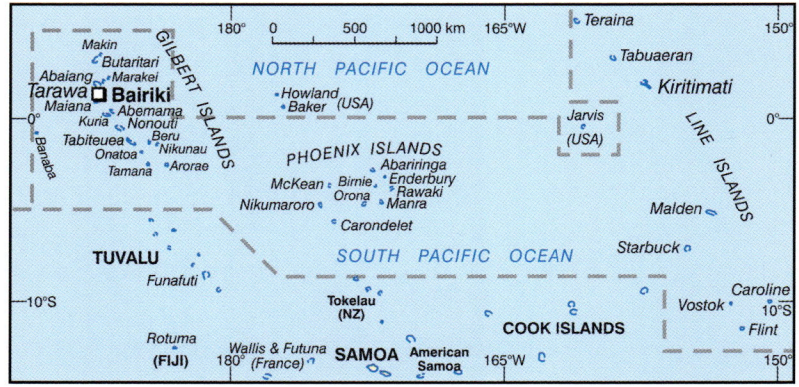

B Bradley, Cartographic Art Company

BACKGROUND

Kiribati is tiny – the total land area of its thirty-three coral atolls is 810 square kilometres – but it spreads over three million square kilometers of ocean. Its three island groups, Gilberts, Phoenix and Line, straddle the equator and the date line. The nation of 100,000 people is a genuine 'global centre'.

The Phoenix and Line groups have never been permanently settled, but for 3000 years Micronesian people have survived on the meagre land and rich sea resources of the sixteen Gilbert Islands. Over most of that time, the atoll dwellers were left alone to harvest coconuts, grow taro in sandy soil and catch an abundance of fish. To passing mariners (including Sir Francis Drake in the 1580s) the islands were only navigational hazards until the nineteenth century when foreigners landed in search of turtle shell, pearls, copra and labour. Between 1830 and 1870 men were taken by blackbirders to slave work in Peru's salt and silver mines and the cattle stations of New South Wales. But the trade did not flourish. Micronesians live by the sea and after a week on the dusty Australian plains the hardy conscripts walked back to the coast and waited for mission ships to bring them home.

A peaceful protectorate

Home was tough and demanding. Competition for land led to frequent inter-island raids, rape, murder and invasion; feuding villages and the few European missionaries and settlers lived in fear of sudden reprisal. In 1892, after sailors from HMS *Royalist* had ended one such battle, the British government declared the Gilbert Islands to be a protectorate and, to widespread satisfaction, fighting and feuding ceased.

Eight years later, the colonial office granted the Pacific Islands Company an exclusive licence to mine recently discovered

Workers digging for phosphate, Banaba; ca 1909
Photographer Lilian Arundel
Colville Collection Alexander Turnbull Library, Wellington, NZ.
PAColl-6044-01

phosphate on nearby Banaba (Ocean Island). Although illegal (Banaba was not included in the protectorate until 1916) this act was to have profound consequences for the future of the Gilberts/Kiribati.

A Micronesian/Polynesian colony

In 1908 British officials moved from their first capital Tarawa to Banaba and in 1916 the Ellice Islands (now Tuvalu) and Tokelau were incorporated into the Gilbert and Ellice Islands Colony (GEIC). For the first half of the twentieth century, the colony's islands were administered by their *unimane* (elders) and *kaubure* (councillors) under the direction of island magistrates and British officials.

Government House, Banaba; ca 1909
Photographer Lilian Arundel
Colville Collection Alexander Turnbull Library, Wellington, NZ.
PAColl-6044-17

Generally regarded as a backwater of Empire, the GEIC was to attract some international attention with the publication of *A Pattern of Islands*, Arthur Grimble's tales of a district officer's life in Micronesia written with what's been described as 'an attractive self-denigration, uncommon in the British Colonial Service' (Snow & Waine 1979: 213)

Phosphate

Others with an interest in the colony were British and Australasian farmers who imported phosphate mined from Banaba. In 1913, the Banabans succeeded in claiming greater compensation and royalties for the benefit of their community while the colonial government also gained by increased mining licence revenue. This arrangement continued after 1919 when the British Phosphate Commission (owned by Britain, Australia and New Zealand) replaced the Pacific Phosphate Company, continuing to employ many Gilbertese (now known as I-Kiribati) as labourers. By 1945, when their island was no longer habitable, Banabans had built up sufficient funds to allow most of them to resettle on Rabi, an island they had bought in Fiji. The colonial government had also put revenue into a development fund, the balance of which would eventually be passed to independent Kiribati.

World War II and its aftermath

On 10 December 1941, three days after the attack on Pearl Harbour dragged the United States into World War II, Japanese forces landed on Tarawa. Most Europeans fled to Fiji; the remaining few were executed. The Gilbertese were forbidden to move from their atolls as battles raged across Melanesia and Micronesia, finally reaching the colony in 1943 when American troops landed on Tarawa's Betio beach and drove out the Japanese. Mementos of that awful battle still remain.

The 1950s brought the first moves towards self-government in the form of a colony conference, at which Gilbertese from many walks of life recommended policies and projects. Control still lay with colonial officials but Gilbertese people were being introduced to government business. Executive and advisory councils were established. In 1965 the Gilbertese National Party was calling for faster change and two years later its leader was first among the eighteen elected Gilbertese and five Ellice Islander members of the new house of representatives.

Separate or together?

Progress to independence was delayed by two questions. The first was whether the Gilbert Islands and the Ellice Islands should remain together and form one nation. In a referendum Ellice Islanders voted for separation and became Tuvalu in 1978, a year earlier than their I-Kiribati neighbours, who still had to resolve the second delaying question: should Banabans (most of whom had become citizens of Fiji) get a larger share of revenue and compensation from the phosphate mining industry, and be represented in the *maneaba ni maungatabu*, the new nation's parliament? 'Yes' was the answer in both cases and in 1979, just as Banaba's phosphate deposits were exhausted, the Gilbert Islands became the independent nation of Kiribati.

LEADER'S STORY: SIR IEREMIA TABAI

Ieremia (later Sir Ieremia) **Tabai** was the first president, or *beretitente* of Kiribati. He was born on the southern Gilbert Island of Nonouti.

KIRIBATI

◆ ◆ ◆

When I was eleven I went to Tarawa as a first former at King George V High School and studied maths, biology, geography, history and English, which is not an easy language. In primary school I had learned how to construct sentences and so on but I am still learning now at my age. I always carry my small dictionary with me in case I hear a word I do not understand. At high school I never came first in my class but I consistently came second, so I was recommended for a New Zealand scholarship to study in that country. I must have been good enough. I went to St Andrew's College in Papanui Road, Christchurch. The Head of the School, Ian Galloway, met us at the airport and took us to his home. We spent about a month there being introduced to the New Zealand way of life. We were taught to sit at the table and which spoon and fork to take first and so on. And never to stretch out to get something you want, always ask. Another guy was with me – he's now a lecturer at Alafua College (the Alafua Campus of the University of the South Pacific) in Samoa. When we got to St Andrew's, there were two other people from Kiribati. One was in the USA for many years and now he's back on Funafuti in Tuvalu. And one is now in New Zealand, I think permanently. He's a very well-known economist, working in the region somewhere.

Ieremia Tabai
PI Forum Secretariat

NEW FLAGS FLYING

In distant New Zealand

I felt very lonely, cut off from home and every evening, at least when I first arrived, I cried in my bed. And every week I stood at the gate waiting for the postman to come and if I didn't get a letter, I was very disappointed and I was beginning to think about all sorts of things, particularly when my classmates were a bit cheeky; that made life that much harder. On a sports day we had to cycle to another school, but I didn't have a bicycle, I couldn't afford it. I tried to avoid having to say that I didn't have a bike to go on. It was not easy and I regard my New Zealand experience as a particularly hard one. I remember that each seven days we were given 30 cents by the school and I gave 5 cents to the offering because we went to church every morning. So I saved 25 cents and by the end of the term I had a few dollars to spend. That taught me to be careful with resources and look after myself and so on.

Changes at home

From St Andrew's I went on to study accounting and graduated. When I returned to Tarawa in the mid-1970s, there must have been only a handful of us with a so-called degree from a Western country so it was easy to get a job. I was posted to the Ministry of Finance. Our country, the Gilbert and Ellice Islands Colony, was at the stage of self-government, with a chief minister leading the government in everything except foreign affairs and defence. They were controlled by a British man on the ground – John Smith. The next step for us would be independence. The people here are by nature very quiet, so there was no harsh push from them for independence. The whole process was helped by the attitude of the British government who were very keen to call it a day. They said it was no longer fashionable to have colonies and their role was to get us organised and ready to be on our own. So it was never a question of having to struggle or fight for independence. Really our masters were very keen to leave us at any time.

After I had been in the ministry for a year, a general election was announced and I decided to contest it. The chief minister was Naboua Ratieta. He had been groomed and in the game for many years and everyone was expecting that he would be the next leader. But when four friends and I were elected to the House, it was obvious that one of us would become chief minister and according to the constitution, that decision had to be made in the House. We five knew we would become members of the new government and we sat down and talked about it. The man we chose to support decided he did not want the job, then the others said they would not stand against me. Being there at the right time is important in politics and when the one we had wanted

Government Buildings, Tarawa; ca 2010
PI Forum Secretariat

had gone, they looked around and that's how I became chief minister. It was then our government's responsibility to negotiate our financial package and constitution and all the rest of it.

A special constitution

Our constitution is not the same as any other in the region, it's very different from what you have in New Zealand and in Australia. And I must admit I am really pleased with the result. It's working, our neighbours now are talking about adopting our system. Recently I heard on the radio people talking about the Tongan election and how it had been won on a 30 percent popular vote. That will never happen here now. You only get in when more than 50 percent of the people want you. It is a first past the post system but with the qualification that you must have over 50 percent of the vote to be elected. That's why I believe our system is good.

Another thing I am happy about is the stability our constitution gives us. I heard that Vanuatu's prime minister had lost a confidence motion, and that's really funny when the leader is actually on his way to Mexico and his friends are back home voting him out. It would never happen here. Compared to the experience of the other countries in the region, politically we are very stable and that's because of our constitution, which we built up after very extensive consultation on all the islands and villages. I was still in Parliament at that time. The results were brought to Tarawa and considered by a national constitution convention. When the nature of the constitution was agreed, recommendations were put to Parliament and gone through again. After that, we went back to our islands again and after that process we got what we've got now. A very extensive process of consultation.

We took the view that you really have to look at the local element and not be bothered about what happens in the UK or Australia or New Zealand. We have an executive president and the way he is elected is different from any other system in the world. We have the concept of a limited term which we have borrowed from the Americans and the French. The limited term is a very good idea, if you ask me. Before we became independent, we saw in places such as Indonesia a guy who had been there for years and years. Even among our neighbours – I don't want to mention their names – but they have been there for years and years. My view is it is wrong for any particular person to be in government for too long. That's why we have a limited term. You can only serve a maximum of twelve years no matter how good you are.

Separate nations – a mistake?

Before I became chief minister, a critical pre-independence decision had been taken by our colonial partners, the people of the Ellice Islands (now Tuvalu). The British gave them the option to remain with the Gilbert Islands or go their own way. They chose to go their own way and I can well understand the reason. They felt they would be outnumbered and dominated by our people and that's why they have to go on their way. When I look back I think it would have been better if we had stayed together as a country. I think we could have been a bigger country with a bigger voice and so on and they are very resourceful with those small atolls there. They seem to be doing well. I look at the statistics and the value of their reserve fund per capita is much better than ours. I guess I am biased because I married a girl from Tuvalu. The decision to separate was probably a mistake of the people at that time, but it's history now and we get on with our Tuvalu neighbours very well indeed.

Banaba kept in the family

Another thing we had to try to resolve was the long dispute over Banaba. They wanted to go their own way and we said no and we ended up with a compromise in the constitution where there is a chapter that deals entirely with Banaba. The whole intent there is that we would not be able to take away their land or do anything on their land without the consent of their Rabi Council. That chapter was really imposed by the British who wanted to leave this part of the world with their reputation intact. Their demand to take Banaba away to Fiji didn't make sense anyway so we stuck to our view that the Banabans should remain with us and I think that was the right decision.

The British decided that phosphate mining would end in 1979 so on Independence Day we lost our main source of income and since then it's affected the level of services we can provide. We've got a budget of about $A18–19 million a year. We accepted that, but it's very hard. And the minister for the budget for 2012 has had to budget for a decrease in income and expenditure because he has no other option. We now have what is called the reserve fund which is the main income earner for the government. It's worth about $A5–600 million and the interest each year we are using as a balancing item in our budget.

Independence celebrations

I can't remember much about our Independence Day but at the celebration on the small soccer field next to State House I was given some pieces of paper which had already been drafted and agreed. It was really a formality, to do with our constitution. I seem to remember the words 'Order-in-Council'. I made a speech but I can't remember what I said. It's a courtesy, that sort of thing. There's not much difference from country to country.

They all say the same sort of thing. The real test is what happens afterwards.

It was a hectic day for me. I had to look after so many VIPs like Princess Anne. I'm sure they all enjoyed it and were happy to see how the locals in a small place like the Gilberts played their games. We are not used to fancy celebrations such as the Fijians have, you know, the kava drinking and the Police Band. I've seen some of them – and they can put on a show. When I became chief minister my predecessor had spent a lot of money on a band and a defence force but the first thing we did in government was to disband it.

Self-reliance

I strongly believe political independence must be accompanied by economic independence and so we gave up, ahead of schedule, the aid Britain had promised to us over a five year period. We weren't economically independent by then but we wanted to show we were on the way towards doing things for ourselves. I cannot be sure that all the people supported that, but they put us back into power at the next election. We kept the main services going and the people were basically happy.

We were the first South Pacific country to have a fishing plan. When the Russians approached us about allowing them to fish in our waters, I said, 'Yes, of course, if we can agree on the terms'. It was big news at that time. I was abused locally, politically, by the church groups, with marches and so on, but I was convinced I was right. I did my homework, studied the law and told Australia and New Zealand 'If you can license Russian fleets to catch your fish, why can't we?' They really had no answer except 'You are too small'. I came back and said, 'Under international rules, they can sail within twelve miles of our beaches without a fishing licence'.

It may have changed the attitude of certain people. It's a funny world. Soon after that I went to Fiji and was surprised to be met at the airport by a senior minister of Ratu Mara's government. He took me to my hotel room and, for the first time, offered to do things for Kiribati. I said 'No, I will not change'. And that's the way it is.

We have also tried to develop our own fishing industry through a scheme called *Te Mautari*. After twenty years it still gives us only a 5 to 10 percent return which is too small. We jointly own a purse seiner with our Japanese friends and there is a lot going on among neighbouring countries working together to exploit Pacific tuna, which is about half of the world's resource. We don't get a fair return from it. It's funny because all the countries that are fishing in our zone are our friends — South Korea, Japan, Taiwan, USA — but when it comes to economics, you don't have any friends, it's the money! It's the way the world works; that's one thing I have learned.

We saw that when Britain, Australia and New Zealand benefited from cheap phosphate and sold it below the world price but the residuals that came to us were very low.

Hard work and success

There's still a lot of work to do here and our problems are immense, but I think Kiribati has earned a pass mark since independence. I still have a strong interest in politics here, which is why I represent my island of Nonouti in the *maneaba ni maungatabu* (our parliament). When you live on the atolls, it's very hard to find a job and without one you're reduced to a very miserable existence. Politics is an area where I can make a contribution.

I may be old-fashioned but one thing holding us back is fast population growth. It's affecting our standards, our environment, everything we value. I talk about this in the villages and in Parliament. Looking at the world's fertility rate, in developed countries like UK, France, Italy, Spain, on average, a woman will give birth to one child in her lifetime. Here in Kiribati it is in excess of five per woman and our population is about 100,000. We cannot afford that and unless we seriously address that question, things will get worse.

It is natural that the small island states will continue to struggle, but the key to the development of each nation is at the door of national leaders. They have to take the hard decisions about moving forward. I hope New Zealand's initiative to expand the work scheme will go ahead because that's one thing that will have an impact on smaller countries. But I understand that in this world you do not have permanent friends, just permanent interests. We

I-Kiribati youth, Tarawa; ca 2010
PI Forum Secretariat

realised it was no longer in the interests of the British to hang around here, and they had to go back and be on their own. We know that we also have to be on our own, and just do what we can afford. When I first came to Parliament the words I used a lot were self-reliance. I still believe in it.

SOME SIGNIFICANT EVENTS SINCE INDEPENDENCE (1979)

1979	Treaty of Friendship allows USA use but not ownership of some Phoenix and Line islands.
1985	Political parties introduced.
1994	Teburoro Tito elected *beretitente*.
1998	Tito re-elected.
1999	Kiribati becomes UN member.
2002	Controversial law allows government closure of newspapers.
2003	Tito re-elected; loses confidence vote; Anote Tong elected *beretitente*; appoints Ms Teima Onorio deputy.
2007	Tong re-elected.
2009	American Association for Advancement of Science identifies Kiribati as 'among the first to feel the impact of climate change'.
2012	President Tong appeals for international help to buy land in Fiji for re-settlement of I-Kiribati driven from their homes by rising sea levels.

◆

REFERENCE:

Snow, P. and Waine, S., *The People from the Horizon*. London: Phaidon Press, 1979.

VANUATU

CHAPTER TWELVE

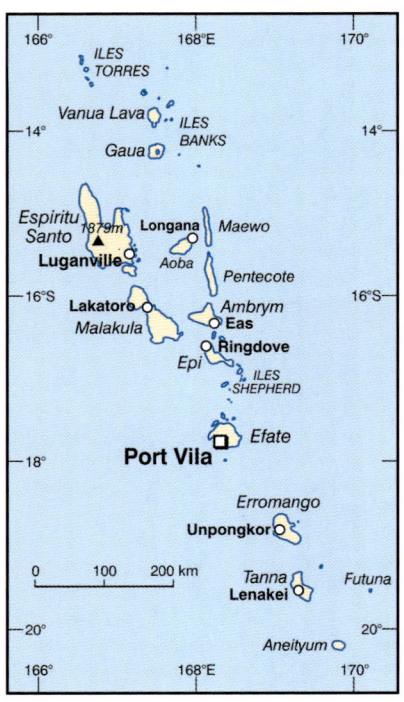

B Bradley, Cartographic Art Company

BACKGROUND

Vanuatu is believed to have been settled by Austronesian-speaking peoples around 4000 years ago. One of the earliest known leaders was the chief, Roy Mata, who united a number of tribes in 1200 AD. The chain of eighty Melanesian islands running north from Fiji and New Caledonia to the Solomon Islands has suffered much from foreigners with conflicting interests. Early seventeenth century Spanish, French, Portuguese and British explorers were followed by nineteenth century raiders and privateers keen to plunder the resources of the group, which had been named the New Hebrides by Captain James Cook.

Early devastating exploitation and the curious 'condominium'

By 1825 every sandalwood tree had been felled and hundreds of islanders had been bullied, killed or dragged away to slavery in Australia by disreputable traders.

Missionaries began arriving in 1839 but early conversion attempts were often thwarted.

VANUATU

Missionary J Williams arrives at Tanna, Vanuatu. He is murdered the next day; 1841. Engraver George Baxter
Alexander Turnbull Library, Wellington, NZ. B-088-015

Many persevered and were allowed to evangelise. Unfortunately, they also introduced smallpox, influenza, pneumonia and other diseases which killed many of the converted.

British and French naval ships dominated the waters off Vanuatu with the sole purpose of keeping out rivals. In 1888, they signed a joint naval agreement, the first of many ill-founded compromises imposed on the islanders, later called the Ni-Vanuatu. In 1906 Britain and France set up the Condominium of the New Hebrides — a unique, absurd colonial construct. Its first court consisted of British and French judges, a Dutch registrar and a Spanish president who spoke little French and less English.

Over the seventy-six years of what soon came to be called the 'Pandemonium', British and French administrators ran separate police, education and other services.

The 100,000 or so islanders, separated already into 110 language groups, were further divided into anglophones and francophones. Chinese, and French 'colon' farmers from New Caledonia, came to buy land despite the New Hebrideans' objections.

In 1958 an advisory council was established, increasing local hopes that land sales would be stopped and decolonisation started, but those hopes quickly fell away. In 1959 President de Gaulle declared France would keep control of her Pacific territories. Soon after, Prime Minister Macmillan declared Britain was to leave her colonies. For a further twenty years, colonial conflict would bedevil constitutional progress.

Pressure for political change

In 1971 returning Ni-Vanuatu graduates began to work for political change, while French officials encouraged land sales to settlers supporting colonial rule. The British (anxious that France support their bid to join the EEC) colluded with French authorities to delay political progress.

In the 1975 election of the first representative assembly, the largely anglophone New Hebrides National Party (NHNP), led by Father Walter Lini, won most Ni-Vanuatu votes but was denied majority control by six members appointed by the British and French resident commissioners. The NHNP boycotted the assembly. When requests for a more democratic system were refused, the party refused to take part in the 1977 election. A minority government was installed and public protests were quelled with tear gas. French officials encouraged disruptive groups on the island of Tanna and a northern secessionist movement, Nagriamel, which would continue to cause trouble after independence.

In the 1979 representative assembly election, the Vanuaaku Party (formerly the NHNP) won 62 percent of votes and twenty-six of the thirty-nine seats. Believing the country's future should be determined at home, it boycotted constitutional meetings in Paris but attended discussions in Port Vila until a new constitution, restricting land ownership to Ni-Vanuatu and entrenching French culture, was agreed by 'Melanesian consensus'.

Independence at last

However, Vanuatu's Independence Day – like its seventy-four years of condominium history – was soured by its colonial masters. On 30 July 1980, cheering crowds filled the capital. But the flag-raising in Luganville on Espiritu Santo was jeered by Nagriamel supporters. Also present were British and French troops, sent at the insistence of the French until the new government guaranteed protection to French interests.

LEADER'S STORY: FR WALTER LINI

Walter Lini, the first prime minister, was the man who had to resolve this colonial interference. An Anglican priest who became known as the father of independence, he was born on Pentecost Island and brought up as an English-speaking New Hebridean.

Land sales to foreigners

When I was a student, I thought Vanuatu's colonial experience, perhaps alone in the Pacific, had been totally negative. That

Walter Lini
PI Forum Secretariat

became more clear in 1960 when Americans came and bought plots of land, lots of land and subdivided it. When the landowners and we Ni-Vanuatu, but mostly members of the advisory council, were beginning to question why the French and the British were doing this, even though at every session of the advisory council the question would be asked, the question was never answered.

We were sitting there and everyone was sitting there but the land was being taken away from under our nose and it was clear that there was no political power and the French and the British were not going to stop it for us so they let it happen legally. They tried to make it a legal deal with the Americans but obviously the churches and the people of Vanuatu, even the missionaries who were in Vanuatu, were totally against what was happening.

I tried to persuade them that this was wrong. The British, that is. Mainly because I was able to communicate with them because I knew enough English to speak with them. The person in charge of the Anglican church at that time was also a member of the advisory council, an archdeacon who then became bishop. So we tried to discuss it with him. We put our thoughts together so that he could take the feeling and the thinking of our people to the advisory council. He was the one who was outspoken against the land sale that had been taking place, and subdividing the land.

It was very dangerous to speak out in those days. But it was perhaps easier for an Anglican church leader to do it ... even a missionary, an archdeacon. I don't think the British would touch him, or the French, so it was right that he should do it.

Differences between Britain and France

It was sad for us to see that the British were hastening Fiji to independence, and ready to do so in the Gilberts and the Solomons, but not in the New Hebrides. But we began to understand that because it is a condominium, the British cannot do it on their own. It also began to dawn on us that the British would be willing to give independence to the New Hebrides but the French were clearly totally against that.

When politics began for me in 1970–1 it was clear I should try and push our thoughts and ideas through English language and put them before the British district agents and other British administrators and missionaries in Vanuatu or New Hebrides at the time.

Political action

The start of our political activity was when we formed what we called the New Hebrides Cultural Association. This was decided upon on Queen's Birthday 1970. It was at the cocktail hour. Three or four of us who were educated in New Zealand had already started this Western Pacific Students' Association, and some of the thoughts we had started here. We stood there together and drank the whole length of time for the cocktail before we realised everyone had already left! The British Commissioner came and almost chased us out, so when we went out we said 'Okay, we will start tomorrow, we will work for a political change, we will form a Cultural, a New Hebrides Cultural Association'. That was in May.

It became a political movement three months after it was formed. We had a meeting and then we considered everything that we did was not enough for an 'association' to raise and question and put forward, and we thought it would be better to form a political party to support what the members of the advisory council were demanding from the French and the British administrators at that time. So in September we became a political party, the New Hebrides National Party.

As soon as we called it the New Hebrides National Party then everyone, including other people in other places too, understood that there was a political group, because our 'cultural association' was not clear. So we maintained the party as the New Hebrides National Party. We waited until 1976. Then we began to discuss that maybe the French and the British now know and are sure that we have political aims and the party that we have set up here is a political party.

To get the word out on what we were doing, we had small pamphlets, about sixteen pages, the first one called the *New Hebridean Viewpoint*. We continued to call it the *New Hebridean Viewpoint* until it became clear to us that the only way that we would be able to deal to the French and the British at the time was to change the name of the party, so they wouldn't understand what it means! So we changed the name. We had a congress at Tauto on Malakula, we decided on various proposed names, and then we came up with Vanuaaku Party which in fact means the same, it means the National Party. Our main effort, our main emphasis at the time, was to try to confuse the British and the French, so they wouldn't know what Vanuaaku Party means.

Civil disobedience

In 1977 there was supposed to be an election. Then we decided we would not participate because we were totally against going to Paris and London to meet. The Vanuaaku Party said that we would meet in Vila, not in Paris or London.

VANUATU

Others had gone to London, the Fijians, of course. And even our opposition, UCNH, the union of moderate parties went. They even bought our plane tickets, they worked out allowances for us in London, we all went and collected them. At the time of boarding the plane we refused to go. So the others went.

It appeared to be a piece of disobedience, but we decided we would not go. We emphatically told them that it is very important to hold a meeting in New Hebrides because we are discussing New Hebrides. We should not hold it in London or Paris. We stood by that and those who went to Paris and London decided on a date of election. Then the election came. We also boycotted the election, saying that if not enough people go to polls, it will be difficult to set up a government. So they held the election and then the government could not work.

Market Place, Port Vila, Vanuatu; ca 1998
Photographer Julia Brooke-White
Julia Brooke-White Collection

We encouraged civil disobedience against the government. I don't know where we learnt it from. In fact we had some influence from Western Samoa, some knowledge of what had happened in that country at one time. That is the only place we could say we had learned from. So we took that stand and we decided not to go to elections and instead we would declare a provisional government. When we declared that provisional government, we paralysed all the services the government can carry out in the rural areas. Even, we would not allow the government officers, especially the British government officers to go, and we arrested a number of British district agents, one in the Banks Islands, another in Tanna. We held them and then we let them go again after discussion – at the threat of arresting all of us we let them go!

We were certainly risking imprisonment and worse. But it was good we did not hide on one of the islands, we were in Vila and we did everything and we communicated every day with the government, both the French and the British. I was in Vila so sometimes I would call the British resident commissioner to talk with him, or one of his officers. And the French, I'd talk to him and his officers.

Protests and risks

At times, I sensed that maybe if I go to that meeting then they'd arrest me, because one time I rang a famous radio person named Jean Masias, he was French and head of that department. He was the head for the whole of Radio Vanuatu. So I rang him and said I have some news I want to report to you, I want to come and give it to you in the office. He said, 'No, don't come to the office but I will be waiting in a car at such-and-such a place with one other officer'. Then as soon as I put down the phone I said to my other two people who were supposed to go and see him, 'We shall not go'. Because they refused to see us in their office, we refused to see them in their car. We will not meet them on the road. If we meet them on the road maybe they will listen to what we say, if not, they will kill us or arrest us. So we didn't go.

There were times when we felt we were in some danger. Another time which was very tense was when we decided to bring a radio transmitter into Vanuatu. It came in the plane through Immigration, passed. As soon as we put that suitcase in a taxi we reached the point where we had all the people ready, one to pick it up, next to pick it up and run with it, then next we were at the point where we could hide it. It was very tense at that time when the person who was bringing it came through Immigration, and then passing through. As soon as it was placed in the car, in fifteen minutes it was in the place where we wanted it to be! You can say it's a kind of treason against the established government – but we had to do it.

Even as a priest I thought it was quite justified because I thought I was doing it for the right of the people.

Then there were changes that put Father Leymang in. He was prime minister and I became his deputy. It was not an election, just a government established by negotiation, to get some members from our side, and some members from theirs.

Citizenship and land

We decided that because of the experience that we had with the New Hebrides identity card, it was alright to have that identity card, but in a number of places we were not accepted. Citizenship was important. We also knew at that time that there were people like the French, who had dual citizenship. So when we looked at the constitution, we decided that it would be very important for us to have only one citizenship. If you are going to have a Frenchman wanting to become a Ni-Vanuatu citizen, he has to renounce his French citizenship. Or the British or New Zealander or others – so it was just one.

On land ownership, we decided – it was one of the key points of our constitutional discussion – to make sure that all lands in Vanuatu returned to the custom owner, to make sure that the Americans and all the other people who bought big masses of land would not take this land away, it would still be Ni-Vanuatu. The land issue was the most controversial and difficult. We were not going to compromise. And we were glad that it was agreed on by every political party, even those other parties who were against independence.

Decentralisation was the very last point to agree on, because the French and the francophone parties insisted that we shall not agree to the constitution until it is clearly indicated that before independence is granted, we have to have a government of Tafea in the south, and a government of Santo. It has to be worked out before, and if it is possible, we must do that before we get independence.

Final negotiations

So we tried from 7 o'clock in the morning until it was 7 at night, we couldn't agree on that point. We continued the next day and about 5 o'clock we decided okay, we'll sign the constitution. We agreed on the constitution. The cocktail that was prepared for us in the French Residency, when all the guests were there at 7 pm waiting, including the members of the UN observing team, all the dinner and cocktail was wasted, none of us went to eat. We were too exhausted.

Afterwards I did write to thank the British and French 'for their patience and tolerance'. I was at times angry. But sincerely, I thought the patience that the British and the French had was in fact sincere. The French and the British in fact did not do anything to develop us. In fact they waited, waited and waited until we saw, ourselves, how we should begin to move to get self-reliance, no, self-government and independence. It was not them forcing us, but our people demanded it from them. In fact I thought that we went to independence because we really wanted it, not because it was forced upon us.

Difficulties with colonial masters and rebel leader Jimmy Stevens

During the time of the work-up to elections, and after elections, I became more frustrated with the French and the British. I became more mad with what the French were trying to do, because all the delays had been mostly by the French. We would sit, for example, in a security council, which was me, the French resident commissioner, and the British, and we would agree if there was a situation of law and order developing in one of the islands. We would agree, the British would send their police immediately, the French would drag their feet and then maybe instead of sending it before the morning, in the middle of the day they'd say 'Oh we've decided not to send police forces'. So those were the incidents or the cases that really made me much madder. I became mad because the French were deliberately trying to tell us lies and deliberately trying to show that they were in control, not us.

When the situation developed in Santo, with Jimmy Stevens, we had to deal right away with it. The French and the British were still there, and I was really frustrated when we were able to get the British army, the British marines to come and stay there, and then the French brought theirs to Vanuatu too, but they wouldn't do anything.

So my experience of having UN forces or different governments' forces as a peacekeeping force in a country which has an internal problem is that it would be very difficult for the police or the security forces to take any action. Especially if someone who is overall commander of the forces has a completely different view and wants to direct things the way he wants, not for peace but perhaps to continue. Jimmy Stevens is a very nice person to talk to, but he's a very devious man. He'll tell you one thing but immediately after you go, he will do something else. I became more dissatisfied when we would work on a programme of work with the British and the French and when we'd finished, the French would send their own person to talk with Jimmy Stevens and then they would come with what Jimmy Stevens had said to tell us.

At one point we did feel that the country might fracture, until we sent the British and the French back then we got the PNG forces to come in with the Australians, to give us the backing, then we were able to give direction, saying, this is what we want, then the PNG people will carry it out, but when the British and the French were there we would not be able to do that.

I felt sad that it was necessary to put Jimmy Stevens into gaol. That was so, and a number of times I personally, would release him, but my fear is that if we began to do that, the constitution and subsidiary laws that have been made to govern the actions of individual political leaders or whatever will begin to erode the respect for law and order. Court judgments about acts of treason will no longer be respected so even though as a priest I felt we should forgive Jimmy Stevens and all his followers for what they had done, again I questioned whether governments are there to forgive. I resolved that governments are not there to forgive. The churches and individual persons are there to forgive, but the governments are there to make sure the law is upheld, and it is seen to be providing justice for all.

Government and Independence

I agree that gaining independence can be easier than making it work. That was true in our case because we had a common cause, we wanted to make sure we did not lose our land in Vanuatu, that's why we struggled and we were able to unify the whole population, of New Hebrideans then but today Ni-Vanuatu. It was easy to achieve independence because we did not want to lose our land but we also wanted to have a constitution to protect our land and all the things that we have. But it was more difficult to govern because we had not experienced the art of decision-making, quick decisions that will have quick results or long-term results, decisions that are very important for national security.

We did not have any experience in that and that is why, after we became independent, I went to Ratu Mara and asked him 'Sir, I put the question to you – what are your views in running a country after independence? What are the most important things you must do?' He said 'Only two. One – make sure you do not take a long time to make a decision. If you have to decide, decide. Secondly – if you find someone in your government is trying to slow down the decisions and the process of implementing what has been decided, get rid of him'. That was very useful – it helped me quite a lot.

SOME SIGNIFICANT EVENTS SINCE INDEPENDENCE (1980)

1980

August	Lini government sends French/British troops home; asks Papua New Guinea to help. Terrorist activity on Santo increases. PNG troops arrest Jimmy Stevens and some foreigners.

September	PNG troops leave. Vanuatu police charge several hundred people associated with rebellion. Jimmy Stevens sentenced to 14.5 years' prison.
1981	Most prisoners released. Vanuatu official denied entry to New Caledonia. French ambassador asked to leave Vanuatu.
1983	Vanuaaku Party re-elected.
1987	Vanuaaku Party splits; Coalition governs under PM Lini.
1991	Coalition of Vanuaaku/Union of Moderate Parties governs under Maxime Carlot Korman (first francophone PM).
1996	Coup d'etat attempt fails.
1997	Asian Development Bank programme; tax/public service reforms.
1999	Father Lini dies. Barak Sope, leader of Melanesian Progressive Party, elected PM.
2002	Sope convicted of forgery.
2003	Sope pardoned.
2004	President Alfred Maseng steps down when criminal record revealed, replaced by K Mataskelekele. Serge Vohor elected PM, replaced by Ham Lini after no-confidence vote.
2008	Coalition governs under PM Edward Natapei.
2009	Natapei survives no confidence motion.

FEDERATED STATES OF MICRONESIA

CHAPTER THIRTEEN

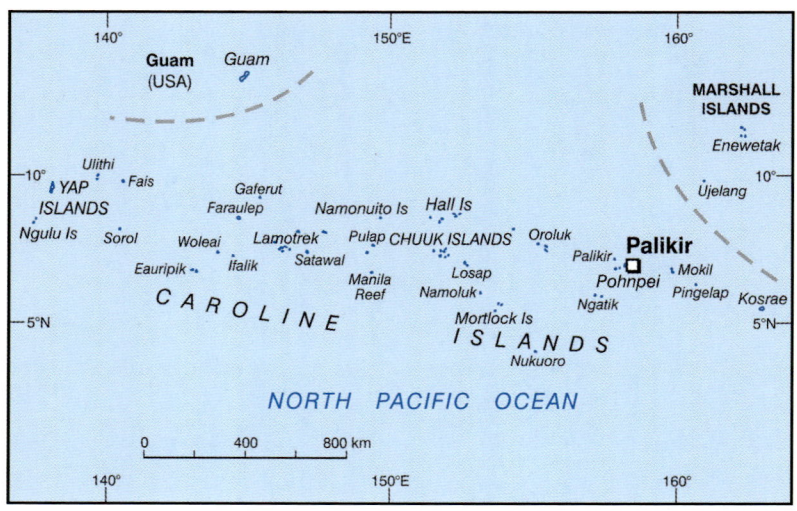

B Bradley, Cartographic Art Company

BACKGROUND

The Federated States of Micronesia comprises the four constituent states of Kosrae, Pohnpei, Chuuk (formerly known as Truk) and Yap and forms part of the Caroline Islands group in the northern Pacific. Its people are divided among a dozen language groups and several cultural traditions. Linguistic evidence suggests ancestors of the present population came from the Philippines and Indonesia over 4000 years ago.

The first European visitors were Portuguese explorers searching for the Spice Islands – in fact some distance away in the Indonesian archipelago. Spanish explorers followed, in 1525 and 1564, leading to Spanish colonisation which lasted until Germany purchased the islands from Spain and raised its own flag in 1899. The Germans are said to have established a lucrative copra trade but had to face and put down a rebellion on Pohnpei. At the start of World War I in 1914 Japan took control. It promoted economic development but excluded islanders from government and imposed the Japanese language. From 1935 Japan developed the island of Chuuk (then known as Truk) as a military base.

World War II

A significant portion of the Japanese fleet was based on Truk and had a major role in the Pacific war against the United States. In 1944 many Japanese vessels were destroyed there in a naval battle. Numbers of sunken ships on the seabed of the Chuuk Lagoon are still dramatically visible from the air. By the end of World War II, the economy of the islands had been largely destroyed.

In 1947 the islands now comprising the Federated States of Micronesia became part of the Trust Territory of the Pacific Islands (TTPI), administered first by the United States Navy and later by the United States Department of the Interior.

Constitutional developments

Protracted constitutional negotiations continued through the 1970s. Eventually agreement was reached with Washington on a 'Compact of Free Association'. It was implemented in 1986 and the Federated States of Micronesia then became an independent state in free association with the United States. Under the compact, the Federated States of Micronesia has full responsibility for internal and external affairs, subject to the security interests of the United States.

Subsistence fishing and farming predominate in the Federated States of Micronesia, although there is a little tourism and some revenue from the licensing of foreign fishing boats. Financial support from the United States is the primary source of revenue, and Washington has agreed that grants will continue until 2023.

LEADER'S STORY: JOHN HAGLELGAM

John Haglelgam was the second president of the Federated States of Micronesia, and served in that office from 1987 until 1991. Now a teacher at the College of Micronesia – Federated States of Micronesia, specialising in the history and economy of Micronesia, he was born in 1949 in the Yap group.

John Haglelgam
Robert and Augustine, MITC, Federated States of Micronesia

The island where I was born, Eauripik, is one of the smallest in Micronesia. After attending an Outer Island junior high school I was sent to an American high school in the State of Oregon. From there I went to the University of Hawai'i at Manoa, returning to the Trust Territory in 1973.

Political involvement

I worked for the Micronesian legal services for a time and then when an election came up in 1974 I ran for the Congress of Micronesia. I barely met the age requirement!

I was interested in politics because I wanted to do something – particularly for the Outer Island people. No matter how you looked at it, the Outer Island people were marginalised, and even now to a certain extent, they are still marginalised politically, socially and economically. I wanted to help them.

Although American nuclear testing was taking place at this time, it was in the Marshalls and didn't affect our islands at all. I became really aware of it after I got into Congress.

But I was fully aware of pro-independence opinion while I was at the University of Hawai'i. When the students at UH were protesting the Vietnam War, those of us Micronesians from the Trust Territories, we would join them. The signs that we held up were not for the Vietnam War but they were 'Free Micronesia' signs. Two students from Palau were our leaders and I was one of the leaders from my part of the Trust Territory.

According to some scholars in Micronesia, pro-independence sentiment can be traced back to the creation of our first high school in the fifties, called the Pacific Islands Central School (PICS). Students there came from all over Micronesia and then some of them went into the government, worked for a couple of years, and then almost all of them went to the University of Hawai'i.

Pressure for change

By the 1960s and 1970s there was a strong popular feeling all over Micronesia for independence. I think it was a realistic feeling and people opted for a 'Compact of Free Association' because the feeling was that the compact would help us develop our economy, and once we developed the economy, then we could become fully independent. That was the mantra at the time. (The compact was negotiated while I was at the University of Hawai'i – I came back only at the end of it.)

We were fully conscious of what was happening further south – Samoa's independence in 1962 and Nauru's soon afterwards. In fact Samoa and Nauru and, to a certain extent, Kiribati, gave us the impetus to push for liquidation of the trusteeship. Of course, we had ended up being one of the last UN trusteeships – we were telling the United States that we should liquidate the trusteeship.

It was becoming embarrassing to have a trusteeship that they administered as one of the last.

Negotiating with the United States

We felt that the United States was dragging its feet because they wanted to hold on to the Trust Territory. It showed in the first negotiations; when they sat down to negotiate the Micronesians made it clear that they wanted free association [with the United States] but the Americans rejected it. What they wanted was for Micronesia to remain American territory. The reason, of course, was strategic. They just wanted to have control over the land so any time they wanted to use land they could move in and just take it by power of 'eminent domain'. That's pretty much like what they're doing in Guam right now.

Of course, that was all during the Cold War. Now we are seeing something of a replay. I just read an article, written by an American, saying that the US is bungling the relationship with the Micronesian Freely Associated States. He is strongly recommending that the relationship should be turned over to the State Department instead of the Department of the Interior, so that the US could talk to the Freely Associated States governments as equals, and not talk down to us.

The quirky thing about the Compact of Free Association with the United States is that bilaterally our relationship is conducted through the State Department, but then all the money comes from the Department of the Interior. So the Department of the Interior has a very big hold on the Freely Associated States. That is basically it under Compact 2, which was negotiated about twelve years ago. So I can come out with it and tell you that Compact 2 is really a neo-colonial system.

Controlling the money

I call the system under Compact 2 neo-colonial because of the difference between it and the first compact. The first compact liquidated the trusteeship and gave us full control. We controlled the money and all we had to do was account for the money we spent. But we did a really bad job with this accounting process. So with Compact 2 a committee was established, called something like the Joint Economic Management Committee, or JEMCo, which comprised three Americans and two FSM citizens. That was the set-up – and when they vote it's always straight along US/Micronesian lines. So the Micronesians, always in the minority, are always defeated.

This really is meddling in the affairs of the FSM. All budgets, year after year, have to be submitted to JEMCo. Not only do they review the budget, they can change it in any way they see fit. This still continues today! Even if we terminate the compact, when it ends – and anyway the economic provision ends in 2023 – JEMCo will still keep going; it stays for ever and ever, amen!

Ending the Compact of Free Association?

There has been some debate in our Congress about the possibility of terminating the compact. I'm certainly one of those who feel we should do that: terminate the Compact of Free Association in totality. We will still be stuck with the 'perpetual denial' right treaty – it means the United States has the right to deny other countries access to FSM. But I think we should terminate the whole thing. Why should we keep it? It is really an unequal treaty. The perpetual denial right is of no benefit to us – it is for the benefit of the US but nothing for us.

Of course, if we terminate that treaty, I don't think we would still get American money. I think that would be it. And the US might switch their attitude and become hostile to FSM, they might just treat us like Iran.

I agree we would become like Kiribati or Tuvalu with really no regular outside support. But I think we would have a full grasp on our sovereignty, our sovereign independence, instead of living in this situation of having Department of the Interior officials coming in and behaving like they are the super-king of FSM.

There would be popular opposition to the loss of American money. But when you go out to the villages, this compact money doesn't filter down to the villages. Most money is spent by the government to support their employees. I think probably most opposition would come from the government.

But I have no intention of going back into politics to campaign for such a change. No, I'm right with three or four more years of teaching and then I will happily retire to my small island of Eauripik. Maybe Eauripik will become independent!

The right to live and work in the United States

Returning to the relationship with the United States, FSM citizens do have the right of entry to the US and they can live and work there. The Americans are putting curbs on that right. The US Congress has passed a law setting up some kind of screening. Maybe it will be based on health, maybe on possible criminal records. Maybe it will restrict the ability to make a living in the United States. If that should be the case, then we would be going back to pre-compact days all over again.

But meanwhile the free access to the United States has caused significant population loss to FSM. There are estimated to be

25–30,000 FSM citizens in the US. Amazingly most of these people who stay in the US have a high school education or less. Educated people stay back here!

Population flight

Our problem seems to be similar to the problem described in Niue and the Cook Islands. We're heading in the same direction. When you go around in the villages in all the states of FSM, some of the villages are like ghost villages. Very few people remain. The number of people staying in the FSM is decreasing. Of course, with the negative reaction from the US on free access, and if they come up with some kind of restrictions, I think some of these people are going to come back. For the nationhood of FSM in the long run, that would be good. These people were fishermen and farmers, they made their

Traditional game in Pohnpei, Federated States of Micronesia; 2009
Photographer Michael Field
Michael Field Collection

living by subsistence living, then they went to the US and they put themselves on welfare. The most important reason for going to the US is to be on welfare! It's too bad that the politicians, instead of thinking about curbing this travel to the US, are encouraging it.

When I was president [from 1987 to 1991], I was working to terminate the trusteeship. [In 1986 the trusteeship was terminated unilaterally by the United States but it wasn't formally terminated by the UN Security Council until 1990.] I found dealing with the Americans, the most powerful country on earth, very difficult. I was lucky I met President Bush – the older Bush. Recent presidents have not been able to meet the president of the United States. Why? Because they consider us a small potato … or a small coconut country! That is the difference between the Americans and China. China makes sure that FSM officials meet the president. And, unlike the Americans, their attitude is not condescending. The American attitude is very condescending, something like 'we gave you the money so what are you talking about?'

From optimism to pessimism

Looking back over the period since independence, I think initially in 1986 and then maybe for about ten years, there was optimism in FSM. But even with the political, social and economic progress we made, everyone was looking forward to more development. But I think right now we seem to be falling into a space where we don't expect anything to be done anymore. It's very depressing when you think that way. That's why I say that if someone really studied the effect of the compact on economic development, I think they would see that the compact was a barrier to economic development, instead of a catalyst. In our mentality too, we became so dependent on the compact money that we don't even want to farm! Everyone's waiting for their relative's pay-cheque.

FEDERATED STATES OF MICRONESIA

Even our businesses are all geared towards services. It is not for manufacturing, things that move the economy along, it is all done to provide service for employees.

I think everybody realises that we can't depend on anyone but ourselves. I think people could start farming. But I don't think this feeling is growing among the people. There are still very few farmers in Pohnpei. In fact most of the farmers in Pohnpei are from the other states in FSM or they're from China or Korea. The most popular thing now is to go to the United States. People realise that if they go to the US they can apply for welfare and be on welfare so they don't have to work to receive money and support.

Building new relationships

I think attendance at Pacific Islands Forum Leaders' meetings is very valuable for FSM. When I was president, I tried to realign FSM foreign policy to bring FSM closer to our neighbours to the south. That is the reason I brought in the fisheries' patrol boats. We ended up getting two patrol boats from Australia, because I wanted to create that relationship with Australia and New Zealand and the other countries in the south. My analogy was ... we attached ourselves to the US. It's like a fishing boat attached to an aircraft carrier. Every time the aircraft carrier increases speed, the fishing boat is about to sink!

I don't think that interest in the forum has carried on since I left the presidency. Even the way of using the patrol boat now disappoints me; instead of doing surveillance they use it as a tour boat for politicians and to carry dead people from one island to another.

Now I'm simply looking forward to two or three years farming on my home island. My feelings about the future of FSM are not very optimistic at present, primarily because I dislike what the United

States is doing. It is bringing back neo-colonialism, not bringing back but creating neo-colonialism in the FSM – not only the FSM but also in the Marshalls.

The Americans are telling us that the region is less strategically important than it was during the Cold War. They say once the compact is terminated in 2023, no more, don't expect any more help. That's why I think it's important for FSM leaders to start the conversation on what we're going to do to oppose the compact. What should we do? To what country should we turn? How should we create our relationships with other countries, like China? China built the headquarters for the regional Fisheries Commission in Pohnpei. They also built the beautiful Pohnpei State Executive Branch building.

I don't think we should expect China to completely replace the United States. What I'm saying is we have to prepare mentally, prepare the FSM citizens mentally, to live with less. I think FSM receives development assistance from the Asian Development Bank, mostly in the form of loans.

I don't know what we get from Australia but the most visible aid from Australia is the patrol boats. My motive for getting the patrol boats was partly to kill two birds with one stone. The first one, I want FSM to establish a good surveillance programme because when I came president our surveillance people were using a sailing boat! That's one reason. But the other reason was to bring FSM closer to Australia, and lure Australia to build an embassy in FSM. The embassy would also be accredited to the Marshalls and Palau. I succeeded. At a forum leaders' meeting in Kiribati, Australia sent one of their VIP airplanes to bring me to Pohnpei because Gareth Evans, the Foreign Minister of Australia, was coming to announce the establishment of the Australian Embassy in the FSM.

FEDERATED STATES OF MICRONESIA

I'm determined not to go back into politics. My island of Eauripik is almost independent! I can always go fishing. All I need is to do that maybe once every month and I'll be happy.

SOME SIGNIFICANT EVENTS SINCE INDEPENDENCE (1986)

1991	Joined the United Nations, UNESCO, World Health Organisations, UN Convention on the Law of the Sea.
1993	Joined the International Monetary Fund.
1995	Joined the Nuclear Non-Proliferation Treaty.
1997	Joined the Comprehensive Test Ban Treaty.
1998	29th Leaders' Meeting of the Pacific Islands Forum in Pohnpei.
2004	Amended Compact with the United States enters into force.
2004	Headquarters of the Western and Central Pacific Fisheries Commission established in Pohnpei.

MARSHALL ISLANDS

CHAPTER FOURTEEN

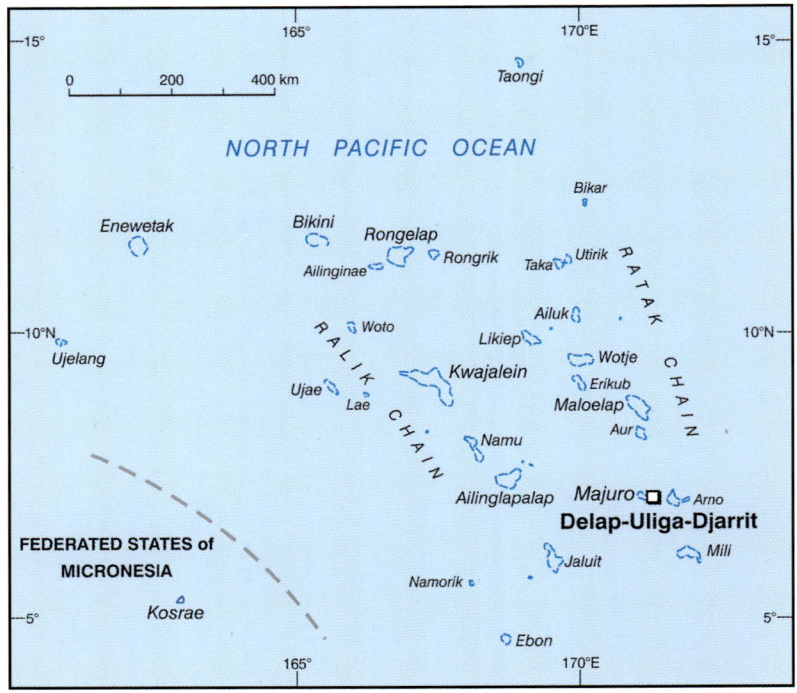

B Bradley, Cartographic Art Company

BACKGROUND

The two Micronesian atoll chains which make up the Republic of the Marshall Islands, named for an eighteenth century English sea captain, have an unhappy record of interference by foreign traders, missionaries and blackbirders and domination by large nations.

Colonised for nearly four centuries

Along with their fellow Micronesians spread across the western Pacific around 10 degrees north, the Marshallese were colonised for nearly four centuries. First to arrive in the sixteenth century was Spain, who later (1874) claimed the islands, then Germany (1885–1914), Japan (1919–44) and USA (1944–86).

Each ruler brought new languages, systems, diseases and religions and took over the Islanders' scarce atoll land to mine phosphates, establish plantations, house troops and test weapons.

Devastation caused by World War II

In the 1940s the demoralised Marshallese, forced to live under Japanese military administration, had to face yet another onslaught when World War II turned their islands into battlefields. By 1944, United States forces had driven out the Japanese at huge cost. The two years of warfare, in which one in every ten Marshallese died, was described as 'among the bloodiest ever seen in the Pacific' (Dibblin,1988, 17). After the battle for Kwajalein, buildings had been reduced to kindling and not one tree or shrub remained alive.

A new 'Trust Territory' but American bases and nuclear testing

In 1947 the United States and the United Nations Security Council signed an agreement putting the 'Trust Territory of the Pacific Islands' (most of Micronesia, including the Marshall Islands), under the wing of America. The United Nations mandate required the United States to protect the health of the inhabitants and promote their economic advancement and self-sufficiency. It also allowed the USA to 'fortify' the islands, an intention declared in a 1945 speech by President Truman: 'Bases which our military experts deemed to be essential for our protection, we will acquire … by arrangements consistent with the UN Charter'. (Dibblin 1988, 19)

Kwajalein atoll; 2009
Photographer Michael Field
Michael Field Collection

The Marshall Islands were the 'Pacific Proving Grounds'. Thousands of troops and their families were based at Kwajalein, headquarters for a missile range, and sixty-six nuclear tests were carried out between 1946 and 1958 on Bikini and Enewatak. The Marshallese had been shifted to other atolls but did not escape the effects of nuclear fallout. Radiation sickness, cancer, birth defects and similar afflictions became commonplace.

Over a fifteen year period, Kwajalein, Roi, Namur, Rongelap, Utrik and Bikini were seriously damaged or changed by military activities. Housing, sanitation and the like on other overcrowded atolls were severely stretched as Marshallese people sought a safe home.

Compensation negotiations long drawn out

After a 1975 referendum, the islands which had constituted the Trust Territory split into the separate states of Palau, the Federated States of Micronesia, and the Republic of the Marshall Islands. It was not an easy decision. Many people thought staying together would give them a stronger position in negotiations with the United States, but the majority voted for separation with the hope of eventual self-government or independence. The three young states continued to consult and cooperate, but each stood alone in putting its case for compensation to the most powerful nation on earth, the United States.

Led by Amata Kabua, a senior *iroij* (chief), Marshallese ministers and officials fought hard for redress over issues such as the consequences of nuclear testing, people's rights to return to their home atolls and social and economic imbalance between wealthy United States bases and poorly resourced Marshallese atolls. Over the years, more than $US700 million has been paid in compensation for the effects of nuclear testing. Some of that has been invested by the Marshalls government, which receives some $US40 million annually in rent and aid.

Eventual self-government and then independence

In 1979, the Marshall Islands became self-governing. In 1983, along with citizens of the other Trust Territory states, the Marshallese responded in three plebiscites to the offer from the United States of a 'Compact of Free Association'. Although many on atolls most directly affected by military activity voted against acceptance, a majority was in favour. President Reagan welcomed the islanders' decision to 'take up your new status in the world as a sovereign nation'. Perhaps bearing in mind the 3000 American troops and support workers still living on the billion dollar Kwajalein Military Base, he ended his speech by saying 'But you will always be family to us'.

In 1986 the Republic of the Marshall Islands adopted a constitution which included a president and a parliament (*Nitijela*) and achieved independence under its first president, Amata Kabua.

LEADER'S STORY: KESSAI NOTE

Hon. Kessai Note, a member of President Amata Kabua's Cabinet on independence, became the Republic's third president in 2000. The first non-chiefly Marshall Islander to achieve that position, he remained in office until 2008. Born on Ailinglaplap atoll in 1950, he completed his tertiary education in Papua New Guinea and returned to his homeland to work as an advocate for the people of Bikini atoll. He still has memories of the nuclear tests carried out there during his childhood.

Kessai Note
Government of the Marshall Islands

Although we lived about 700 miles away from where the testing took place, we could hear the sound of the explosions and see the light from the explosions in the sky, every day and every night.

It was frightening because we didn't know what it was, and we didn't know what to expect. When you see the bright light lighting up on the other side of the road, you really get confused. You don't know what to make of it. At the time there was very little information, we didn't know what it was, there was nothing on the radio. We were left on our own. I didn't know what to expect.

Everybody on the island, and not just the islands we were living on, the entire Marshall Islands, even as far as 800 miles away, everyone was confused, we didn't know what it was. All of a sudden we'd see the bright light and explosions and all that.

So far as health consequences were concerned, you know, when the testing took place on Bikini they had to move the people away several hundred miles to some of the neighbouring islands. The expectation was that the explosion impact, the consequences, would be minimal, but later we found out that that was not the case, people were affected even if they lived on faraway islands.

Compensation for victims of nuclear tests

A lot of my political and professional life involved the consequences of all that. As soon as I came back from college I became the spokesman for the Bikinian people, the victims of the nuclear testing. I guess that's where I started my public or political career, when I started working for them and started protesting or claiming for compensation or treatments from the US government.

In 1970 the Australian government provided scholarships to Micronesian students to go to Papua New Guinea or other colleges or universities. At the time Australia was still the administrative authority in Papua New Guinea. (Papua New Guinea became independent in 1975, after I left.) They had to pick students from each of the six districts in Micronesia, Palau, Saipan, Ponape, Truk, Marianas and Yap and I was fortunate to be the recipient of that scholarship from Marshall Islands in 1970. That was how I got there.

Studies in Papua New Guinea

I studied basically traditional agriculture. Well it was an agricultural college.

It was kind of a cultural shock for me, coming to Papua New Guinea from an atoll way up north. At the time even Papua New Guinea was unknown to this part of the Pacific. We were mostly associated with the American way of life you know, to some extent, so to speak, but Papua New Guinea was eye-opening for me, a young man from Marshall Islands to travel all the way to Papua New Guinea.

This experience of being in a country that was getting ready for independence must have influenced my thinking because when I came back the Marshall Islands people and all Micronesia, were already talking about getting more autonomous in the running of the government in their countries, rather than continue to be a territory of the US. Not just Papua New Guinea but other countries in the Pacific were doing the same thing, like Kiribati and other countries.

So I got back to the Marshall Islands in 1974 or '75 and there was already discussion about some kind of independence, autonomous government or something like that. You know what, when I was in Papua New Guinea, Chief Michael Somare was there, the chief minister at the time, and he later became prime minister. After twenty-seven years, when I became president, I got to work with Michael Somare, we became good friends over the course of seven or eight years that I served as president of the Marshall Islands.

Connections made across the Pacific while young men became very valuable as we became senior men. I've known Julius Chan also.

MARSHALL ISLANDS

Independence and Micronesian neighbours

The sentiment in favour of possibilities for independence or real self-government very strongly came from the Marshall Islands, under the leadership of one of our traditional leaders at the time, Amata Kabua, paramount chief who later became the first president of the country. He served for like sixteen years, he died in office. But he led the movement to break away from the rest of Micronesia. We were part of the Micronesian Trust Territory of the Pacific Islands, the TTPI.

And we were not just breaking away from that but we were also breaking away from the rest of Micronesia, towards being independent. The Solomon Report that was authorised by President Kennedy at the time, tried to determine the future for Micronesia and what was missing in the report was that there was very little input from the local people. I read the report several times. It was anticipated that Micronesia would continue being dependent on the United States. It was strongly recommended that the US continue to administer the Micronesian people. But it was the local people that started the movement away.

It was tough for us, dealing and negotiating with the mightiest nation on earth. And not only tough, it took a very long time, the negotiations went on for fourteen or fifteen years before we started getting back on track and to work on our free association compact with the United States, but it took a very long time. We had to bring in consultants and lawyers and economic experts and all that.

I was a supporter of the Marshall Islands breaking away from the rest of Micronesia. I was still in Papua New Guinea when I thought that the Marshall Islands could well be on its own rather than being part of a Micronesian country. But of course I was only a student at the time, I didn't have all the information I would have needed to form a very firm position on that. On the surface I thought if other countries in the Pacific similar to the Marshall Islands could become independent then why couldn't we.

Claims to Washington

Well, as soon as I got back from college my father's older brother was one of the senior officers of the Bikinian community on Kili Island. And as soon as I got back they brought me to the council, the Bikini Atoll Council. I started off as the translator for them. At the time they used to go to the US for a congressional hearing in Washington and they needed somebody to translate for them. I filled that position. Actually I started only a few months after I came back from Papua New Guinea. We started going to Washington on a regular basis, asking for compensation and treatment.

My father died of liver cancer as a result of the testing. It was found that it started, it was caused by radiation.

Later on, we established the nuclear claims tribunal and during the first negotiation the United States set up a trust fund of $US250 million, at the same time establishing the nuclear claims tribunal to process claims, to make sure they're legitimate and make sure the claims are based on the nuclear-induced sickness. There was a certain level of compensation that the claims tribunal provided to the families or the victims that were afflicted or affected by nuclear testing in the Marshall Islands.

So far as childbirth problems were concerned, one of the presumed conditions given by the nuclear claims tribunal, up to as late as 1958, was that a child born with certain kinds of sickness was eligible under the nuclear claims tribunal. We had a lot of that, a lot of thyroid, a lot of cancers. We have the highest cancer population in the world. So the problem is out there.

Marshall Islands constitution

My first entry into political life ... I started working for the Marshall Islands government, still under the Trust Territory at the time in 1975 and I was at the Ministry of Agriculture, agricultural economy and extensions, and in 1966 the Marshall Islands decided to have their own constitution. In 1977, they had a countrywide election for members of the first constitutional convention of the Marshall Islands. That is the convention that would draft the Marshall Islands constitution. I stood for that, I ran, and I got elected to that convention. I was one of the forty-six members of the convention that drafted the Marshall Islands constitution. I was there for two years and it took three years to write the constitution and present it to the people for approval in a referendum. I was there and that was my first exposure to politics.

When the constitution was drafted we had in mind that ultimately one day the Marshall Islands would become a full independent country. At the same time we were negotiating with the United States on a relationship rather than a territory. So that's how the Compact of Free Association was also structured, to give the Marshall Islands ultimate independence. We had in mind that the Marshall Islands would become a full independent country. So we drafted the constitution and subsequently we approved the free association agreement with the United States, and after several years we became a member of the United Nations as a full sovereign country.

As to whether total independence has happened yet, we consider ourselves a sovereign country and I think the United States and also the United Nations, you cannot become a member of the UN

Marshallese dancers in Pago Pago, American Samoa; 2008
Photographer Julia Brooke-White
Julia Brooke-White Collection

if you are not a sovereign country. We have full responsibility of our foreign affairs, except in the agreement with the US in the compact, the US continues to have security and defence responsibility for the Marshall Islands, in exchange for the Marshall Islands to give rights to use some of the land in the Marshall Islands.

We are full members of the Pacific Islands Forum and so on, while we continue to depend on the US to provide financial assistance and other opportunities.

Back when I was a member of the constitutional convention and we were thinking about full independence, I believe people saw us as revolutionaries at the time because not many in the Marshall Islands population were ready for independence. After some forty years of being under the Trust Territory, people became to be so dependent on the United States to provide everything, you know, food through the USDA program, free schools and free hospital visit treatments, everything was free. The US started off with the US Navy running Kwajalein and that's where half the Marshallese population was living, they got everything free, even school lunches. So we had become so dependent on those handouts from the United States. It was not easy to change people's mentality, dependency – we had to convince them.

Unlike the situation in most territories across the Pacific, we were swamped by the governing power. Even the administrators and teachers and classroom teachers and just about everybody were Americans. To think that you are going to get rid of them would be unthinkable.

Marshallese nowadays under the new amended compact can travel to the US without visa requirement. They can move to the US and live and work and study and whatever without a visa, and without a green card for employers. Also Marshallese citizens can serve and join the US Armed Forces. There are several hundreds of them in the US Armed Forces now. I don't think there's the need to be a US citizen for me I don't think, I don't know why. Anyway, personally, I'm proud of being Marshallese!

In the early eighties, we were fighting on two fronts, first of all the rest of the Micronesian leaders did not want the Marshall Islands to be separated from the rest of Micronesia, and at the same time we were negotiating to get out of the Trust Territory with the United States and become an independent country. It was kind of a multilateral discussion under different spheres and different purposes. There were obstacles and challenges from every corner. I think that's why it took so many years to come to the negotiation with the US and the rest of Micronesia.

Keeping our people informed was important. We were doing a lot of public education, we would get on the radio and go to outer islands and local communities like church groups and youth groups and all that to try to explain what it is all about, you know, that Marshall Islands wanted to be a separate and independent country.

The constitution we ended up with is a mixture of the Westminster system and we adapted some of the functions and the separation of responsibilities that are based on the United States constitution. It's a mixture of both. We had very good legal counsels and lawyers working on that. Alison Quentin-Baxter was one of those. A very bright constitutional lawyer, she helped us on the draft of the constitution.

We decided the name of our parliament would be the *Nitijela*. The name of the Marshall Islands, we got that from some European captain that came through years ago. There were names that we looked at when we were drafting the constitution; we thought they were too ancient and probably too complicated to get the rest of the world to even pronounce them, so we ended up stuck with the words Marshall Islands.

Well we had a public contest for the national flag and several proposals were presented and we finally landed on that one. We set up several committees to look at that, and even for the national anthem. Actually the one we have, we've gone through several national anthems, but the latest one we have was composed by the president, Amata Kabua, himself. We kind of officially adopted that; it is the current official national anthem now.

The president is elected by the *Nitijela*. The current president, Jurelang Zedkaia, is the fifth president we've had since we became independent in 1979. Not independence, but we've had our constitutional government since 1979. [Full independence came in 1986.]

Constitutional government and independence

I well remember that day in 1979. We decided early on that May 1st would be the effective date of the constitution, so on May 1st 1979 we had a huge celebration in the Marshall Islands and in Majuro. That's when the new constitutional government was installed, with the president and with the first Cabinet and with the first *Nitijela*. After being officially elected, we took the oath of office and that's how we started off on the first day of May 1979. We had the ceremony outside of the courthouse, it was quite a large area, I remember wearing those suit and ties, we looked very formidable – then it started pouring rain like crazy and we all became wet. It was raining like – man, I remember how cold it was wearing a soaked wet cold suit. That's how we started, we took our positions and I happened to be one of the first ministers of the Cabinet at the time, I remember sitting out in the rain soaking wet, so cold. The mood and the spirit, people were so happy and excited about it. It was a new day in the history of the Marshall Islands. I think with a lot of anticipation and anxiety and expectation and all that.

There was a lot of uncertainty. Even the compact with the US had not been worked out at that time; we didn't know how much funding support we were getting from the US and all that. But yet we were excited to be a new country and I was excited.

I was the third president of the Marshall Islands and the first one who was a commoner. Amata Kabua and his cousin were paramount chiefs. Actually he died in office so his cousin was elected to complete the term for almost three years. Then I was elected president in 2000. I was there for eight years. Then I was replaced with another leader – Litokwa Tomeing.

My election to president demonstrated that it was no longer just the chiefs who were in charge. The constitution gave the Marshallese the right and freedom to choose whoever they want for leadership in the Marshall Islands, not just for president but for other offices like members of parliament, local government, mayors and all that.

It would be very difficult for us to manage without American money coming in as rent for the military bases and to support us. People would continue to live on subsistence levels, making copra and fisheries and running livestock and things like that. We don't have much in the way of natural resources or minerals, we continue to depend on outsiders to provide some level of support and that's going to be a fact of life … for many years to come …. But I think for the Pacific Island countries we should really focus on what we have, the water, the ocean fisheries, agriculture, for our sustenance but we need to develop some industries that we can export, [and] provide for the local communities.

SOME SIGNIFICANT EVENTS SINCE INDEPENDENCE (1986)

1990	UN officially ends Trusteeship.
1991	Republic of the Marshall Islands joins United Nations.
1996	President Amata Kabua dies.
1997	Imata Kabua elected president.
1999	Kessai Note elected president (first commoner).
2003	Some provisions of Compact of Free Association renegotiated.

2007	RMI joins International Labour Organisation. Litokwa Tomeing elected president. Prolonged drought; state of emergency declared.
2009	Jurelang Zedkaia elected president.

◆

REFERENCE:

Dibblin, J., *Day of Two Suns*. London: Virago, 1988.

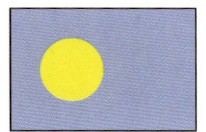

PALAU

CHAPTER FIFTEEN

B Bradley, Cartographic Art Company

BACKGROUND

The Republic of Palau comprises the most western of the Caroline Islands in the north-west Pacific. Ancestors of the present Caroline Islanders are thought to have come from South-east Asia between 3000 and 4500 years ago. Archaeological evidence confirms the existence of early specialised shell and stone technology and extensive agricultural terracing.

As with its neighbouring states of the Marshall Islands and the Federated States of Micronesia, Palau's first colonisers were Spanish, who called the islands Los Palos. One European visit attracted much attention: the British ship *Antelope* was wrecked on an island in the group and the encounter led to the introduction of a chief's son, Lee Bo, into fashionable London society.

Spain maintained its sovereignty over the islands until Germany purchased them in 1899.

At the start of World War I in 1914, Japan took over the Caroline Islands and, as a Japanese colony, Palau gained a modern infrastructure and an expanded copra industry. By 1935 one of the most populous islands, Koror, had more than four times as many Japanese as locals.

During World War II Palau became a significant military base and a launching pad for Japanese attacks on the Philippines. Following United States military rule at the end of the war, in 1947 Palau became part of the US-administered Trust Territory of the Pacific Islands (TTPI). Independence was only achieved many years after Palau's Micronesian neighbours.

Nuclear-free

An important factor behind the delay in agreement with the United States on a 'Compact of Free Association' was the Republic of Palau's 1981 adoption of a nuclear-free constitution. Washington considered the nuclear-free provisions to be incompatible with American security interests.

In 1986 a draft compact was agreed giving the islands independence subject to defence remaining a United States responsibility for fifty years. But successive referenda in Palau failed to produce the required 75 percent vote in favour of the compact. In 1987 Palau voted to amend the constitution to allow approval of the compact by a simple majority. In a subsequent plebiscite, 73 percent supported the draft compact, but in 1988 the Supreme Court ruled that was unconstitutional.

This was one of the more troubled periods in Palau's long experience of colonial rulers. As well as the pressure from Washington, in Palau itself there were unprecedented political scandals involving even murder and suicide. Eventually Washington's concerns were met and Palau achieved self-government in free association with the United States on 1 October 1994.

Economy

The country's economy continues to rely largely on subsistence agriculture and fishing, with increasing revenue from tourism. In 2009, Palau announced it would follow the United States' request and accept seventeen of the remaining Uyghur detainees in Guantanamo in return for substantial financial recompense. China's angry reaction was ignored by Palau, one of the diminishing number of states according full diplomatic recognition to Taiwan.

LEADER'S STORY: SANDRA SUMANG PIERANTOZZI

Palau is one of the few Pacific countries where major public positions have been held by women. One of the most significant is **Sandra Sumang Pierantozzi**. Over the protracted period of negotiations culminating in the 1994 achievement of self-government in free association with the United States, Ms Pierantozzi was appointed or elected to posts from relatively lowly secretary to cabinet minister, senator and vice president.

PALAU

◆ ◆ ◆

I was born in 1953 in Koror, former capital of Palau. I describe my family — the Sumangs — as his and hers and theirs. My father's first spouse passed away, leaving him with four girls and my mother's first spouse passed away, leaving her with five children. Then they married and produced six of us. Altogether, four boys and eleven girls.

Sandra Sumang Pierantozzi
Private collection

My father was a village chief and before World War II when we were still under the Japanese mandate, he felt if he got himself to Japan he would be able to go to school. Unfortunately he was of the wrong colour so he couldn't get into any Japanese schools. He learned to drive and was a taxi driver in Tokyo for five years. When he came back to Palau he spoke a little English and excellent Japanese. Marine biologist researchers were coming to Palau then and they needed a guide and interpreter. I was fascinated when they came to the house, so impressed that my father could speak English. He was a great observer and environmental man and earned the nickname 'the scientist'.

By then Palau was part of the Trust Territory of the Pacific Islands, mandated by the UN to USA to help develop the islands to eventual independence. We had a common government in Saipan, so we were aware of what the other Micronesians were doing. Fortunately we were not subjected to the nuclear tests, but we were close enough.

Even though my father was chief of a village, we were poor and my mother made our clothes and sewed dresses to make money to put us through school. I was called in to help and learned the art of sewing and when I went to college I made dresses for myself and was able to get by. Mom and Dad sent us to Seventh Day Adventist schools and I graduated from a high school which was considered one of the best in Palau. It had about an equal number of boys and girls, but every time I got my record card I always came out on top. My dad went around telling everybody 'My daughter made straight As!' He had promised the family that whoever got straight A grades would get ice cream so he would beg $2 from my mother and I would walk half a mile to the store and bring back a gallon of ice cream in a can and that would be a treat for everyone in the family. It also encouraged everybody to do their best because there was always a good reward. My father was such a strong supporter of the family; I think I had a very good upbringing.

United States education

Our courses at school were basically the same as in the United States. I remember once thinking, 'I am a Pacific Islander, why have I to learn about things that a student in Kansas City has to know?' Every Monday we had to stand in line and pledge allegiance to the United States, and as I was growing up I started to question why I was doing that. I think my education at home prepared me more for life in the United States – but it also taught me how to live in the world, how to get on with and respect others, to know my place and take responsibility.

I grew up in a maternal culture. I didn't feel oppressed per se, but I knew that as a woman there were certain roles I had to play. Sure I heard some people say, 'Don't bother going to school and college because you're a woman, you'll come home and be a mother and a housewife so it's enough to just finish high school'. But my father was very different. Traditionally, when kids went away to school, if somebody in the family died they'd have to come home. My dad was different and said to me, 'Don't bother coming home, let this be our last goodbye, the next time we see each other will be in heaven'. I said 'No Dad, if something happens I want to come back'. He said, 'If you came back how could we talk? My eyes would be closed. But you stay at school because that would be more important for you in your life than coming home to see a dead man.' Well it actually happened that way. A month after I went back to college he died, and in spite of his instructions, I came home to find they had buried him. I cried, then his words came to my mind and I said, 'Enough, I'm not going to cry any more', and I turned around and ran right back to school.

Seventh Day Adventist missionaries had helped me apply to Union College in Lincoln, Nebraska and they awarded me a scholarship and I was also fortunate enough to get a two-year Congress of Micronesia scholarship. So I went to Nebraska for two years and got my degree. I was the first Palauan at the college but there was a Palauan family and two other girls living close by the campus. When I stayed in the dorm and got homesick or lonely, I would visit them and that really helped me.

Sometimes when I got up at 7 am to go to breakfast and classes the snow would be up to my knees. I'd be so cold I'd say 'At home I would be sleeping and warm, why am I torturing myself, what am I here for?' But I thought, if others have done it I should be able to do it, too.

Some others who had gone to study in the USA decided to stay and live and work there, but I was always taught, and believed, I had such strong ties to Palau that I should go home and stay home and be a Palauan first. I don't think I was ever strongly influenced by American feminism.

Being Palauan

Palauan women rule the home, we just appoint male members of the family or the clan to be chiefs and we have the power to remove them from those positions if they do not listen to, or follow, the wishes of the women in the home. So it never was an issue for me. Because I had been brought up to 'be whatever you want to be', it never dawned on me that my horizons should be limited, in fact I always thought that the sky is the limit. When we were growing up, I got tired of being poor and I thought, when I grow up I'm going to work hard to make sure I'm never poor again!

When I was still going to school in Palau, a young Italian man living in Palau and earning a good income knocked on the door and proposed marriage. I said, 'Are you out of your mind? I'm still going to school!' He came in and asked my father who said 'Fine, but she should finish high school'. So when I finished high school my suitor came knocking again and again I said 'Are you out of your mind!? I just got scholarships and I have to be a housewife!? Forget it!' And when I came back he was still waiting so we married and I started teaching at the Micronesian Occupational College.

After that they gave me a further scholarship to go to the University of Hawai'i and get a four-year degree, and my then husband, still my husband today, who had waited all those years for me, said, 'OK, I will not stand in your way' so he let me go to the University of Hawai'i. I was on my own there and I didn't quite know what to do with all the freedom that I had. My upbringing kept my head straight so I did my studies and I wanted to graduate right away so I carried up to twenty-one credits at a time and graduated early. Initially I didn't know what to do with that freedom, but you learn eventually, as an individual, what to do with what you have.

Government work

In 1979 when I came back to Palau I started another career, working for the legislators who had begun to write a constitution for the country. Because of my training at Nebraska, somebody recommended that I get into the constitutional convention as a stenographer. There was a bunch of us and someone was needed to take minutes of the meetings. The seasoned ones were smart, they said 'My shorthand is rusty, send somebody else' and since I was the newest one, as naïve as I was, I was sent there. All the deliberations were in Palauan and since I didn't know who to ask for advice, as they talked in Palauan I took it down in English, and had a journal ready for them the next day of the convention.

Those were the days of typewriters, no computers, so when they complained about small technical errors I really got scared, thinking I was going to get fired. Then out of the corner of my eye I saw one of our former presidents, Mr Lazarus Salii, raise his hand and say 'Mr President, I have no corrections to offer. On the contrary, I have nothing but compliments to the person who did this journal, because although we conducted deliberations all in Palauan yesterday, it comes out in English and the English is excellent. When you delivered your opening speech yesterday it was in Palauan, on the record now it is as if you had spoken in English. The prayer that the pastor delivered to open the convention is as if he had prayed in English.' The secret was that the pastor had been my high school teacher, so when he prayed 'Our Heavenly Father', I wrote 'who art in heaven', using the old English, so they were very impressed. From then the tide turned; everything I did was just great!

That's why to this day I have a very good working knowledge of our constitution. I became secretary to the committee on civil liberties and fundamental rights, which wrote our bill of rights in the constitution and I learned about the foundation of how our government works. After that I started work for the old Congress and learned what the politicians did.

Then an interim legislature of one year came in and I didn't like their politics so I went to a private company and worked for one year. When our government came into office again in 1981 I was recruited to work for the Senate and eventually became clerk of the Senate. I really enjoyed the job, recording top leadership meetings for Palau. After working for the Senate for quite a long time, I travelled with the members of Congress and the Association of Pacific Island Legislatures, which consisted of legislative bodies of the North Pacific.

Ministerial appointment

Then various financial problems developed and the US Department for the Interior was breathing hard on Palau to bring in financial reforms. President Etpison asked if I would become minister of Finance – we called it minister of Administration because it covered more than just finance. I was kind of scared but somebody advised me not to be scared because the technicians were all there, they knew what to do but needed somebody with a good head on his or her shoulders to make the right decisions. So I jumped in and was appointed minister of Administration in 1992.

It was a four-year term but in the first two years the Congress would not pass the government structure that the president wanted. It was difficult because his former vice-president wanted to handle the money. But we were on the verge of bankruptcy and the United States said we had to bring in reforms. Right away I started making improvements, and two years later I told my president, 'When I first took this office, you asked me for $10,000 of the money donated to you to help a school that had been devastated by a typhoon. It took me two weeks to produce a cheque. Today you can ask me for up to $3 million and I will issue a cheque without blinking an eye'. I was able to pay off financial deficits with current monies and still balance the budget. I left a surplus of $2.5 million, which may sound small, but for us that was big money.

Running for office

In 1992 I offered to run for the Senate of Palau. While I was campaigning for that election, some women got up and declared me their vice-presidential candidate. I thought, 'Why not?' That became my slogan. It was the first time I ever ran for office, but because of my reputation as minister of Finance I won big and got into the primary with two others. I beat them, became candidate for vice-president and later was elected to that position.

I was extremely pleased, because I never thought a woman would have a chance. But we were lucky to be under United States Trusteeship for fifty years so I grew up where there was really no discrimination against women that you might find in other Pacific nations or other countries. So there was never a time when I tried to get into something and they said 'No, that's only for men'.

Gender differences in Palau

Culturally speaking, Palauan women like to sit in the back and control things. They didn't bother putting themselves forward, they'd say, 'Let the men do the fighting and all of that, we have better things to do'. In reality it's the women who keep things going, who go house-to-house campaigning for their husbands, their uncles, their brothers. The men sit at home. In fact when I ran for vice-president and got in, a presidential candidate had headquarters across the street so I went over to say hello. The women were outside, preparing food, organising and so on and they said 'Go and meet the candidate inside'. And there was a table full of men sitting under the air conditioning, supposedly strategising. You know how it is. They were just passing time. It hit home to me that as a woman you really have to work twice as hard.

In the early days my Italian husband and I got in a lot of arguments. He wanted me to sit at home and just be there when he came home. I started climbing the walls and told him, 'I didn't go to school to sit at home!' I read books, made clothes, baked, I did everything, and I was bored. So finally he let me go teaching and when I came home he would say, 'What should we eat tonight?' I would say 'I don't know I haven't ….' He'd reply, 'When I came home, my mother had food on the table'. Finally I said 'OK, I'm not your mother! She didn't teach eight hours a day, and so when you came home, she could have everything ready for you. But I'm not your mother!'

We sat down and talked about it and before long he became a very understanding husband, telling me 'I don't want to be in the way of what you want to do for your country, so do whatever you have to do'. When I needed billboards for campaigning, he would get them all done. He's been a big support in my life and helped me when I went into government administration, held three ministries and then the post of vice-president.

Advancement of women

Every time I have the opportunity I try to inspire young women to put themselves forward and take responsibility. We have done well in terms of employment of women in the civil service, but not so well in political leadership. However, my cousin was our first woman minister of Community and Cultural Affairs and another woman holds that position now. We have two senators who are women, and currently four women governors.

We also have many businesswomen in Palau. I have had several successful businesses, from restaurants to flower shops to small personal finance and because I don't have any children, I consider all the children of Palau mine, and I go out of my way to help them. Women like the former New Zealand prime minister, Helen Clark, inspired me and who knows, being the first woman president of Palau is always a possibility. I can't say anything right now, but the future is open. The sky is the limit. We'll see.

Population flight

Unfortunately, the number of Palauans at home is dwindling. Many are migrating to the USA and elsewhere to work and we are increasingly becoming a minority in our own land. But I tell women in Palau, and elsewhere, never give up. If you have aspirations to get into leadership, please do and give it all you can, but if you're going to get in there, don't be a token woman. Be a woman that makes a difference and if you want to help people, it doesn't matter if you're in politics or other places of leadership, you help because you want to help your country.

SOME SIGNIFICANT EVENTS SINCE RATIFICATION OF THE COMPACT OF FREE ASSOCIATION (1994)

1994	Palau admitted to the United Nations.
1998	Becomes 'off-shore' financial centre.
2001	Bank regulations and anti-money laundering laws passed.

2005 Palau leads land and ocean conservation program 'Micronesia Challenge'.

2009 Diplomatic and trading ties with Malaysia formalised. Palau bans commercial shark fishing and establishes world's first shark sanctuary.

2010 US agrees to provide further $US250 million aid.

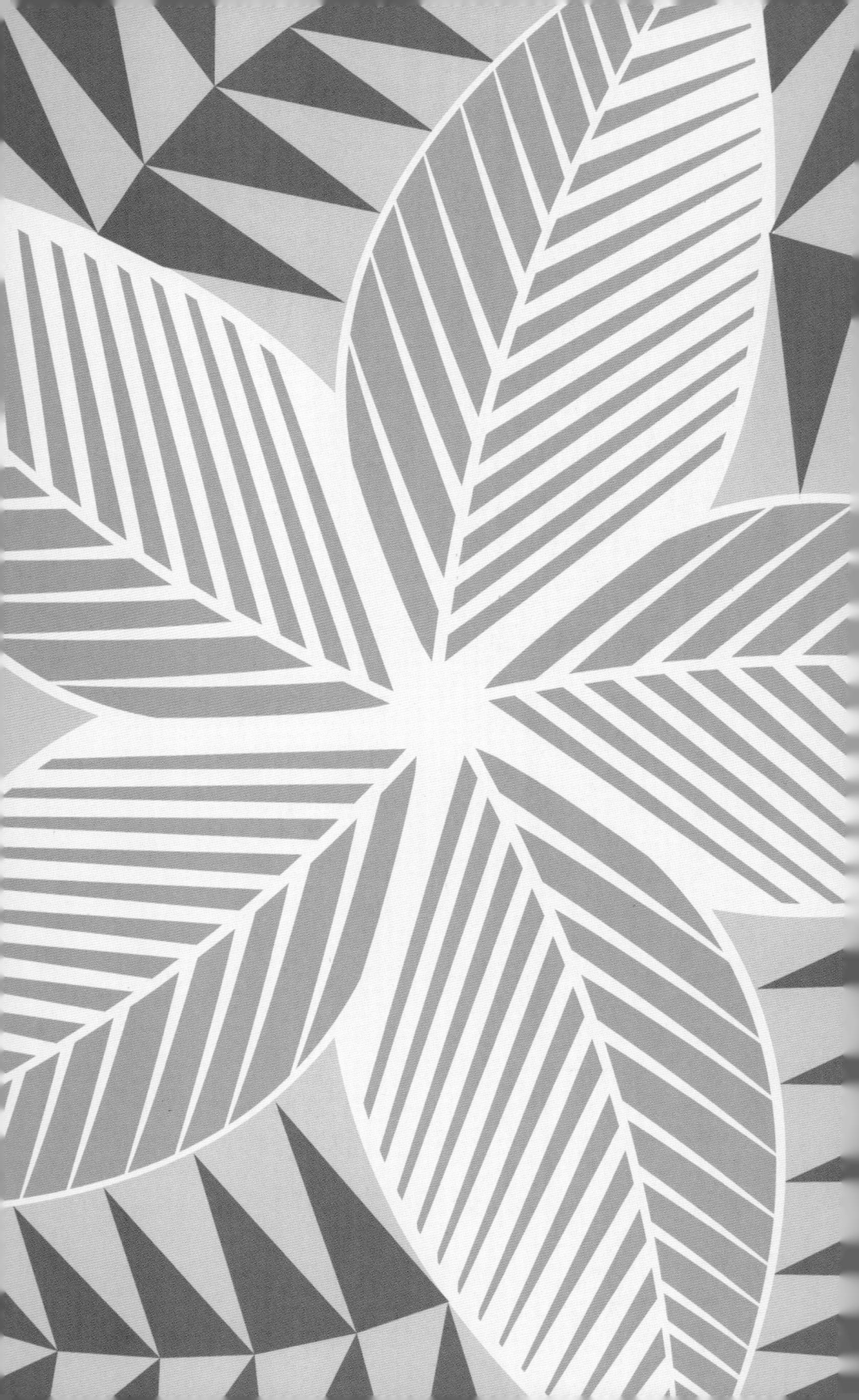

PERSPECTIVES OF PACIFIC WOMEN

CHAPTER SIXTEEN

BACKGROUND

None of the Pacific Island leaders who brought their countries to independence or self-government were women. By international standards, that was no surprise; in the 1960s and 1970s there were few women leaders globally and most positions of political power were held by men.

Across the Pacific, male domination of politics had long been the norm, which is not to say that women were without authority. In countries with chiefly traditions, women of high rank carried — and still carry — great influence, though only a very few — such as the much admired Queen Salote of Tonga — have governed in their own right and name.

Women housekeeping, Samoa
Photographer Julia Brooke-White
Julia Brooke-White Collection

Women preparing meat, Fiji
Photographer Julia Brooke-White
Julia Brooke-White Collection

In mostly matrilineal Micronesia, men are chosen by women to be chiefs, while Samoa's *matai* system ensures a role for women in awarding, and receiving, titles. And, as in all human relationships, the most powerful influences often work behind the scenes. As Dame Carol Kidu remarks about Papua New Guinea 'women are powerful in the private sphere, very powerful, but that power was not translated into the public sphere. The men took the power in the public sphere ….'

As new flags were set flying from 1962 onwards, there might have been some hope that independence or self-governance would bring more opportunities for women and more encouragement for them to move into 'the public sphere'.

Women preparing vegetables, Cook Islands
Photographer Julia Brooke-White
Julia Brooke-White Collection

In their first national elections, voters in Samoa, the Cook Islands, Fiji, Solomons and Papua New Guinea elected some women parliamentarians, but their male prime ministers and colleagues did not see fit to appoint or elect them to Cabinet. Outside Parliament, as expatriate administrators departed, women made some gradual advances into national and regional advisory posts. Few in number, they nonetheless exercised considerable influence in fields like administration and education.

Meanwhile, across most of the developed, democratic world, 'Women's liberation' as it was popularly known, increasingly encouraged women to step beyond their traditional role within the family, and make the most of new opportunities in business, the professions, and politics.

By the 1980s, politicians such as Indira Gandhi, Margaret Thatcher, Corazon Aquino and Benazir Bhutto were leading major countries and among smaller nations women presidents and ministers were becoming common.

Regrettably, the political advancement of Pacific women has yet to reach similar levels. While women (in groups or as individuals)

Women preparing to vote, Fiji
Photographer Julia Brooke-White
Julia Brooke-White Collection

have taken advantage of more opportunities to prosper in commerce, the professions and public service, the numbers standing for and being elected to Parliament have fluctuated. Fifty years after Samoa led the way into independence in 1962, no Pacific Island nation has had a woman president or prime minister and the women interviewed here are among only a handful who have held senior or leadership positions.

In the twenty-first century, efforts are being made to change that, and advance gender equality in politics. These include projects sponsored by the Commonwealth Parliamentary Association, United Nations Women, and a major current project 'Vital Voices', supported by the Australian and New Zealand governments and the Asian Development Bank.

In Palau, the United Nations Development Programme and the Pacific Islands Forum have sponsored a 'Mock Congress' introducing women to governance and executive processes.

Action is also proposed in Samoa, where the number of women in the forty-nine member Parliament fell from four to two in the 2011 elections. The prime minister then called for an amendment to the Electoral Act to bring about a better balance between men and women in Parliament by 2015.

In December 2011, Papua New Guinea's Parliament passed the first stages of a bill which will reserve some parliamentary seats for women only. The prime minister of the Solomon Islands has spoken of similar action.

Chapters fifteen and sixteen carry the stories of three women who decided years ago that it was time for them to step into the male-dominated world of politics, and take women's power from the private into the public sphere.

Overcoming mistrust, suspicion and sometimes misguided assumptions about the roles of women, Hon. Sandra Pierantozzi (see chapter fifteen), Hon. Fiame Naomi Mata'afa and Dame Carol Kidu have made major contributions to political life in their countries and across the Pacific.

LEADER'S STORY: HON. FIAME NAOMI MATA'AFA

Naomi Mata'afa was born in 1957. She has been a Samoan MP since 1975 and was the country's first woman cabinet minister, serving as Minister of Education and Minister of Labour and now Minister of Justice. Her extended family awarded her the title *Fiame*, previously held by her father, Samoa's first prime minister. Fiame Naomi has strong childhood memories of the early days of independence in Samoa and the guests who were welcomed to her parents' home.

There was a whole range of them, from relatives and friends to colleagues of my parents and overseas visitors. If they were Samoan, there would be Samoan protocols and sometimes it was appropriate to have kids around and sometimes not. But with the *palagi* visitors, it was often appropriate to be introduced as the child, so to speak. Up to a certain age, you're literally dancing around the ankles. But then there's a transition when you are slightly older, around eight, nine, and then you begin to be part of the family who are serving, doing the work around the place.

Fiame Naomi Mata'afa
Private collection

We often saw the New Zealand High Commissioner, who played a significant role. And I recall a visit by Governor-General Sir Bernard Fergusson. His son George later became UK High Commissioner to New Zealand, also seconded to Samoa, and when he was here recently he made a point of contacting me and passing over lovely photos of when we were kids and he had visited our home with his parents.

Although my father had other, older children with different mothers, essentially I was the only child at home most of the time. I don't think you could describe me as being special, but I know I had a privileged home background, with more access to resources and stuff. We spoke mostly Samoan, and I thought I spoke English quite well until I went to school in New Zealand and discovered my English was not as good as I had thought it to be.

My first school was the village school, in the community house opposite our house. My mother could see me walking around looking like I was one of the teachers! Because I was the daughter of the chief of the village the teachers thought they'd better just let me do what I wanted. So my mum pulled me out of that school and put me into another where a relative of hers was the principal. And when she came to pick me up later on, I was sitting on the principal's lap! So, finally she took me to Malifa, a bigger government school with a bigger pool of kids, and I just sort of settled in.

Independence

I was aged four and a bit when Samoa became independent. My recollection of it, I'd have to be honest, is mostly about what people told me. And I've seen films of it. In fact, there's a great photo of me sitting there with my mum. Obviously it's hot, so she has taken my top off. I'm sitting there topless waving at the camera. My mum also tells the story that it was an overcast, rainy day but right over Mulinu'u, where we were holding the ceremony, was this ring of clear weather.

I had a sense that my dad was involved. I had overheard his discussions with his first cousin Malietoa, a regular visitor to our place. They were both *tama'aiga* (heads of Samoa's four ruling families) and members of the constitutional group which worked out the complex solution of two joint heads of state, which is a very Samoan sort of thing. The three titles, the *Mata'afa*, the *Tupua*, the *Tumalele Fano* covered, as it were, one part of the country and the *Malietoa* covered the other bits. Two of them shared the head of state position. My dad was more interested in the active political side, and was a member of Parliament under his *Fiame* title, so he became prime minister and the fourth *tama'aiga* became a member of the Council of Deputies.

Education in New Zealand

It was mostly my mum's idea that I should go overseas to secondary school. She was in the first group of Samoan scholarship students who went to New Zealand in 1945. In fact, she and most of her siblings got scholarships to study in New Zealand, they came from that kind of family. I actually went to Samuel Marsden Collegiate School in New Zealand as a boarder when I was eleven. It was a big wrench but fortunately I went with a cousin so there were two of us. My mother's younger sister had gone to Marsden while my mum and her older sisters had gone to Wairarapa College in Masterton. They put the Samoan students all over the place.

My cousin and I were the only Samoans in the class. I can't remember feeling alone and frightened because, you know, I'm five foot nine, and I think I was five foot seven when I was eleven. The others kind of had a go at the two girls who were different, and being Pacific kids we could hold our own so we knocked a few heads around and that sorted it out and they left us alone and we came to an understanding. I was lucky because it is an excellent school with great pastoral care so they recognised straight away that my English needed fixing. So, cousin Pamela and I had one-on-one English tutorials twice a week for two years. Our guardians were the Kellers, family friends for a long time, so multi-generational, and lots of *palagi* family friends, as well as relatives so there wasn't any shortage of contact if we needed to talk to people.

I liked sports and all the extracurricular things, debating, plays, social and cultural activities, you name it, I was doing it. And I enjoyed going off with some of the girls to stay with them, 'specially the girls from farming families. That was a whole side of New Zealand that I suppose most Samoans don't get to see.

Preparation for political life

From a very young age I was aware I wanted to be active in politics. When my dad passed away, in my last year at school, that's why I put up my hand for the titles that had become vacant and I got one of three titles that he had, *Fiame*. I knew I needed to have that ticket to get into politics. I suppose that we always take our role models from people around us, so of course my mother and her sisters were big role models for me. All were very strong women, brought up that they could really do anything. Two of them were MPs, and other women had been in Parliament, too. If you do a profiling of the women that have been in politics here, most have been older women, so they've done the child-bearing,

Minister Fiame Mata'afa at UNESCO launch, Apia
Private collection

child-rearing thing. Most have held senior ranking titles, either the chief leader or orator titles. Most of them have been professional women, so they've also gained some profile in their respective communities. And the other thing, quite common for people in politics, is that they come from families with some association with politics. You have families of doctors and lawyers where the profession is seen as a norm and you understand it so I think for me because I was around politics from such a young age, I didn't see it as anything strange.

In Samoa we don't believe there should be parliamentary seats set aside for women. That's my personal position, too. But I think some women in Melanesia have said that probably would be one of the only ways they could ensure some level of participation. I know our colleague Carol Kidu in PNG is having an uphill struggle. She has been trying for a number of years to get their government to agree to have a set number of seats in terms of a quota arrangement. Before Carol came in, there were only one or two women in the PNG Parliament and they really haven't had another one since Carol has been there. So I think in some countries you do need to have it otherwise it won't happen.

The only place in the Pacific is Bougainville, where the autonomous government set up, I think, three seats, for women. But women thought that was the only opening for them, and that they couldn't challenge the open seats. So they need to do a bit of education around the participation of women in the electoral process.

Here in Samoa we had a bit of a relapse this last election because there were four of us in Parliament, with three of us in Cabinet. Now there are only two women MPs and only myself in Cabinet. The first thing is to make sure there are no barriers to women going into politics. The second thing is that people need to be choosing to do that. You know, you can set all these things up but if women don't put up their hands, it's not going to happen. Women are quite pragmatic. I was talking to a group of senior public servants recently and they said politics isn't seen as a very secure job so they won't necessarily be choosing it. In this election less women ran for Parliament than last time and I think it's because when you're in an economic crunch you're more pragmatic and you go for the more secure opportunity. Sometimes people interpret it as having to be about your personal money, but it's really organising around resources and support and women are good at pushing other people but not really about pushing themselves.

Becoming a *matai*

After my seven years at Marsden School I chose to go to Victoria University in 1976 because I was interested in politics and elements of law and Wellington was like my home town. Early in 1977 I got word from here that court cases for my father's titles were due so I came home for two years because I was involved in those processes and received the *Fiame* title in 1978. I went back in 1979 to pick up my studies – essentially I was doing my second year. Then I got notification from the Lands and Titles Court that I'd been taken to court by some of my family for being an absentee *matai*. I was told (not formally, they didn't write it down on a piece of paper) but they said, 'Listen kiddo, if you want to keep your title, you better stay put and look like you're serious about it'. I thought that was quite unfair because other people were getting their titles and going off and doing other things. It probably would not have happened if I had been a man!

Older people were vying for the title and were not very happy when it was given to a twenty-one-year-old girl. During the court case they were even talking about my suitability for it because I wore jeans and went to the pub and drank beer with *palagi* men – all that sort of stuff. So I said, let's get some equal treatment here. I know this person, he holds a title, quite senior, he goes out drinking with *palagi* men, wearing jeans! What's the difference?!

Fortunately I had a few family people in my corner. But even as I was going through it I could understand what was happening, and I took that message on board. I went and lived in the village for seven years, got involved with the community and with my family. Essentially I became the quintessential Samoan *matai*, doing what *matais* do. I was organising the boys to go to the village, and people to do the fishing, you know, all that sort of thing, getting involved with education projects. I became a deacon of my church, which was a really big thing – if you're going to do it, you have to do it properly! Whatever your beliefs, the important things are how you engage and interact.

A really good Samoan *matai* is probably one of the best feminists you'll ever come across because he's looking after his family and he's making sure people are engaged and reach their potential and stuff like that. When you see a really good *matai* in action, utilising all the human resources at his fingertips, which include the women, then you can say he's a great feminist.

Interestingly, they don't do Women's Studies at the University of the South Pacific. But they have been pushed along. Recently, in the Cook Islands, we conferred an honorary degree on Marjorie Crocombe, a pioneer in establishing USP. At a lunch put on by her family after the graduation, she said they complained bitterly to the management of the university in the early days that the university had no Pacific spirit. There was no Pacific content, most of it was the traditional *palagi*

Matai Fiame Mata'afa with church elders
Private collection

university thing. So a lot of Marje's life's work has been to ensure that the university has had Pacific people writing about the Pacific, recording historical and traditional and cultural elements. I still see it now, USP is still challenged to build on that. It's not just about women, it's the whole gender thing and utilisation of the human resource. And if they're not using it, we're all the poorer for it.

I held the Education portfolio for fifteen years, and when I was first appointed minister, my prime minister, Tofilau, said if you don't do anything else you should get the Samoan national university off the ground. Colin Aikman had come in and done a review for the government and he recommended essentially the establishment of what would be a community college which could be built up, by steps, to a university. But what's in a name right? So we said, whatever it is, we want to call it a university.

If I was talking to young women, I'd say, if you want to affect people's lives, I think public office is unparalleled in terms of the opportunity to influence and make changes. But you don't do it from a vacuum, you have to be engaged, you have to expose yourself to it. First and foremost women have to take the step. I think for most of the Pacific the quality of life has got to the stage where some women could be making the decision to move into these areas of leadership, and especially into national politics. You won't know until you step up. You may fail, but you won't know until you step up.

I have been lucky because I knew from an early age that this is what I wanted to do. So if there were people there that could further my understanding of politics, I'd get to understand them better, move around the circles of it. Sometimes it's not like that for other people, but if you're interested, politics is not the kind of thing you can do as a hobby. I'm interested in leaders and leadership, so I'd read up on particular leaders, see how their lives transpired, how they got to where they went, but essentially, the political thing is about the politics where you're at. So for me it's Samoan politics.

Minister Fiame Mata'afa with US Secretary of State Rice
Private collection

I'm quite a sensible girl. I like to pace myself and I'm very good at saying no. I like to do things and to do them well, so I pick the things I want to do. And I'm quite good about suggesting other people do things that I can't quite manage, or don't want to do.

My dad died when he was fifty-three. A lot of people think he was older because he looked it. But he died quite a young man, and a lot of that had to do with the burden of work at that stage of our development, so I'm very mindful of that too. I am happy to serve my country, but I want to do it well, and keep well. Public service is often seen as giving up your life for the public. I'm quite happy to do that, but on my terms.

LEADER'S STORY: DAME CAROL KIDU

Carol Kidu, the widow of Papua New Guinea's first citizen Chief Justice, was elected to Parliament in 1997, soon after Sir Buri Kidu's death. She became Minister for Community Development and has worked tirelessly to increase opportunities for women to enter political life. Dame Carol believes her upbringing in Brisbane has remained a strong influence in her life.

Minister Dame Carol Kidu
Private collection

My family was working-class with a very strong social conscience, not a Christian-based family but one based on social justice. In the times of the 'White Australia' policy, Dad and I went to some Aboriginal meetings and things like that. I was taught that there are no differences. That background perhaps made my mind ready for what was ahead of me. When I was sixteen I went to a holiday fitness camp where I met this Papua New Guinea student called Buri Kidu and fell madly in love. He was my first boyfriend. I was only sixteen, sweet sixteen, never kissed. Before long, neighbours started to criticise my parents. I learned later that my mother and father got hate letters in our mailbox which they never showed me. They were worried, undoubtedly, what our future would be, but once they met Buri, they knew he was a fine person, and they stuck by us. How could they go back on what they had taught me all my life?

Racism

This was the time of the 'White Australia' policy and I remember being moved on by police when I was sitting with Buri in a Brisbane park, and an old man spitting at me in the street when I was walking along with Buri and calling me a filthy woman. I felt pity for that old man, that he could be so bitter. I had some other unpleasant experiences when I first went to PNG. I went as a university student with my sister, to have a look at the place, and we were billeted with a colonial Australian family. Undoubtedly fine people, but they had a very clear picture of where people fitted in life. When Buri came to visit me and they realised he was my boyfriend, things became very cold, they basically didn't speak to me from then on. They would not allow Buri in the house to visit me. They said natives go through the back door. Their daughter obviously had more liberal ideas and used to try to talk to me, but when the father of the household dropped me at the airport, he said 'The best advice that I can give you, young lady, is to get that monkey off your back, he'll bring you no good'.

Choice and change

Buri and I remained very close but he never broached the issue of marriage, so I did. He would avoid it, so I'd broach it more. Then he said, 'There've been some marriages at home, Australian men to Papua New Guinean women, and what happened was that people become Australian you know, they go that way.' Ours was one of the very few relationships between a Papua New Guinea man and a woman from outside, so he didn't know what would happen. When, eventually, I talked about marriage he said, 'You've got to understand Carol, if we get married don't ever ask me to choose'. I said, 'What do you mean?' He said, 'Don't ever ask me to choose between you and my people, because I tell you now I would have to choose my people, I've been educated for my people.' So we married on that understanding, and I always knew that. He made it very clear and was very honest and I knew my future would be spent in Papua New Guinea.

MP Dame Carol Kidu revisiting her Motu waterfront house
Photographer Jason Smith
Private collection

I married into *Motu* society, lived village life with the women, went gardening and shell-fishing, washing clothes in a dish with water that you had to carry from a communal tap, carrying firewood and making the fire – I'm useless at that so I'd let the other ladies make the fire – cooking huge pots of flour and rice and tapioca, as well as school teaching.

I'd studied a bit of anthropology at university and had always been interested in other people and other cultures, but I won't pretend it was easy, it was hard going. I think the thing that has made me be able to survive politics is the fact that I went through a long induction as a *Motu* wife. I would never pretend to fully understand *Motu* society, or other societies at home and the multiplicity of tribes, but I think I possibly understand them a little bit better than some of the experts.

My mother-in-law was a wonderful mentor, only two years' formal education, but a great woman and a great leader within the family. She was the boss in the household. In traditional society at home, *Motu* society particularly, but I think in all societies, women are powerful in the private sphere, very powerful, but that power was not translated into the public sphere. The men took the power in the public sphere, and this is where we've got to make that quantum leap, to give women the space in the public sphere. She always supported me, when I'd been in tears or things, she'd sit with me and say to the relatives in the household, 'Poor one, she's thinking about her mother and father'. She'd know in her heart, that I was just not coping with it all. Sometimes Buri would say, 'Look Carol you knew the arrangement, if you can't take it, if it's too hard ... ' But I'm so glad I stuck it through! If I had not done that, I would have brought shame to him and his mother.

She never suggested her son might have made a mistake by marrying a foreign woman, but other female relatives did not support the idea of my becoming Buri's wife. I found out later they had asked how can she live our life, how can she help in the gardens, what use will she be? For them, a white woman was someone who had servants, that's all they knew. They also worried that I would take their son away from them, pull him away.

People saw me as a submissive wife, probably because within the village, I'd play the role of a hard-working, non-complaining *Motu* woman but in the privacy of our own home Buri happily shared the burden of household chores. I'm always conscious that I'm 'a part of' but 'apart from' as well. I can never pretend. I suppose I learned that if you are going to lead people, you have to live with them.

Leadership

I always based my campaign on society relationships. I was a teacher, I was involved with YWCA, and getting the preschool going, so I was doing things, involved with organisations, but never from a political perspective. I was never part of the Council of Women or women's political lobby. Before Buri died I established the Port Moresby Business and Professional Women's Club and the girls' scholarship scheme, and things of that nature. I was facilitating, but I never saw myself as a leader. I see myself now as a politician, a facilitator and a catalyst for change, but I don't actually see myself as a leader. It's strange, but you will know what I'm getting at.

Politics

Buri's death put me into politics. I had the sympathy vote. A new chief justice was appointed in 1993 after the Cabinet did not renew Buri's contract. He was starting to plan his life after the judiciary and people were pressuring him, not just people of our own tribal group, but all the Papuan region, the southern coast, asking him to stand for politics. He often said to me, 'I don't know if I really want to do this'. He was getting things in place to go into private legal practice. I said, 'I don't think you have much choice, there's so much pressure from the people for you to stand'. In 1994 he suddenly died. We blamed the politics of the day for his death. The next election was June 1997. Motivated, I suppose, by love and anger about the things that had happened to him and about injustices we were seeing around us, I thought if Buri can't do it, I'll do it. I campaigned with his name very much, but I used to say 'I cannot be Buri but maybe I can contribute in some way'. I was so well known amongst the *Motuans* that I was regarded as a *Motu* woman and I concentrated on going into the settlements of the people that had moved from the rural areas and villages. I worked very hard, with a passion to try to change things, that's a positive passion I guess, but also the negative passion of anger which can drive you as well. But, without the sympathy vote, I don't think I would have been elected. And if Buri had still been alive I would never have dreamt of standing for politics, that's his role in that society.

Our children backed me, but politics doesn't make for a good life for family and children. In PNG the expectations of a politician are huge and if you don't have a good financial base you can't fulfil those expectations. It is assumed that politicians' children are wealthy and privileged, and people will demand money of them. But my personal life didn't change. I still lived at the beach on customary land with extended family, no running water, carrying water every day.

In 1997 there were two women in Parliament – myself and Dame Josephine Abaijah. We were on opposite sides of the floor because she was part of the late Sir William's party. I did ask her one time, could we form what you'd call a women's caucus, just two of us, but that put her in a compromising situation because I don't think her party leader would have entertained the idea. I could see the value of us working together but that was difficult.

I didn't have a clue what went on in Parliament and how I should behave. In some ways it was harder than learning to be a *Motuan*. You know the saying about boiling the frog – get the frog in the water and as it gets hotter you gradually adjust. With this, I was thrown into the boiling water. I found it very challenging. At first I was regarded as Buri's widow, and there was a certain hands-off approach by my political opponents. I was in the opposition to start with and the first time a government minister threw a rude comment at me, I thought, 'Yes! It's time I started being seen not as the widow of Sir Buri Kidu'. That was something that had to be done, I had to establish myself in my own right.

Women and politics

It is very hard for Papua New Guinean women to move into politics and attract support. For example, in my first campaign I gave a very good speech in *Motu*, which is hard and I think Buri was helping me, if there's such a thing, from the other side. Afterwards I heard this old man from the same tribal village as us, saying 'OK, because she's a European she understands these things, but we'll never vote for our own women'. That's never left my mind.

Even preferential voting did not help women. I decided we really had to throw ourselves at the problem. We got involved and enlisted women. The UN and Ausaid backed us up and so did Sir Michael Somare, who said right from the beginning, 'Carol, you must get more women into politics'. I feel sad that he has not been given credit for the progress we have made. A huge amount of work went into it, but it was really difficult getting a proposal up and running on the floor of the House. It was just a blessing for women, that power politics among the men meant they had to announce a critical piece of legislation for Parliament to be recalled unexpectedly, and the legislation creating separate seats for women was sitting waiting already on the notice paper.

Because it was brought in that way, they had to vote for it and hopefully they've had a genuine mind change and they'll take it to the end. The present prime minister's party is headed by a woman and she and other women organised a big rally and spent money bussing women in and buying them uniforms. It was populist politics that brought this legislation to a new level. Men who have supported it will find it very difficult to back off from it now.

It is good to see women have made some progress politically in our region. When Bougainville came out of their ten-year civil war they introduced reserved seats for women in their new constitution. In Samoa some women who had earned local and family authority through the *matai* system have been able to move into national politics. The prime minister of the Solomon Islands, which had no women in Parliament, has made a statement that they will have reserved seats by the next election in 2013. If our bill goes through in PNG it will be a huge impetus for other countries to follow suit.

Parliamentary seats have been set aside for women in many countries such as Rwanda and Uganda where they have come out of civil war, or genocide, and had to write a new constitution. Women were often so prominent in those wars and fights that they demanded their right to have a voice in the new constitution. I hope that does not mean other countries will have to suffer severely before women are fully and fairly represented, but that has been a tendency – and Bougainville was the same, let's face it. They came out of the war, the women had been the peacemakers, and the women were given a voice; they fought for it. I think maybe PNG are going to break that, because male politics has catapulted it forwards.

Women who are considering going into politics have to be extremely strong, and have extremely supportive husbands and families. Sometimes, women who have succeeded in the political sphere have been viewed by society, not just by men, as the women who are perhaps divorcees. That's used against them with the background suggestion that a good wife shouldn't really be in this field, so they've got to really be ready for that as well. Women have also to go through all the cultural hoops, like I did. I asked family permission, first an elder that I thought would be sympathetic, then we asked the immediate family. After that we went to Buri's grave and the elders spoke to Buri and said 'This is what's going to happen, please help her and support her'. Then we went to the clan and so on.

I guess, also, the negativism of so many male colleagues inspired me to keep going. Plus the efforts of the technical working group, the reference groups, all those people just persistently keeping it going; that had never happened before. So I couldn't drop it, no matter what.

Now that I am no longer in Cabinet, I may be at the rather bittersweet end of a long hard road. When our bill was presented in Parliament, the incumbent deputy prime minister yelled at me, 'You'll never be given credit for this law, we're the ones who've passed it'. Quite unnecessary, I thought, and I said, 'I beg your pardon, I never claimed this law, it doesn't belong to you, it doesn't belong to me, it belongs to the women of Papua New Guinea'.

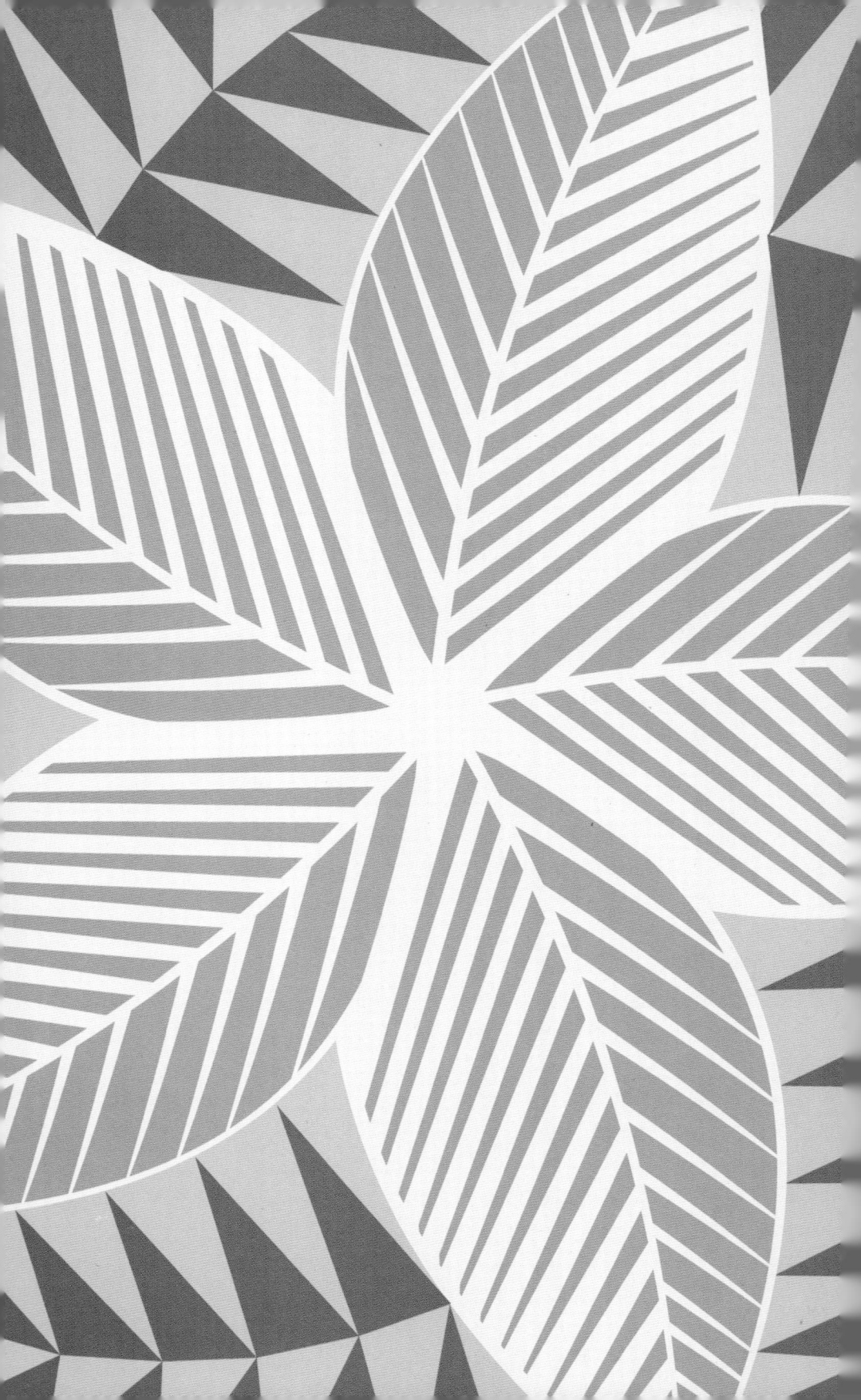

CONCLUSION

CHAPTER SEVENTEEN

Ian Johnstone and Michael Powles

> *We know we have to be on our own and just do what we can ...*
>
> Sir Ieremia Tabai

> *Conquerors come, conquerors go, the ocean remains, mother only to her children. Oceania is vast ... hospitable and generous. We are the sea, we are the ocean ... We must not allow anyone to belittle us again, and take away our freedom.* (Hau'ofa 1993: 11, 16.)

It is obvious from their stories that the leaders who set new flags flying in the Pacific faced huge and daunting tasks. With little experience of national, let alone international, governance and politics they had to negotiate with much larger nations to whom they had long been subservient. The arrangements and constitutions that would frame their new countries' futures had to be agreed quickly and finally, even though the notion of statehood was relatively new to the Pacific.

At the same time, the new leaders had to lift their own peoples out of that subservience and lead them into self-government or independence. Perhaps the most testing and important task was to overcome what Sir Peter Kenilorea identified as 'fear of the unknown'. Assuming a confidence often unwarranted by the resources available to them, they had to chart a way through uncertain undercurrents towards an uncertain destination. They had to persuade their people to see their country as a vibrant new nation, setting out with confidence and determination on a path it had chosen for itself, even though – as Terence Wesley-Smith points out – in most cases the preparation for nationhood and independence had been inappropriate and inadequate:

CONCLUSION

It is difficult to overstate the enormity of this move in Pacific island places often characterised by small size, arbitrary colonial boundaries, rudimentary modern infrastructure, and limited market economies. Tuvalu, with a population of less than 8,000, for example, had almost no administrative infrastructure in place when it achieved independence in 1978, and only limited capacity to generate revenue for government services. In 1975 leaders in Papua New Guinea faced a population of three million people speaking more than 850 languages, a secondary education system less than a decade old, and no roads connecting the capital city to other centres of population. Although the idea was to liberate colonised peoples, those peoples were obliged to take up that freedom in the context of institutions, ideologies, and expectations that were themselves legacies of colonialism. (Wesley-Smith 2006: 122–3.)

Courage

Taking on those tasks took courage, with which these descendants of master ocean navigators were certainly well endowed. Many probably sensed their own 'fear of the unknown' but pushed it to the back of the mind as they negotiated with their colonial power and did what they could to instil confidence in their people. Courage must have been very necessary for leaders like Walter Lini when bullied and deceived by powerful France and Britain, or Kessai Note and John Haglelgam, going from their tiny Micronesian atolls to Washington to try to get a fair deal from the mightiest nation on earth. Some seemed to sail through with confidence because of heritage, or ambition, or love of the battle – particularly the Samoans and Tongans and Albert Henry, Hammer DeRoburt and Michael Somare. Others, like Ratu Mara and Walter Lini, who told us they'd rather have been somewhere else, probably had to work hard to keep going.

But they all showed courage – certainly to overcome intractable disappointment, as Ratu Mara experienced when required to negotiate, 'for the destiny of my own country' with Britain, a nation he had trusted and admired – and, as Bikenibeu Paeniu recalls, when Tuvalu's leaders realised they were being left to go it alone with minimal resources and separated from their Polynesian kin by a misguided colonial oversight. Some leaders displayed their courage more dramatically; nowhere better than in the Cook Islands where Albert Henry and Tom Davis both relished jousting challenges, and in Nauru, where Hammer DeRoburt exploited to the full the phosphate ace in his hand. But perhaps the most effective courage was shown by those leaders, for example in Samoa, Papua New Guinea, Kiribati, Niue and Solomon Islands, who steadfastly and quietly tried to take their people towards the democratic goal well described by Samoa's Tofilau Eti Alesana: 'the stability of the country ... that really is an asset ... developed countries abroad ... won't waste their resources with a country that is not resting peacefully'.

Re-assessment and change

As the euphoria of their new status carried them through the early years of nationhood, many leaders and people – and others watching from beyond the Pacific – may have thought stability and peace had been successfully established. But often that view was too optimistic. Within a decade of self-government or independence, it was becoming obvious that some of the political systems negotiated with the old colonial masters and introduced at independence were inadequate or unsuitable and re-assessment and change were needed. The institutions, methods and practices

CONCLUSION

inherited from the colonial period demanded increasing critical scrutiny. Unlike other critical observers of the Pacific, the late Greg Urwin, Secretary-General of the Forum Secretariat, saw this as a positive and necessary process:

> After all, what is essentially going on is that people, a quite broad range of people, are trying to redefine what it will take to run their countries into the long-term future. I don't think it is stretching reality to say that this analysis has applicability even in situations where serious breakdowns have taken place, such as Solomon Islands and Bougainville. It is far from being a negative process, except where it exceeds certain bounds, as in the cases I've mentioned or unless you take the — to me — quite unrealistic view that we are drifting away from some mythical past golden age. It will often be a somewhat messy process — genuine change is like that. It may well be a sign of ongoing political maturation, and as such the cause for considerable optimism. (Urwin 2004.)

Britain and the Westminster system

The constitutional arrangements acquired at independence seemed particularly unsuitable in many former British possessions. Only in Kiribati was the trouble taken to devise and install a constitution designed to meet the needs and wishes of the newly independent state.

Solomon Islands, Vanuatu, Tuvalu and Fiji had all adopted Westminster-style constitutions, either because that was what Britain suggested, or because, as Ratu Mara explains, 'It was the only parliamentary system I knew. If we were to move to independence, it had to be with this system. There had to be an opposition and a government side'. Through Pacific inexperience and British failure to examine other options, most

Solomon Islands rebels attempting to depose government, Honiara; 2009
Photographer Michael Field
Michael Field Collection

former British possessions were now forced to try to build new nations with, it can reasonably be claimed, unsuitable constitutions which ignored long-standing local traditions of consensus government and instead enshrined parliamentary division and required elected leaders to challenge and oppose each other, rather than consult and co-operate. With no robust public service to support and advise them, many inexperienced politicians began to make up their own rules, rig elections, and bring down governments. Although Fiji managed to avoid such pitfalls for a while, after seventeen years of independence it was plunged into serious disharmony, ensnared in the consequences of two other British colonial policies, the import of immigrant labour and over-militarisation of the Fijian population.

Britain's hasty departure from its poorly equipped Pacific colonies provoked this rueful comment from Kiribati's President Tabai: 'But

CONCLUSION

Soldiers enforce Fiji's fourth coup d'etat, Suva; 2006
Photographer Michael Field
Michael Field Collection

I understand that in this world you do not have permanent friends, just permanent interests. ... it was no longer in the interests of the British to hang around here; they had to go back and be on their own'.

Surprisingly, as evidenced by the pictures of Queen Elizabeth II on the walls of Fiji homes and the royal names still attached to Pacific schools, there remains considerable affection towards the departed British.

Australia, Nauru and Papua New Guinea

As with Britain, Australia was very willing to hand over control in the territories it had governed. Its departure from Nauru, though complicated by phosphate compensation negotiations, was amicable and in the end satisfactory to both parties. Like its

Melanesian cousins, Papua New Guinea soon found its constitution to be no great help in uniting its diverse mixture of highland, island and coastal peoples and tribes. With few reliable systems to regulate the exploitation of resources and fairly distribute the wealth earned, the country was soon affected by stresses and conflicts and even a civil war on Bougainville. Fortunately, former administering power Australia was also a close neighbour and, despite some sensitivities founded in its colonial past and its modern big power status in the South Pacific, it has been in a position to offer support in troubled times to Papua New Guinea and other Melanesian countries.

New Zealand, Samoa, Cook Islands, Niue

New Zealand, the other colonial power to cede its authority between 1960 and 1980, was able to draw on its South Pacific

Fijians celebrate in their new home, Wellington; ca 1998
Photographer Julia Brooke-White
Julia Brooke-White Collection

CONCLUSION

nearness, its own Polynesian heritage and communities, and small-scale familiarity. These factors all helped negotiations about the timing and form of independence or self-government with Samoa, the Cook Islands and Niue. In all three cases, leaders knew that when constitutions were devised and introduced, the main desires of their people had been considered and addressed. The requirement by the people of Niue and the Cook Islands that they retain the right to live in New Zealand was accommodated within the self-government framework. Although, as former premier Young Vivian points out in chapter seven, the long-term value to Niue of that decision can be questioned, there seems no doubt that, in 1974, it was regarded by the majority in Niue, as it had been nine years earlier in the Cook Islands, as essential in the arrangements for self-government.

Samoa had become independent and signed a 'Treaty of Friendship' with New Zealand in 1962. Its new constitution, in a departure from the internationally endorsed 'one person, one vote' principle, granted the right to vote only to Samoa's *matai* (title holders selected by each family). In a peaceful, satisfactory transition, universal suffrage came later. In similar vein, as explained by Tofilau Eti Alesana and Fiame Naomi Mata'afa, an intricately balanced system maintained the *fa'a Samoa* tradition of leadership by four high ranking families. This carefully constructed constitution helped Samoans to put behind them harsh memories of early inept New Zealand colonial administration, and move ahead confidently as not only the first, but also the most peaceably successful, independent nation in the Pacific.

The Cook Islands began life as a self-governing country in association with New Zealand with a constitution much closer to the Westminster pattern. Questions were soon raised about the suitability of such a competitive system in a small country whose traditional leaders, the *ariki*, had been stripped of authority in colonial days, and where family and clan loyalties have always run deep. Within thirteen years of self-government, nepotism and corruption had seriously damaged the country and its people. The 1978 prosecution of Premier Sir Albert Henry for electoral bribery cleared the air. Since then Cook Islanders have been able to select or dismiss their political leaders with all their traditional exuberance but, most importantly, in relative peace and harmony.

United States of America and the former Trust Territory of the Pacific Islands

Independence did not come to the island groups governed by the United States that made up what was formerly called the 'Trust Territory of the Pacific Islands' (TTPI) until 1986 (Marshall Islands and Federated States of Micronesia) and 1995 (Palau). But pro-independence sentiment was fuelled by events to the south. Former Federated States of Micronesia president John Haglelgam remembers a real impetus for independence coming from word of the developments in Samoa and Nauru especially. During the 1960s he was at the University of Hawai'i and remembers joining local students protesting against the Vietnam war; however 'the signs we held up were not about the Vietnam War, but "Free Micronesia"' (chapter thirteen).

Before the leaders of the three countries signed 'Compacts of Free Association' with the United States they had to resolve a number of difficulties. The first was national identity. The United States had governed the UN-mandated Micronesian islands as one group – the Trust Territory of the Pacific Islands – but when Marshall Islanders voted to leave the group and become a nation with its own constitution, Palau and Federated States of Micronesia followed suit. A second complication, particularly

CONCLUSION

demanding for the Marshall Islands as explained by Kessai Note in chapter fourteen, was the need to present hundreds of cases seeking compensation for radiation sickness to the Nuclear Claims Tribunal. And although independence was by now inevitable, the citizens of the three new nations needed reassurance from their leaders that they would not lose the many subsidies and comforts they had enjoyed while being, as Kessai Note comments 'swamped by the governing power'.

The major complicating factor in constitutional negotiations was that, unlike Australia, Britain and New Zealand, the United States did not intend to leave the islands it had controlled, but to stay, retaining responsibility for defence and renting islands like Kwajalein as military bases housing hundreds of US service personnel. Indeed, as John Haglelgam believed, the United States dragged its feet in the negotiations simply because it wanted to hold onto the old Trust Territory for strategic reasons. After years of negotiations, constitutions carrying elements from both Westminster and Washington models were signed and continue to serve the needs of the three small nations and their colossal tenant. But a cloud, similar to that over Niue and the Cook Islands, hangs over the Federated States of Micronesia, Marshall Islands and Palau. Under the compacts according self-government to the three former territories, their citizens have continuing right of access to the United States. '... some of the villages are like ghost villages,' says John Haglelgam in chapter thirteen, 'Very few people remain'.

From village to city

Although population flight worries politicians in many small island states, Epeli Hau'ofa argues that the movement of peoples in and around the Pacific should be regarded more positively:

The new economic reality [since World War II] made nonsense of artificial boundaries, enabling people to shake off their confinement and they have since moved, by the tens of thousands, doing what their ancestors had done before them: enlarging their world as they go ... Everywhere they go, to Australia, New Zealand, Hawai'i, mainland USA, Canada and even Europe, they strike roots in new resource areas, securing employment and overseas family property, expanding kinship networks ... The world of Oceania may no longer include the heavens and the underworld; but it certainly encompasses the great cities of Australia, New Zealand, the USA and Canada. And it is within this expanded world that the extent of the people's resources must be measured. (Hau'ofa 1993: 10, 12.)

Aid and governance

Other challenges to the exercise of independence in many of the smaller Pacific Island countries include heavy reliance on foreign aid, which inevitably affects their freedom of choice on the international stage. Eyebrows are frequently raised when the Federated States of Micronesia, the Marshall Islands and/or Palau line up with the United States in United Nations votes while the rest of the developing world takes the opposite position.

More damaging to ordinary Pacific Islanders, however, have been attempts by Western aid donors to impose their own definition of 'good governance'. Although the need for better governance has long been accepted in the Pacific, as elsewhere, external solutions imposed as conditions to the grant of aid are increasingly unpopular. Respected Pacific academic, Vijay Naidu,

CONCLUSION

has said: 'While reform is certainly needed to address some of the region's long-standing problems, solutions need to be internally decided through national level processes involving broad-based and inclusive consultations focused on the rights and the well-being of ordinary islanders.' (Naidu 2005.)

Terence Wesley-Smith of the University of Hawai'i is even stronger:

> For the first time, the sovereignty of Pacific states has become attached to performance-criteria and the pressures to conform are acute. ... (Wesley-Smith 2006: 121)
>
> The idea of somehow engineering the wholesale transformation of the central values and practices of Oceanic societies to fit the mould of western style administration is deeply troubling. ... According to former Guam Congressman Robert Underwood, any moves that smack of re-colonisation are simply unacceptable. (Wesley-Smith 2006: 126.)

Fortunately, current evidence suggests these messages are being heard by aid donors. The leaders who led their countries to political independence would have adamantly opposed any recolonisation, however it might be disguised.

Leadership

In the countries where new flags now fly, the tasks of leadership took their toll. Tupua Tamasese Mea'ole, Hammer DeRoburt, Solomon Mamaloni, Tofilau Eti and Walter Lini all died too young. Albert Henry left in disgrace and Kamisese Mara in disappointment. Young Vivian, Bikenibeu Paeniu, Kessai Note, Tom Davis stepped back from politics to lead in other fields.

A surprising number – Tui Atua Tupua Tamasese Ta'isi Efi, Ieremia Tabai, Peter Kenilorea, Michael Somare, Carol Kidu, Fiame Mata'afa and Sandra Pierantozzi – have kept on working in parliaments, councils and cabinets.

Old flags still flying

The Pacific's remaining significant colonial powers are France and the United States. France withdrew from Vanuatu along with Britain but has kept control of French Polynesia, New Caledonia and Wallis and Futuna. The United States retains principally American Samoa and Guam.

American Samoa; 1996
Photographer Julia Brooke-White
Julia Brooke-White Collection

In most of these territories there is strong support for independence. American Samoa's present governor, Togiola Tulafono, has spoken of growing incompatibility with the United States and has reached out for closer relations with both the state of Samoa and the Pacific Islands Forum. In October 2011, the Guam legislature held a 'Decolonisation Forum'. In New Caledonia the indigenous *Kanak* people continue to press for independence. And in French Polynesia, where, incredibly,

CONCLUSION

'We must not allow anyone to belittle us again, and take away our freedom.' (Hau'ofa, 1993: 11)
Photographer Julia Brooke-White
Julia Brooke-White Collection

the teaching of the indigenous languages is still severely restricted, President Oscar Temaru lobbies vigorously for independence when and wherever possible.

In these still-colonial territories, leaders will be strengthened, as were their predecessors who have spoken in these chapters, by this deep certainty expressed by Epeli Hau'ofa:

> Conquerors come, conquerors go, the ocean remains, mother only to her children. (Hau'ofa, 1993: 11.)

REFERENCES:

Hau'ofa, E., 'Our Sea of Islands' in Hau'ofa, E. (ed). *A New Oceania: Rediscovering our Sea of Islands*. Suva: University of the South Pacific and Beake House, 1993, 2–16.

Naidu, V., 'The Pacific Region's Global Challenges: Beyond the Doom and Gloom.' Inaugural Lecture, 20 September 2005, Victoria University of Wellington, Wellington.

Urwin, G., Secretary-General, Forum Secretariat, 'South Pacific Success Stories.' Address to 32nd Annual Congress of the Fiji Institute of Accountants, 21 May 2004, Nadi, Fiji.

Wesley-Smith, T., 'There Goes the Neighbourhood: The Politics of Failed States and Regional Intervention in the Pacific', in Jenny Bryant-Tokalau and Ian Frazer (eds) *Redefining the Pacific?* Ashgate, 2006, 121–126.

ADDITIONAL READING

DECOLONISATION AND LATER

Bertram G, 'The political economy of decolonisation and nationhood in small pacific societies' in Hooper A, et al (eds), *Class and culture in the South Pacific*, University of the South Pacific Institute of Pacific Studies, 16–29, 1978

Bryant-Tokalau J, and Frazer I (eds), *Redefining the Pacific? Regionalism Past, Present and Future*, Ashgate, 2006

Campbell IC, 'Attaining independence', in his *A history of the Pacific Islands*, University of Queensland Press, 197–211, 1989

Campbell IC, 1998, 'Anthropology and the professionalism of colonial administration in Papua and New Guinea', *The Journal of Pacific History*, 33, 1, pp. 69–90

Crocombe R and Ali A (eds), *Foreign forces in Pacific politics*, University of the South Pacific Institute of Pacific Studies, 1983

Darwin, J, 'Decolonization and the end of empire' in Winks RW (ed), *Historiography of the British Empire: Vol V*, Oxford: Oxford University Press, 541–57, 1999

Davison J, 'The decolonisation of Oceania', *The Journal of Pacific History*, 6, 133–50, 1971

Denoon D, Mein-Smith P and Wyndham M, 'Decolonisation?' in Denoon D et al (eds) *A history of Australia, New Zealand and the Pacific,* Blackwells, 390–408, 2000

Firth S, 'The rise and fall of decolonisation in the Pacific', in Denoon D (ed), *Emerging from empire? Decolonisation in the Pacific*, Australian National University, 10–21, 1997

Firth S, 'Sovereignty and independence in the contemporary Pacific', *The Contemporary Pacific*, 1, 1, 75–96, 1989

Firth S, 'Decolonisation' in Borofsky R (ed), *Remembrance of Pacific pasts: an invitation to remake history*, University of Hawai'i Press, 314–31, 2000

Fry G, 'Political legitimacy and the post-colonial state in the Pacific: reflections on some common threads in the Fiji and Solomon Island coups', *Pacifika Review,* 12, 3, 2000, 295–304

Grimble A, *Return to the Islands*, John Murray, 1957

Henderson J and Watson G (eds), *Securing a Peaceful Pacific,* Canterbury University Press, 2005

Lamour P, 'Whose initiative: getting out or pushing out?' in Denoon D (ed), *Emerging from empire? Decolonisation in the Pacific*, Australian National University, 204–8, 1997

Macdonald B, 'Decolonisation and beyond: the framework for post-colonial relationships in Oceania', *The Journal of Pacific History,* 21, 115–26, 1986

Morton H, 'Remembering freedom and the freedom to remember: Tongan memories of independence' in Mageo JM (ed), *Cultural memory: reconfiguring history and identity in the postcolonial Pacific*, University of Hawai'i Press, 37–57, 2001

Quanchi M, 'End of an epoch: towards decolonization and independence in the Pacific', *Agora,* Vol 43, 4, 18–23, 2008

Naidu V, 'The path to independence' in Quanchi M and Adams R (eds), *Culture contact in the Pacific,* Cambridge University Press, 126–44, 1993

Powles M (ed), *Pacific Futures,* Pandanus Books, Australian National University, 2006

Robie D, *Blood on Their Banner – Nationalist Struggles in the South Pacific,* Pluto Press, 1989

Scarr D, 'Searching for sovereignty in the South Pacific 1962–80' in his *The History of the Pacific Islands*, Macmillan, 310–33, 1990

Teaiwa T, 'Microwomen: US colonialism and Micronesian women activists' in Rubinstein D (ed), *Pacific History*, University of Guam, 125–42, 1992

Thompson R, 'Winds of change in the South Pacific' in Lowe D (ed), *Australia and the end of empires*, Deakin University Press, 161–72, 1996

Wesley-Smith T, 'Changing patterns of power' in Rapaport M (ed), *The Pacific Islands: environment and society*, Bess Press, 144–55, 1999

www.rnzi.com/newflagsflying

NEW ZEALAND AND ITS PACIFIC NEIGHBOURS

Chapman T, et al, *Niue: a history of the island,* University of the South Pacific Institute of Pacific Studies, 1982

ADDITIONAL READING

Crocombe RG, 'New Zealand and other Pacific Islands: changing economic, social and political relations' in Rubinstein D (ed), *Pacific History*, University of Guam, 293–310, 1992

Crocombe RG, *Pacific neighbours: New Zealand's relations with other Pacific Islands*, University of the South Pacific Institute of Pacific Studies, 1992

Davidson JW, *Samoa mo Samoa*, Oxford University Press, 1967

Field MJ and Mau: *Samoa's struggle for Freedom*, Polynesian Press 1991

Gilson RP, *The Cook Islands 1820–1950*, University of the South Pacific Institute of Pacific Studies, 1980

Haas A, 'New Zealand: Pacific Island or metropolitan power?' in Crocombe R and Ali A (eds), *Foreign forces in Pacific politics*, University of the South Pacific Institute of Pacific Studies, 99–111, 1983

Hempenstall P and Rutherford N, 'The contest for colonial authority in Samoa' in Hempenstall P and Rutherford N (eds), *Protest and dissent in the colonial Pacific*, University of the South Pacific Institute of Pacific Studies, 18–42, 1984

Henderson J, 'Microstates and the politics of association: the future of New Zealand's constitutional links with the Cook Islands and Tokelau', in vom Busch W et al (eds), *New politics in the South Pacific*, University of the South Pacific Institute of Pacific Studies, 99–112, 1994

Henningham S, 'The limits on power: Australia and New Zealand and the region', in his *The Pacific Island states: security and sovereignty in the post-cold war world*, Macmillan, 114–36, 1995

Hooper A and Huntsman J (eds), *Matagi Tokelau: history and traditions of Tokelau*, University of the South Pacific Institute of Pacific Studies, 1991

Howe KR, 'Samoa', in his *Where the waves fall*, Allen and Unwin, 230–54, 1984

Ihimaera W, 'The long dark tea-time of the south: New Zealand's search for a Pacific identity' in Thakur RT (ed), *The South Pacific: problems, issues and prospects*, Macmillan, 133–44, 1991

Liua'ana B, 'Who made Western Samoa independent?' in Denoon D (ed), *Emerging from empire? Decolonisation in the Pacific*, Australian National University, 40–46, 1997

Meleisea M et al, 'Preparation for independence' in Meleisea M (ed), *Lagaga: a short history of Western Samoa*, University of the South Pacific Institute of Pacific Studies, 1983

Macdonald B, 'Towards a Pacific community: geopolitical and regional perspectives on New Zealand's relationships with the small states of Oceania', in Rubinstein D (ed), *Pacific History*, University of Guam, 313–22, 1992

Ross, A (ed), *New Zealand's Record in the Pacific Islands in the Twentieth Century*, Longman Paul, 1969

Wesley-Smith T, 'Australia and New Zealand' in Howe KR, Kiste RC and Lal BV (eds), *Tides of history*, Allen and Unwin, 195–226, 1994

AUSTRALIA, NAURU AND PAPUA NEW GUINEA

Davison J, 'The republic of Nauru', *The Journal of Pacific History*, 3, 145–50, 1968

Downs I, *The Australian Trusteeship: Papua New Guinea 1945–75*, Australian National University Press 1980

Fry G, 1992a, 'Australia and the South Pacific' in Boyce RJ and Angel JR (eds), *Diplomacy in the marketplace: Australia in world affairs 1981–90*, Longman Cheshire 1992

Fry G, 1993b, 'At the margin: the South Pacific and the changing world order', in Richardson JL and Leaver R (eds), *The post-cold war order: diagnoses and prognoses*, Sydney, Allen and Unwin, 1993

Fry G, 1996, 'Framing the Islands: knowledge and power in changing Australian images of the South Pacific', Working Paper, Dept of International Relations, Canberra, Australian National University.

Fry G, 1997a, 'The South Pacific experiment: reflections on the origins of regional identity', *Journal of Pacific History*, Vol 32, 2, 180–202

Fry G, 1997b, 'Australia and the South Pacific: the rationalist ascendency' in Cotton J and Ravenhill J (eds), *Seeking Asian engagement: Australia in world affairs 1991–95*, Melbourne, Oxford University Press, 291–308 (Note: published each five years, various authors)

Fry G, 1997c, 'Framing the Islands: knowledge and power in changing Australian images of the South Pacific', *The Contemporary Pacific*, Vol 9, 2, 305–344

Hasluck P, *A time for building: Australian administration in Papua and New Guinea 1951–1963*, Melbourne University Press 1976

Parker RS, 'Appraising the colonial record: Australia in Papua New Guinea', in Lal BV and Nelson H (eds), 'Lines across the sea: colonial inheritance in the post colonial Pacific', *Pacific History Association*, 9–24, 1995

Pollock N, 'Nauru's post-independence struggles' in Lal BV and Nelson H (eds), 'Lines across the sea: colonial inheritance in the post colonial Pacific', *Pacific History Association*, 49–56, 1995

ADDITIONAL READING

Pollock N, 'Nauru: decolonising, recolonising – but never a colony' in Denoon D (ed), *Emerging from empire? Decolonisation in the Pacific*, Australian National University, 102–6, 1997

Shand D, 'Australia: the intermediate umbrella' in Crocombe R and Ali A (eds), *Foreign forces in Pacific politics*, University of the South Pacific Institute of Pacific Studies, 87–98, 1983

Thompson R, *Australia in the Pacific Islands in the Twentieth Century*, Scholarly Publishing, 1998

Wesley-Smith T, 'Australia and New Zealand' in Howe KR, Kiste RC and Lal BV (eds), *Tides of history*, Allen and Unwin, 195–226, 1994

FRANCE AND THE PACIFIC

Aldrich R, *Greater France: a history of French overseas expansion*, Macmillan, 1996

Bensa A and Wittersheim E, 'Nationalism and interdependence: the political thought of Jean-Marie Tjibaou', *The Contemporary Pacific*, 10, 2, 1998, 369–90

Chafer T and Sackur A, (eds), *Promoting the colonial idea: propaganda and visions of empire in France*, New York, Palgrave, 2002

De Dekker P, 'France' in Howe KR, Kiste RC and Lal BV (eds), *Tides of history: the Pacific Islands in the 20th century*, Allen and Unwin, 258–79, 1994

Henningham S, 'France in Melanesia and Polynesia', in Howe KR, Kiste RC and Lal BV (eds), *Tides of history: the Pacific Islands in the 20th century*, Allen & Unwin, 119–45, 1994

Henningham S, *France and the South Pacific: a contemporary history*, University of Hawai'i Press, 1992

Martins G, 'France as a South Pacific actor' in Thakur RT (ed), *The South Pacific: problems, issues and prospects*, Macmillan, 105–16, 1991

Scarr D (ed), *France in the Pacific: past, present and future*, (special issue of *The Journal of Pacific History*, 26, 2, 1991)

BRITAIN AND THE PACIFIC

Douglas B, 'Imperial flotsam? The British in the Pacific Islands' in Winks RW, (ed), *Oxford History of the British Empire: Historiography*, Oxford University Press, 366–78, 1999

Howe KR, 'Fiji', in his *Where the waves fall*, Allen and Unwin, 255–80, 1984

Lal BV, 'Managing ethnicity in colonial and post-colonial Fiji' in Lal BV and Nelson H (eds), 'Lines across the sea: colonial inheritance in the post colonial Pacific', *Pacific History Association*, 37–48, 1995

Laracy H (ed), *Tuvalu: a history*, University of the South Pacific Institute of Pacific Studies, 1983

Latukefu S, 'Tonga at independence and now' in Lal BV and Nelson H (eds), 'Lines across the sea: colonial inheritance in the post colonial Pacific', *Pacific History Association*, 57–68, 1995

Macdonald B, 'Grimble of the Gilbert Islands: myth and man' in Scarr D (ed), *More Pacific Island Portraits*, 211–30, Australian National University, 1978

Norton R, 'Accommodating indigenous privilege: Britain's dilemma in decolonising Fiji', *The Journal of Pacific History*, 37, 2, 2002, 133–56

Wood-Ellem E, 'Queen Salote and the British dual mandate policy' in Denoon D (ed), *Emerging from empire? Decolonisation in the Pacific*, Australian National University, 22–25, 1997

USA AND THE PACIFIC

Hanlon D, 'Patterns of colonial rule in Micronesia', in Howe KR, Kiste RC and Lal BV (eds), *Tides of History*, Allen and Unwin, 93–118, 1994

Petersen G, 'Why is Micronesian independence an issue' in Lal BV and Nelson H (eds), 'Lines across the sea: colonial inheritance in the post colonial Pacific', *Pacific History Association*, 69–82, 1995

Sunia FIF, 'American Samoa: Fa'a Amerika?', in Afeaki E, et al, *Politics in Polynesia*, University of the South Pacific Institute of Pacific Studies, 115–30, 1983

BIBLIOGRAPHY

Asby G, *Guide to Pohnpei,* Rainy Day 1983

Bennett JA, *Wealth of the Solomons: A History of a Pacific Archipelago, 1800 – 1978*, University of Hawai'i Press, 1987

Boyd M, 'The Record in Western Samoa to 1945', in *New Zealand's Record in the Pacific Islands in the Twentieth Century,* Ross A (ed), Longman Paul

Boyd M, 'The record in Western Samoa Since 1945', in *New Zealand's Record in the Pacific Islands in the Twentieth Century,* Angus Ross (ed), Longman Paul, 1969.

Burns, Sir Alan, *Fiji,* H M Stationery Office, 1963

Crocombe R, *The South Pacific,* University of the South Pacific, 2001

Crocombe R and Ali A (eds), *Politics in Polynesia,* University of the South Pacific Institute of Pacific Studies, 1983

Crocombe R and Ali A (eds), *Politics in Melanesia,* University of the South Pacific Institute of Pacific Studies, 1982

Crocombe R and Tuza (eds), *The First Ten Years of Solomons Independence,* University of the South Pacific, Honiara and Institute of Pacific Studies, 1992

Dean and Ritova, *Rabuka – No Other Way,* Marketing Team International, 1988

Dibblin J, *Day of Two Suns,* Virago, 1988

Field M, *Swimming with the Sharks*, Penguin, 2010

Gina LM, *Journeys in a small canoe,* University of the South Pacific Institute of Pacific Studies and Pandanus 2003

Griggin, Nelson, Firth, *Papua New Guinea,* Heinemann, 1979

Grimble A, *A Pattern of Islands,* John Murray, 1952

Harris NV, *The Tropical Pacific,* University of London Press, 1966

Hau'ofa E, 'Our Sea of Islands' in Hau'ofa E (ed), *A New Oceania: Rediscovering our Sea of Islands,* Suva, 1993, University of the South Pacific and Beake House

Howe KR, *Where the Waves Fall,* Geo. Allen & Unwin 1984

Kennedy T, *An Ocean of Islands,* Nandina Press, 2004

Lal BV and Fortune K, *The Pacific Islands – an encyclopedia,* University of Hawaii Press, 2000

Laracy H (ed), *Tuvalu – a History,* Institute of Pacific Studies and Government of Tuvalu, 1983

Leibowitz AH, *Embattled Island,* Praeger, 1996

Mara, Ratu Sir K, *The Pacific Way,* University of Hawai'i Press, 1997

Naidu V, 'The Pacific Region's Global Challenges: Beyond the Doom and Gloom', Inaugural Lecture, Victoria University of Wellington, Wellington, 20 September 2005

Pointer M and Folau K, *My Heart is Crying a Little, Tagi tote e loto Haaku*, Government of Niue and University of the South Pacific Institute of Pacific Studies, 2000

Prasad R, *Tears in Paradise,* Glade Publishers, 2004

Shennan J and Tekenimatang M (eds), *One and a Half Pacific Islands*, Victoria University Press, 2005

Snow P and Waine S, *The People from the Horizon,* Phaidon Press, 1979

Todd I, *Papua New Guinea: Moment of Truth,* Angus and Robertson, 1974

'Tonga Constitutional and Electoral Reform Commission Final Report', EastWest Center, 2008

'United Nations Trusteeship Agreement, Agreement approved by the General Assembly of the United Nations', 13 December 1946 http://untreaty.un.org/cod/repertory/art85/english/rep_supp3_vol3-art85_e.pdf accessed 1 March 2012

Urwin G, Secretary-General, Forum Secretariat, 'South Pacific Success Stories', Address to 32nd Annual Congress of the Fiji Institute of Accountants, Nadi, Fiji, 21 May 2004

Van Trease H (ed), *Atoll Politics,* University of Canterbury and Institute of Pacific Studies, 1993

Various, *Cook Islands Politics,* Polynesian Press and South Pacific Social Sciences Association, 1979

Viviani N, *Nauru – Phosphate and Political Progress*, Australian National University Press, 1970

BIBLIOGRAPHY

Wesley-Smith T, 'There Goes the Neighbourhood: The Politics of Failed States and Regional Intervention in the Pacific', in Bryant-Tokalau J and Frazer I (eds) *Redefining the Pacific?,* Ashgate 2006

Williams M, Macdonald B and Macdonald B, *The Phosphateers,* Melbourne University Press, 1985

INDEX

Bold page numbers refer to main passages. Italic page numbers indicate photographs.

A
Abaijah, Dame Josephine 285–286
Africa 131–132
aid 113, 144, 219, 224, 228, 242, 262, 303
    reliance on 109, 243, 246, 302
Aikman, Colin 26, 112, 278–279
Alebua, Ezekiel 159
Alliance party (Fiji) 93, 96, 97, *98*, 102, 104
American land-buyers 204, 210
American Samoa 12, 31, 71, 304, *304*
Anglo-German Convention 55
Antelope (ship) 251
Asian Development Bank 228, 269
Ausaid 286
Australia 165, 212, 227–228, 237, 269
    independence from 7, 57, 62, 123, 133, 297–298
    mandates and trusteeships 55–56
    phosphate exploitation 56–58, 60–61, 64, 66
    place in colonialism 13, 121
Awai, Joseph 135

B
Bainimarama, Voreque 104–105
Baker, Rev Shirley 76
Banaba (Ocean Island) 12–13, 167, *183*, *184*, 184–186, 192
Barnes, C E *63*
Bavadra, Timoci 104
Berlin Conference (1889) 19
Bikini 234, 236–237, 240
Billy Hilly, Francis 159
blackbirding *see* slave trading
Boas, Obed 129
Bogotu, Francis 149

Bougainville 124, 137, 148, 275, 287–288, 295, 298
Bougainville, Louis-Antoine 18
Britain
    attitudes to independence 7, 62, 143, 147, 165, 169, 170, 188–189, 202, 205
    colonisation and control 12–14, 71–78, 86–87, 108, 120–121, 140–141, 158, 164, 167–170, 183–185, 201–204
    phosphate mining 55–56, 61, 185
British Phosphate Commission 55–57, 60, 185
Brown, Doug 102
Bugotu, Francis 152

C
Cakobau, Ratu Edward 90, 101, 102–103
Cakobau, Ratu George 90
Cakobau, Ratu Seru 86–87
Campbell, Jack 147
Caroline Islands 218, 250–251
Carter, D J *63*
Chan, Julius 124–125, 134, 136–137, 238
Charles, Prince of Wales 100, *100*
Chaudhry, Mahendra 104
chiefs (incl. matai, ariki) 27–28, 36–37, *37*, 50–51, 70, 104–105, 151–152, 235, 245–246, 277
    as independence leaders 5, 21, 56, 59, 239
    status lost 37, *39*, 42, 300
    status retained 72, 87, 89–90, *90*, 272–273

317

China 66, 226, 228, 252
Chinese immigrants 141, 159, 202, 227
churches 5–6, 76, 115, 204
Chuuk 55, 218–219
citizenship 111, 153, 186, 209–210, 243
    New Zealand 50, 110, 168
Clark, Helen 32, 261
climate change 166, 175–176, 196
Colonial Sugar Refining Company
    (CSR) 88, 95–96
colonisation 11–14, 19, 120–122, 158,
    218–219, 232–233, 251
Commonwealth Parliamentary
    Association 269
Compacts of Free Association
    (with US)
    Marshall Islands 235–236, 239,
        241–243, 246
    Micronesia 219, 221–224, 228–229
    Palau 251–252
connections among leaders 6–7, 79,
    134, 150, 155, 238
constitutions 295–296, 299–300, 301
    Bougainville 287
    Cook Islands 11, 47–48, 50,
        299–300
    Fiji 97–99, 295
    Kiribati 190–192, 295
    Marshall Islands 236, 241, 244–246,
        301
    Micronesia 219, 301
    Niue 11, 299
    Palau 251–252, 257–258, 301
    Papua New Guinea 127, 132, 298
    Samoa 10, 21, 23–25, 28–30, 31,
        272, 299
    Solomon Islands 145, 149, 152–154,
        156, 295
    Tonga 72–74
    Tuvalu 171, 173–174, 295
    Vanuatu 203, 209–210, 295
Cook, James 36, 108, 200
Cook Islands 10, **36–51**, 108–109, 294,
    299
    constitution 11, 47–48, 50, 299–300
    women in 268, *268*, 277

Cook Islands Party 38, 41, 44, 47
Cripps, Sir Stafford 23
Crocombe, Marjorie 277
Curacao, HMS 140

D

Davidson, Jim 26, 62–63
Davis, Sir Tom 5, *44*, **44–51**, *49*, 294,
    303
de Robert, Henry 135
Democratic Party (Cook Islands)
    44, 47
DeRoburt, Hammer 4–5, 56–57, *57*,
    59–66, *63*, 293–294, 303
discrimination 27, 44–45, 112, 150–151,
    170, 281
diseases 19, 22, 87
Dowiyogo, Bernard 64, 66
Drake, Sir Francis 182

E

economic development 28, 47–49, 81,
    116–117, 165, 174–175, 226–227, 252
    under colonial rule 153, 158, 211,
        219, 251
education 2–3
    in Australia 77, 126–127, 135
    in Britain 93–95
    under colonial & trusteeship rule
        13–14, 25, 126–127, 135, 153,
        169–170, 187, 254
    development of 28, 115, 116
    in New Zealand 2, 6, 44–45, 93,
        111–112, 144, 149–150,
        186–187, 205, 271, 273–274,
        276
    in Pacific 169, 177, 236–238
    in United States 46, 220–221, 255,
        256
Ellice Islands 164, 184, 186
    see also Tuvalu
Enewatek 234
epidemics *see* diseases
Eri, Vincent 132–133
Etpison, Ngiratkel 258

INDEX

F

Falvey, John (J G) 92–93, 99, 103
Federated States of Micronesia *see* Micronesia, Federated States of
Fergusson, George 271
Fiji 79, **86–105**, *99*, 185–186, 194, 296–297, *297*
   constitution 97–99, 295
   women in *267*, 268, *269*
Fiji Labour Party 104
fisheries 65, 193–194, 219, 227–229, 262
flags *30, 63*, 149, 171–173, 244, *304*
Foster, Sir Robert 101
France 13, 18, 214, 304–305
   colonisation by 12–14, 158, 201–202
   delaying practices 6–7, 12, 205, 211
   treaty with Tonga 70–71, 74, 81
Fraser, Peter 7, 20
Freegard, Douglas 146
French Polynesia 6, 13, 304–305
Fugui, Rev (1970s) 147

G

Ganilau, Ratu Sir Penaia 104
George Tupou I, King 70–71, 76
George Tupou II, King *72*, 77
George Tupou V, King 73, 81–82
Germany 12–13, 71, 218, 233, 251
   in Nauru 55
   in New Guinea 120–121
   in Samoa 19, 22–23, 26–27, 75–76
   in Tonga 74–76
Gilbert and Ellice Islands Protectorate/Colony 12, 164, 184–186, 188
Gilbert Islands 165, 182–183
   see also Kiribati
Goff, Phil 117
Golon, Aser 149
Gordon, Sir Arthur 87
Grimble, Arthur 185
Guadalcanal 159
Guam 13, 303, 304
Gudgeon, W E 37
Guise, John 124, 132

H

Haglelham, John *220*, **220–229**, 293, 300–301
Hasluck, Sir Paul 125–126
Hau'ofa, Epeli 14, 301–302, 305
Henry, Albert 40–45, *41*, 47, 50–51, 300, 303
   in campaign for self-government 4–5, 7, 38, 41–42, 45
   personality 5, 47, 293–294
Henry, Sir Geoffrey 48, 51, 111
Hughes, Tony 151

I

Ielimia, Apisai 178
Iloilo, Ratu Josefa 104–105
immigration 79, 87–89, 111, 296
imperial rivalries 13, 19, 55, 71, 75, 140
Indian nationalists 23
Indo-Fijians 87–89, *89*, 93, 95–103
Indonesia 120, 135
Irish nationalists 23

J

Japan 219, 233, 251, 253
   postwar relationships 64, 80, 165, 194
   WWII invasions and attacks 55, 60, 122, 165, 185–186
Johnson, Les 126, 133
Johnston, Sir Charles *63*

K

Kabua, Amata 235–236, 239, 244, 245–246
Kabua, Imata 246
Kabui, Joseph 137
Kaputin, John 124, 127
Kausimae, David 147
Keating, Paul 64
Keke, Dr Ludwig *59*, **59–66**
Kemakeza, Sir Allan 159
Kenilorea, Sir Peter 5–6, **149–157**, *150*, 159, 292, 304

Kidu, Dame Carol 267, 275, *280*, **280–288**, *282*, 304
Kidu, Sir Buri 280–285
Kiki, Albert Maori 124, 127–129
Kiribati 109, 166–167, **182–196**, 221
  constitution 190–192, 295
  see also Gilbert Islands
Kisan Sangh union 88, 96
Korea 165, 227
Korman, Maxime Carlot 214
Kosrae 218
Kwajalein 233–234, *234*, 236, 243, 301

L

land 27, 87–89, 101, 124, 141, 153, 157, 202–204, 210, 213, 222
Lange, David 47
languages ix, 120, 140–141, 167–168, 202, 218
  colonial policies 13, 219, 305
  preservation 117
Latasi, Sir Kamuta 171
Lauti, Sir Toaripi 171
leadership 101–102, 144, 156, 158–159, 177, 191, 213, 292–296, 299–300, 303–305
  pre-independence 2–9, *10*, 61, 93–94, 126–128, 151–152
League of Nations mandates 19, 27, 55, 121, 253
Lee Bo (Carolines chief) 251
Lee Kuan Yew 102
Lester, Joan 147
Levers (company) 141
Leymang, Father Gerard 209
Line Islands 182, 196
Lini, Ham 214
Lini, Father Walter 5–6, 12, 155, **202–214**, *204*, 293–294, 303

M

Ma'afu, Enele 86
Maasina Rule 142–143
Mainu, Leonard 149
Makea, Queen *37*, 37
Malaita 159

Malaysia 81, 262
Malietoa Tanumafili *10*, 272
Malietoa Tanumafili II 21, 32
Mamaloni, Solomon 4–5, *144*, **144–149**, 151, 155, **156–159**, 303
Maoate, Terepai 51
Mara, Ratu Sir Kamisese 5, *93*, **93–104**, *98*, *100*, 293–294, 295, 303
  noble rank 3, 9, 93–94, 155
  regional leadership 134, 155, 213
Mara, Uluilakeba 105
Marching Rule (Solomon Islands) 148
Marshall Islands 109, 220, 228, **232–247**, 300–302
Marurai, Jim 51
Maseng, Alfred 214
Masias, Jean 208
Massey, W F 22
Mata'afa, Fiame Naomi **270–280**, *274*, *278*, *279*, 304
Mata'afa Mulinu'u II, Fiame *10*, 21, 62
Mataio Tuitoga, King 108
Matane, Sir Paulius 126–127, 131, 132
Mataskelekele, K 214
Mataungan Assn 136
Mathieson, J *10*
Mau movement 19, *20*, 22
McEwen, Jock 112
McGregor, Sir William 121
Melanesian Progressive Party (Vanuatu) 214
Mendana de Neira, Alvaro de 36, 140, 164
Menzies, Bob 126
Micronesia 12–14, 267
Micronesia, Federated States of **218–229**, *225*, 235, 300–302, *302*
military forces *92*, 92, *110*, 193
  coups *93*, 104, 296, *297*
  see also peacekeeping forces
missionaries 22, 36, 70, 76, 81, 108, 115, 141–142, 200–201, *201*, 255
Momis, John 137
Morauta, Mekere 137
Moss, Frederick 36–37
Moti, Julian 160
Muldoon, Robert *134*

INDEX

N

Nagriamel 203
Nailatikau, Ratu Epeli 105
Naisali, Henry 174
Namaliu, Rabbie 136
Namur 234
Narokobi, Bernard 135
Nash, Walter 46
Natapei, Edward 214
Natera, John 135
National Federation Party (Fiji) 104
nation-building 98–100, 116–117, 123–124, 154, 168–169, 171, 292–293, 296, 298, 300
natural disasters 32, 117, 137, 160, 176
  see also climate change
Nauru 12–13, **54–66**, 109, 165, 221, 294, 297
Nauru Phosphate Commission 57
Nelson, Olaf Frederick 22–23
neo-colonialism 222–223, 228
Netherlands (Holland) 12, 120–121
New Caledonia 6, 13, 214, 304
New Hebrides 200–211, *201*
  see also Vanuatu
New Hebrides National Party 202–203, 206
New Zealand 195, 269
  colonial role 13, 22, 37, *38*, 45–46, 108
  decolonisation 7, 38–40, 42–43, 62, 112–114, 298–300
  Labour governments 7, 19–20
  phosphate exploitation 55, 58, 61
  relationship with Tuvalu 165–166, 168
  role in Samoa 19–20, 22–28, 32
  in WWII *122*, *143*
  see also under education
Niue 11, **108–117**, 299
Niue People's Party 115
Note, Kessai 5, *236*, **236–246**, 293, 303
nuclear testing 12–14, 220, 229, 234–237, 240–241, 301

O

Ocean Island *see* Banaba
Onorio, Teima 196

P

Pacific Islands Company 183–184
Pacific Islands Forum 227, 242, 270, 295, 304
  Smaller Island States Unit 109, 117
Pacific Phosphate Company 185
Paeniu, Bikenibeu 5, 9, 12, *166–167*, **166–177**, 294, 303
Palau 235, **250–262**, 270, 300–302
PANGU party 123, 125, 129, 135, 136
Papua New Guinea 14, **120–137**, *130*, 212–214, 237–238, 293, 298
  women in 267–268, 270, 275, 280–288
Patel, A D 93, 97, 99
Patel, S P 97
peacekeeping forces 211–212
People's Progressive Party (PNG) 125, 136
Philip, Danny 160
Phoenix Islands 182, 196
phosphate mining 12–13, 55–58, 60–62, 64–66, 167, 183–186, 192, 194
  photos *56*, *57*, *58*, *183*
Pia, Alesala 170
Pierantozzi, Sandra Sumang **252–261**, 270, 304
Pohiva, Akilisi 74
Pohnpei 218, *225*, 227
population
  growth 65, 194–195
  losses 22, 55, 87, 110–111, 116–117, 224–226, 261, 301–302
Powles, Sir Guy *10*, 26
Puna, Henry 51

Q

Qarase, Laisenia 104
Quentin-Baxter, Alison 244
Quentin-Baxter, R Q 112–113

R

Rabi 185, 192
Rabuka, Sitiveni 79, 104
racism *see* discrimination
Ranfurly, Lord 38
Raroa, Oala 127–128, 131
Ratieta, Naboua 189
Rea, Gavera 127
refugees 66
Rex, Sir Robert 5, 109, 113–114, *113–114*, 117
Rini, Snyder 159–160
Robati, Pupuke 51
Roi 234
Rongelap 234
Roy Mata 200
Royalist, HMS 183
Russia 193

S

Salii, Lazarus 257
Salote Tupou III, Queen 72, *73*, 266
Samoa 4, 10, **18–32**, *30*, 71, 75–76, 208, 221
    constitution 10, 21, 23–25, 28–30, 31, 272, 299
    women in *266*, 267–268, **270–280**, 287
Santo 210–211, 213
Secretariat of the Pacific Community 6
Seddon, Richard 37, *37*, *109*
Seveli, Feleti 81
Siku, Derek 160
Skate, Bill 137
slave trading (blackbirding) 87, 121, 141, 164, 182–183, 200, 232
Smith, John (Gilbert & Ellice Islands, 1970s) 188
Smith, John (Solomon Islands, 1974) 150
Sogavare, Manasseh 159–160
Solomon Islands **140–170**, 287, 295, *296*
    constitution 145, 149, 152–154, 156, 295
    women in 268, 270

Somare, Sir Michael 4–5, **123–137**, *125*, *134*, 238, 286–287, 293, 304
Sope, Barak 214
South Pacific Commission 6–7
South Seas commercial syndicate 121
Spain 11, 218, 233, 251
Speight, George 104
Sri Lanka 132
Stevens, Jimmy 211–214
Stinson, Charles 102
sugar industry 88, *88*
Sukuna, Ratu Sir Lala 90, *91*, 94, 97

T

Tabai, Sir Ieremia 5, 9, **186–196**, *187*, 292, 296–297, 304
Taiwan 66, 252
Tamasese Lealofi III, Tupua 19, *20*, 21–22
Tamasese Lealofi IV, Tupua 5
Tamasese Mea'ole, Tupua 9, *10*, 21, 31, 303
Tamasese Ta'isi Efi, Tui Atua Tupua 9, **21–26**, *22*, 32, 304
Tanzania 131
Tarawa 184–186, *189*
Taufa'ahau Tupou IV, King 3, 5, *74*, **74–81**
Temaru, Oscar 305
Tito, Teburoro 196
Tofilau Eti Alesana 21, **26–31**, *27*, 278, 294, 303
Toganivalu, David 111
Togia, King *109*
Tokelau *11*, 167–168, 184
Tomasi, Sir Puapua 174
Tomeing, Litokwa 246–247
Tong, Anote 196
Tonga **70–82**, 108, 168, 266
tourism 66, 109, 219, 252
trade 80–81
traditions and customs 10, 21, 27, 89, 115, 151–152, *153*
    see also chiefs
Truk 55, 218–219
Trust Territory of the Pacific Islands (TTPI) 219, 235, 239, 251, 253, 300–301

INDEX

trusteeships (UN) 7, 19–20, 55–56, 60, 121, 123, 129, 221–222, 226, 233
    see also Trust Territory of the Pacific Islands
Tuilaepa Aiono Sailele Malielegaoi 32
Tuitoga, King Mataio 108
Tu'ivakano, Lord 73, 82
Tulafono, Togiola 304
Tupou VI, King 82
Tuvalu 5, 12, 14, 109, **164–178**, 191, 293–295
    see also Ellice Islands

U

Ulufa'alu, Bartholomew 157, 159
Underwood, Robert 303
United Nations 7, 20–21, 25, 29, 43, 113–114, *114*, 171, 286
    see also trusteeships
United Nations Development Programme 270
United Nations Women 269
United Party (PNG) 136
United States 19, 71, 74, 196, 304
    attitudes to independence 7, 221–222, 239
    forces in WWII 78–79, 142, 164–165, 185–186
    security and control 12–13, 219, 222, 233, 235–236, 242–243, 251, 300–301
    see also Compacts of Free Association; nuclear testing
University of the South Pacific 277–278

Urwin, Greg 295
Utrik 234

V

Vanuaaku Party 203, 206–209, 214
Vanuatu 12, **200–214**, *207*
    constitution 203, 209–210, 295
Vivian, Mititaiagimene Young 5, **110–117**, *111*, 299, 303
Vohor, Serge 214

W

Wallis and Futuna 6, 304
Webb, John 11, **39–44**, *40*
Whitlam, Gough 123
Wiari, Kipling 135
Williams, J *201*
Wingti, Paias 136–137
women 252, 254, 256, 259–261, *266–269*, **266–288**
Woonton, Robert 51
World War I *110*, 121, 219, 251
World War II 3, 77–79, *122*, 122–123, 142, *143*, 164–165, 219, 233, 251
    Islander soldiers 90–92, 122
    Japanese occupation and invasion 55, 60, 122, 185–186

Y

Yap 218

Z

Zedkaia, Jurelang 244, 247

THE EDITORS

IAN JOHNSTONE

After a tour of duty as a District Officer in Northern Rhodesia (now Zambia), Ian Johnstone moved to New Zealand in 1961 and began work in broadcasting. Among his early assignments were TV reports about preparations for independence in Fiji and self-government in the Cook Islands. Later, based in Suva and working for the South Pacific Commission (now the Secretariat of the Pacific Community), he set up radio exchanges among Pacific countries approaching or achieving independence and moderated election debates and coverage. A founding member of the Pacific Islands News Association and a Jefferson Fellow of the East West Center, he established Radio New Zealand's new International Service in 1990 and later joined co-editor Michael Powles on the board of the Pacific Cooperation Foundation. In 1995 he recorded many of the interviews featured in *New Flags Flying* and continues to write and broadcast about South Pacific affairs.

MICHAEL POWLES

Michael Powles has had a long association with Pacific Island countries, including a childhood in Samoa, serving as New Zealand high commissioner to Fiji, accredited also to Kiribati, Nauru and Tuvalu and later accompanying New Zealand prime ministers at Forum meetings and on visits in the region. He served also as ambassador to Indonesia and China, as a deputy secretary of foreign affairs, and then as New Zealand's ambassador to the United Nations. He chaired regional fisheries negotiations and served as a human rights commissioner. In 2002, he founded the Pacific Cooperation Foundation in New Zealand. He later served on the Council of the National University of Samoa and has written widely on international and Pacific affairs. He is a senior fellow of the Centre for Strategic Studies and recently enjoyed re-engaging with the Pacific through involvement in training for young diplomats in Papua New Guinea.

NEW FLAGS FLYING — PACIFIC LEADERSHIP: AUDIO CD

(Audio CD for use in a computer or CD player)

Interview 1   Tui Atua Tupua Tamasese Efi (Samoa)

Interview 2   Tofilau Eti Alesana (Samoa)

Interview 3   J H Webb (Cook Islands)

Interview 4   Sir Tom Davis (Cook Islands)

Interview 5   Dr Ludwig Keke (Nauru)

Interview 6   HM King Taufa'ahau Tupou IV (Tonga)

Interview 7   Ratu Sir Kamisese Mara (Fiji)

Interview 8   Robert Rex and Hon. Young Vivian (Niue)

Interview 9   Chief Sir Michael Somare (Papua New Guinea)

Interview 10   Hon. Solomon Mamaloni (Solomon Islands)

Interview 11   Sir Peter Kenilorea (Solomon Islands)

Interview 12   Hon. Bikenibeu Paeniu (Tuvalu)

Interview 13   Sir Ieremia Tabai (Kiribati)

Interview 14   Fr Walter Lini (Vanuatu)

Interview 15   Hon. John Haglelgam (Federated States of Micronesia)

Interview 16   Hon. Kessai Note (Marshall Islands)

interview 17   Hon. Sandra Sumang Pierantozzi (Palau)

Interview 18   Fiame Naomi Mata'afa (Samoa)

Interview 19   Dame Carol Kidu (Papua New Guinea)